*This volume is one of a series that explains and demonstrates
how to prepare various types of food, and that offers in each
book an international anthology of great recipes.*

Candy

BY
THE EDITORS OF TIME-LIFE BOOKS

TIME-LIFE BOOKS/ALEXANDRIA, VIRGINIA

Cover: A plump grape, half-covered with snowy fondant and dusted with sugar, is lifted from a dish of dipped confections. Many different sweets can be dipped in fondant, caramel or chocolate for a smooth finish. The chocolate-coated selection here includes marzipans, caramels, nut clusters and fondants.

Time-Life Books Inc.
is a wholly owned subsidiary of
TIME INCORPORATED

Founder: Henry R. Luce 1898-1967
Editor-in-Chief: Henry Anatole Grunwald
President: J. Richard Munro
Chairman of the Board: Ralph P. Davidson
Corporate Editor: Jason McManus
Group Vice President, Books: Reginald K. Brack Jr.

TIME-LIFE BOOKS INC.

Editor: George Constable. *Executive Editor:* George Daniels. *Director of Design:* Louis Klein. *Editorial Board:* Roberta Conlan, Ellen Phillips, Gerry Schremp, Gerald Simons, Rosalind Stubenberg, Henry Woodhead. *Editorial General Manager:* Neal Goff. *Director of Research:* Phyllis K. Wise. *Director of Photography:* John Conrad Weiser. *Design:* Ellen Robling (assistant director). *Copy Room:* Diane Ullius. *Production:* Anne B. Landry (director), Celia Beattie. *Quality Control:* James J. Cox (director), Sally Collins. *Library:* Louise D. Forstall.

President: Reginald K. Brack Jr. *Senior Vice President:* William Henry. *Vice Presidents:* George Artandi, Stephen L. Bair, Robert A. Ellis, Juanita T. James, Christopher T. Linen, James L. Mercer, Joanne A. Pello, Paul R. Stewart

THE GOOD COOK

The original version of this book was created in London for Time-Life International (Nederland) B.V.
European Editor: Kit van Tulleken. *Photography Director:* Pamela Marke. *Planning Director:* Alan Lothian. *Chief of Research:* Vanessa Kramer. *Chief Sub-Editor:* Ilse Gray. *Production Editor:* Ellen Brush. *Quality Control:* Douglas Whitworth

Staff for *Candy:* *Series Editor:* Gillian Boucher. *Series Coordinator:* Liz Timothy. *Text Editor:* Norman Kolpas. *Anthology Editor:* Josephine Bacon. *Staff Writers:* Alexandra Carlier, Sally Crawford, Jane Havell, Thom Henvey. *Designer:* Mary Staples. *Researchers:* Margaret Hall, Deborah Litton. *Sub-Editors:* Kathy Eason, Charles Boyle, Aquila Kegan, Sally Rowland. *Design Assistant:* Sally Curnock. *Editorial Department:* Steven Ayckbourn, Kate Cann, Debra Dick, Philip Garner, Theresa John, Lesley Kinahan, Debra Lelliott, Linda Mallett, Molly Sutherland, Julia West, Helen Whitehorn, Sylvia Wilson

U.S. Staff for *Candy:* *Series Editor:* Ellen Phillips (acting). *Designer:* Ellen Robling. *Chief Researcher:* Barbara Fleming. *Picture Editor:* Christine Schuyler. *Text Editor:* Mark Steele. *Staff Writers:* Leslie Marshall, Fran Moshos. *Researchers:* Patricia Kim (techniques), Karin Kinney (anthology). *Assistant Designer:* Peg Schreiber. *Copy Coordinators:* Nancy Berman, Tonna Gibert, Bobbie C. Paradise. *Art Assistant:* Robert Herndon. *Picture Coordinator:* Alvin Ferrell. *Editorial Assistants:* Brenda Harwell, Patricia Whiteford

CHIEF SERIES CONSULTANT

Richard Olney, an American, has lived and worked for some three decades in France, where he is highly regarded as an authority on food and wine. Author of *The French Menu Cookbook* and of the award-winning *Simple French Food,* he has also contributed to numerous gastronomic magazines in France and the United States, including the influential journals *Cuisine et Vins de France* and *La Revue du Vin de France.* He is a member of several distinguished gastronomic societies, including L'Académie Internationale du Vin, La Confrérie des Chevaliers du Tastevin and La Commanderie du Bontemps de Médoc et des Graves. Working in London with the series editorial staff, he has been basically responsible for the planning of this volume, and has supervised the final selection of recipes submitted by other consultants. The United States edition of The Good Cook has been revised by the Editors of Time-Life Books to bring it into complete accord with American customs and usage.

CHIEF AMERICAN CONSULTANT

Carol Cutler is the author of a number of cookbooks, including the award-winning *The Six-Minute Soufflé and Other Culinary Delights.* During the 12 years she lived in France, she studied at the Cordon Bleu and the École des Trois Gourmandes, and with private chefs. She is a member of the Cercle des Gourmettes, a long-established French food society limited to just 50 members, and is also a charter member of Les Dames d'Escoffier, Washington Chapter.

SPECIAL CONSULTANTS

Richard Sax, who was responsible for many of the step-by-step demonstrations in this volume, was for two years Chef-Director of the test kitchens for *The International Review of Food and Wine.* Trained in New York and in Paris, where he served an apprenticeship at the Hotel Plaza-Athénée, he has run a restaurant on Martha's Vineyard, contributed articles to a number of publications and conducted cooking courses.
Pat Alburey, a member of the Association of Home Economists of Great Britain, has wide experience in preparing foods for photography, teaching cookery and creating recipes. She was responsible for making candies for a majority of the step-by-step demonstrations.

PHOTOGRAPHER

Tom Belshaw was born near London and started his working career in films. He now has his own studio in London. He specializes in food and still-life photography, undertaking both editorial and advertising assignments.

INTERNATIONAL CONSULTANTS

GREAT BRITAIN: *Jane Grigson* has written a number of books about food and has been a cookery correspondent for the London *Observer* since 1968. *Alan Davidson,* a former member of the British Diplomatic Service, is the author of several cookbooks and the founder of Prospect Books, which specializes in scholarly publications about food and cookery. FRANCE: *Michel Lemonnier,* the cofounder and vice president of Les Amitiés Gastronomiques Internationales, is a frequent lecturer on wine and vineyards. GERMANY: *Jochen Kuchenbecker* trained as a chef, but worked for 10 years as a food photographer in several European countries before opening his own restaurant in Hamburg. *Anne Brakemeier* is the co-author of a number of cookbooks. ITALY: *Massimo Alberini* is a well-known food writer and journalist, with a particular interest in culinary history. His many books include *Storia del Pranzo all'Italiana, 4000 Anni a Tavola* and *100 Ricette Storiche.* THE NETHERLANDS: *Hugh Jans* has published cookbooks and his recipes have appeared in several Dutch magazines. THE UNITED STATES: *Judith Olney,* author of *Comforting Food* and *Summer Food,* received her culinary training in England and France. In addition to conducting cooking classes, she regularly writes articles for gastronomic magazines.

Correspondents: Elisabeth Kraemer-Singh (Bonn); Margot Hapgood, Dorothy Bacon (London); Miriam Hsia, Susan Jonas, Lucy T. Voulgaris (New York); Maria Vincenza Aloisi, Josephine du Brusle (Paris); Ann Natanson (Rome). Valuable assistance was also provided by: Janny Hovinga (Amsterdam); Judy Aspinall (London); Bona Schmid (Milan); Carolyn T. Chubet, Christina Lieberman (New York); Mimi Murphy (Rome).

CONTENTS

Frivolous Fare

Go on to the Useless Presents," an audience of children asks the narrator in Dylan Thomas' lyric memoir, *A Child's Christmas in Wales*. The storyteller replies with an enchanting catalogue of the candies of his own childhood, from "bags of moist and many-colored jelly babies" to "hardboileds, toffee, fudge and allsorts, crunches, cracknels, humbugs, glaciers, marzipan, and butterwelsh for the Welsh." Useless presents, indeed—and therefore wonderful. Candy is a frivolity whose only purpose is delight. Because of this, candymaking, more than any other branch of cookery, includes a vast array of decorative and fanciful preparations—crystal-clear lollipops, dense and creamy truffles, and fluffy marshmallows, to name only a few.

Even the most elaborate of these confections is within the reach of the resourceful cook. Some candies are simply and easily made—uncooked nut pastes *(pages 56-57)*, for instance, or balls of dried fruit and honey *(pages 46-47)*. Many other candies require precision and dexterity in their preparation. Boiled-sugar candies, for example, demand hot syrups that must be cooked to exactly the right temperature and handled with due caution. And it takes practice to get good results when dipping candy centers in coatings of syrup, fondant or chocolate. But none of these skills is difficult to learn.

This book offers a comprehensive guide to the making of candy. It begins with explanations of the properties of basic ingredients—sugar, nuts and chocolate—and guidelines for selecting flavorings and colorings. The introductory section concludes with instructions for preparing various molds used to contain candies while they set.

Four chapters follow, the first three dealing with broad categories of candy. Chapter 1 covers confections made from boiled-sugar syrups—nut brittles and chewy caramels, creamy fondants, and hard candies such as lollipops. The second chapter focuses on fruits—explaining how to candy pieces of fruit by saturating them with sugar syrup, and how to produce firm fruit pastes or clear fruit jellies. The third chapter deals with confectionery pastes formed from nuts or chocolate, including two classic candies: marzipan and chocolate truffles. In the fourth chapter, you will learn the techniques of dipping and molding. Having mastered all these lessons, you will be able to prepare any of the 253 recipes in the anthology that begins on page 87, as well as to create a myriad of confections of your own.

The confectioners' art

Candy is by its nature sweet. The word itself comes from *qand*, Arabic for sugar, but honey was long the primary sweetener for much of the world. As prehistoric cave paintings attest, Stone Age hunter-gatherers sought and stole the honey of wild bees. By 2500 B.C., the Egyptians not only had tamed bees, but also had developed various molds and other equipment needed to form the yield of the hives into primitive confections.

India, however, had another source of sweetness—sugar cane, a tropical grass whose sap could be turned into a sweetener much more versatile than honey. A method of extracting and evaporating sugar-cane sap to make sugar was known as early as 3000 B.C., and the Indians of that period made boiled-sugar candies such as nougat and nut pastes such as marzipan. From India, sugar cane and candymaking gradually spread east into Indochina and west into the Arab countries. During the Eighth Century A.D., Arabic influence extended the cultivation of the cane along the shores of North Africa, to Sicily—still famous for its candies—and even to the South of France.

Sugar nonetheless remained rare and expensive in the Western world throughout the early Middle Ages: Access to it was confined to the rich and powerful, and its very appearance on a table signified that the owner was wealthy. Among the most inspired exploiters of this "white gold" were the cooks of the papacy, which in the 14th Century established a court at Avignon so extravagant that the poet Petrarch called the city "the Babylon of the West." Papal cooks made bonbons (literally, "good goods") by candying the abundant fruits of Provence in sugar syrup. Then they took the excess syrup, pulled it to make it thick in much the same way taffy is pulled today *(pages 26-29)*, and cut it into short lengths resembling gold ingots. The candy thus formed was called *berlingots* and, like candied fruit, it remains a specialty of southern France *(recipes, pages 91-92)*.

Books devoted to the opulent art of making candy and other sweet confections began to appear in France in the 15th and 16th Centuries. Among the earliest was *The French Confectioner*, by a Provençal physician and astrologer named Michel de Nostredame, better known as Nostradamus. He called his tome an "Excellent and Most Useful Book Necessary to All Those Who Desire to Know a Few Exquisite Recipes." These recipes included clear instructions for the cooking of sugar syrups and various candies, such as candied fruit and marzipan, all of which, the author emphatically warned, were "both expensive and difficult to make."

Renaissance cooks used—and improved upon—the recipes of Nostradamus and his contemporaries, and the work of one of these innovators served to preserve his patron's name in candy. The chef of César du Plessis-Praslin, a 17th Century French general, had the happy idea of toasting almonds, then coating them with sugar. The general presented the confections to the ladies of the court of Louis XIII; they promptly honored the giver by naming them praslines. The word—minus the *s*—now has a number of meanings. Throughout continental Europe, for instance, praline refers to any candy with a coating. In English and American cookery, the term usually means a nut brittle *(page 35)* that is crushed to a fine powder, then used as an ingredient in other preparations. In New Orleans, praline denotes a rich candy often formed from brown sugar and nuts— pecans being the favorite *(recipes, pages 99, 103, 119 and 120)*.

During the late Renaissance, sugar became widely available, even to the common man. This was due at least in part to Christopher Columbus, who on his second voyage to the Americas in 1493 carried cane seedlings to Santo Domingo, launching the sugar-cane industry of the West Indies. By the 16th Century, sugar refining had become a commercial process and candies began to appear in bewildering variety, to no one's displeasure. "Let it hail kissing comfits and snow eringoes," Falstaff shouted enthusiastically in Shakespeare's *The Merry Wives of Windsor.* Comfits (the name came from the French *confit,* or confection) were candied spices; Elizabeth I was said to have chewed them constantly in her later years to sweeten her breath. Eringoes were candied sea holly, thought to be an aphrodisiac. Both were among the many "banqueting conceits"—or assortment of decorative and edible confections that followed a meal—prescribed by Gervase Markham in his cookbook *The English Hous-Wife,* published in 1615. Markham offered recipes for candying fruits and vegetables of all kinds (his technique differs little from the modern method shown on pages 50-51) and he also gave instructions for creating a variety of paste candies.

In the years that followed, candy became a treat not just for banquet guests, but for everyone who had a few pennies to indulge in a treat. It could be made at home, and it could also be bought at the proliferating *confiseries* (confectionery shops) of France, the *Zuckerbäcker* (sugar bakers) of Germany, and the sweet shops of England and America. The ever-increasing production of cane sugar was chiefly responsible for this abundance, but during the 18th and 19th Centuries, sweeteners from other sources were discovered. All of these serve the purpose of the contemporary candymaker.

Understanding sugar

No ingredient used in candymaking is more important or more widely used than cane sugar, made by extracting the juice of sugar cane, processing it until it crystallizes, then whirling it in a centrifuge to separate the liquid from the crystals. The results are dark brown granules of raw sugar and thick, syrupy molasses. The raw sugar may then be refined to make white granulated sugar, and these crystals in turn may be ground to produce easily dissolved superfine sugar or powdery confectioners' sugar. Granulated sugar flavored with molasses is sold as moist, light brown or dark brown sugar, depending on the proportion of molasses it contains.

Granulated sugar can also be made from sugar beets; it tastes the same as white cane sugar but is not as widely used in the United States. Another source of sweetness is the maple tree, whose sap produces the pale brown sugar used to give some candies a distinctive mellow sweetness. Corn, too, yields a valuable range of sweeteners: The long, chainlike starch molecules that make up corn kernels are broken down to yield sugars and syrups of various strengths and degrees of purity.

All these sweeteners, along with honey, have much in common in terms of chemistry. Ordinary white sugar—technically known as sucrose—has a molecular structure consisting of two distinct parts, glucose and fructose, joined by a chemical bond. Each part can exist as an independent sugar. Fructose is sweeter than sucrose, glucose less sweet than either. Corn syrup is mainly glucose; in fact, liquid glucose, which can be bought at pharmacies and candymaking-supply stores, is made from corn. Honey owes its sweetness to fructose. Maple sugar, like cane and beet sugar, is composed chiefly of sucrose. But, unlike white sugar, maple sugar and brown sugars are not pure sucrose; it is the small proportion of substances other than sucrose that give maple and brown sugars their distinctive flavors.

Sugar can be treated in many ways to produce a diversity of candy textures. The fundamental skill of the candymaker lies in

the handling of a sugar syrup—a solution of sugar in water. If you add enough water to sugar to dissolve it completely, the result is, of course, a liquid. However, if the syrup is boiled to drive off most of the water, the syrup will solidify at room temperature. Depending on how much water you allow to remain in the sugar syrup, you can produce textures ranging from soft to extremely brittle.

A sugar syrup has a strong inclination to return to its original crystalline structure, forming relatively large, jagged granules. This tendency can be the bane of cooks. Some candies, such as lollipops, are meant to be clear and glassy, with no crystals at all. Others, such as fondant, are crystalline—but the crystals must be tiny if the confection is to have the desired smooth texture. To inhibit the formation of large crystals, a sugar syrup is normally boiled with certain additives that are known as interfering agents.

The logic of adding an interfering agent is that, before crystallization can occur, molecules must line up in an orderly pattern; any foreign molecule that gets in the way of the sucrose molecules will make it difficult for the sugar to crystallize. A sugar other than sucrose will perform the interfering function well: Corn syrup, liquid glucose and honey are all good choices. Present in small quantities, these sugars result in the formation of fine, small crystals; in high concentration, they can prevent crystallization entirely. Other substances, particularly fats such as butter or cocoa fat, can also serve as interfering agents: They inhibit crystallization by making the syrup thicker. And acids such as lemon juice or cream of tartar will also control crystallization, because they break sucrose down into its glucose and fructose components (a mixture often described as "invert sugar"), thus providing an interfering agent at second hand. It is largely through the assistance of interfering agents that candymakers can ensure that their lollipops will set clear and brittle, their fudge fine-grained and creamy, and their caramels smooth and chewy.

An irresistible ingredient

If sugar is the staple of confectionery making, chocolate is the ingredient that, for many people, symbolizes the luxury of candy. Its smoothness, its richness and its intense flavor can be appreciated in chocolate coatings, molded confections, and combinations of chocolate with cream. It is perhaps surprising to find that this archetypal confectionery ingredient derives from hard and extremely bitter little beans that became available to candymakers only in comparatively recent times.

The beans grow in pods on the cacao tree, a native of the equatorial regions of the Americas. After harvesting, they are allowed to ferment for several days, a process that tempers their bitterness and turns them a light brown color. The beans are cleaned, then dried, roasted and ground to a thick, fatty paste.

Rich in the aroma of chocolate though the beans may be at this point, they are neither sweet nor smooth. The smoothness will be conferred in part by extra cocoa fat—obtained by pressing other batches of beans. To make chocolate, the pale yellow cocoa fat is combined with the cocoa bean paste; the mixture may be sweetened with varying amounts of sugar, or made milder in taste by the addition of milk. Further refining and molding turn the paste into perfectly smooth chocolate, ready to eat or to use in the preparation of confections.

In Central and South America, the cacao tree was cultivated more than 3,000 years ago by the Mayas, Toltecs and Aztecs. They used the beans as currency and consumed chocolate in the form of a thick, slightly bitter drink. Columbus brought cacao beans back to Spain after his fourth voyage in 1502, but it was his fellow countryman, Hernando Cortez, who recognized the commercial potential of the plant. Cortez was introduced to drinking chocolate at the court of the Aztec emperor Montezuma in 1519, and he sent back to Spain not only beans but also recipes for the preparation of chocolate. The Spaniards sweetened the drink, and in this form it gained high esteem.

Chocolate was introduced into Italy during the first decade of the 17th Century, and it became popular in France after the marriage of the Spanish princess Maria Theresa to Louis XIV in 1660. At about the same time, chocolate was gaining popularity among the wealthy in England—the beverage is mentioned in the diary of Samuel Pepys in 1664—and chocolate houses serv-

ing the drink soon became favorite meeting places throughout Europe. It was not until the 19th Century, however, that processes for preparing chocolate for use in confections were devised. When that occurred, the candymaker's larder was complete.

Essential candymaking equipment

The prime requisites for candymaking are a dexterous pair of hands and a cool, dry atmosphere: Heat and humidity can interfere with the preparation of many boiled-sugar confections and prevent the proper setting of chocolate. As for required equipment, the list is short. First of all, you need a cool, smooth work surface for working with hot candy mixtures; marble is ideal, but you can use a metal baking sheet. Good-quality, deep pans are necessary, particularly for cooking sugar syrup. Heavy vessels of aluminum or unlined copper are best, because they will cook syrups evenly and will safely withstand the high temperatures involved. If the syrup contains acidic ingredients—fruit juice, for instance—use a pan made of nonreactive material such as stainless steel to prevent the syrup from discoloring due to chemical interaction. The volume of the pan should be at least four times that of the syrup you are making so that there is no danger of the liquid boiling over the rim. To measure syrup temperatures accurately, buy the best candy thermometer available; it should be clearly marked for ease of reading.

Well-stocked kitchen-equipment shops or candymaking-supply stores carry more specialized equipment, but you can easily improvise from materials readily at hand. To dip delicate candy centers in chocolate, for example, most professionals use specially designed forks (page 69), but you could do some dipping with an ordinary table fork. For starch-casting—a process used to form thin, hard sugar shells around liquid centers—candymakers have special trays, molds and pouring equipment. As shown on pages 80-83, however, you can achieve professional results using a baking pan, some wood and a modeling compound, a kitchen funnel and a wooden spoon. A set of four steel bars (pages 18-19) to enclose candy mixtures as they set will save guessing about volumes—but you will produce an acceptable result with a baking tray.

Small delights

There was a time when candies were believed to have medicinal value. Marshmallows, for example, were originally made with an extract of the roots of the marshmallow plant, sold by apothecaries as a remedy for chest ailments. The 19th Century French epicure Jean Anthelme Brillat-Savarin observed that partakers of chocolate "enjoy unvarying health, and are least attacked by a host of little illnesses which can destroy the true joy of living." The millionaire American gourmand of the Gilded Age, Diamond Jim Brady, always ate two pounds of chocolates after his gargantuan meals; he said it made the food "set better."

None of these beliefs is warranted. Candy is not particularly good for the body: Eaten in large quantities, it can be bad for the teeth and for the figure. Candy is, however, good for the spirit. Offered in modest amounts—as a grace note at the end of a meal, for instance, or as a reward for a virtuous child—it proves the most delightful of treats, food provided for pleasure alone.

Sugar Syrup: The Elemental Ingredient

The transformation of sugar and water into syrups and caramel is the foundation of candymaking. When a sugar-and-water solution is boiled *(below)*, the water evaporates and the concentration of sugar increases. The higher the sugar content, the higher the boiling point, so you can check the concentration by taking the temperature of the syrup with a candy thermometer. Curtailing the boiling at different stages produces syrups with a range of moisture contents.

The less moisture a syrup contains, the harder it will set when it cools. Thus the degree to which the syrup is cooked has a marked effect on the texture of the finished candy. Syrup boiled to a relatively low temperature yields soft candies such as caramels; syrup boiled to a high temperature yields hard candies such as lollipops. The diagram on page 10 lists the temperature ranges for candy syrups; the tests shown allow you to check the temperature readings at each stage.

Since the ultimate concentration of the syrup is controlled by evaporation of the water, the initial proportion of water to sugar is not crucial. There should, however, be enough water to dissolve the sugar easily, and it is best if the resulting syrup requires only brief boiling to reach the desired temperature. A good proportion is about ⅔ cup [150 ml.] of water to 2 cups [½ liter] of sugar. To make caramel, you can either boil all of the water out of a sugar syrup, or carefully melt the sugar without water *(box, right)*.

Throughout syrup making, you must take precautions against crystallization, the formation of sugar crystals that ruin the syrup's texture. Rough surfaces can cause crystallization: Make syrups in a smooth, nonporous metal pan. Because even a single grain of sugar can trigger crystallization in boiling syrup, it is essential to dissolve all of the sugar over low heat and to clear away sugar grains clinging to the pan *(Step 3)* before the syrup boils. Agitation can cause crystallization: Do not stir a syrup once it boils.

In addition to these few precautions, a substance that will chemically interfere with crystallization is specified in many candy recipes as an addition to the sugar-and-water solution. The usual interfering agents are corn syrup and glucose —

sugars whose molecular structures differ from white sugar and therefore prevent white-sugar molecules from aligning for crystal formation. Acids such as lemon juice and cream of tartar have a similar effect. They convert some white sugar molecules into substances that inhibit crystallization. In some sugar syrups, milk solids and fats act as interfering agents: These make the syrups so viscous that sugar molecules cannot align.

Crystallization must be under control while a syrup cools as well as when it cooks. Because boiling water can hold more sugar in solution than water at lower temperatures, a cooling syrup becomes supersaturated with sugar, and tends to re-form into crystals. For certain candies, such as a clear, glossy barley sugar *(pages 24-25)*, it is necessary to prevent recrystallization; for others, for instance fudges and fondants *(pages 38-39 and 30-31)*, controlled crystallization is actually induced. The control of this crystallization depends largely on handling a syrup properly as it cools, but also on adhering to the type and amount of interfering agent called for in the recipe.

1 **Forming a syrup.** Warm a candy thermometer by placing it in a jug of hot water *(box, far right, top)*. Put the required amounts of cold water and granulated sugar into a heavy saucepan. To regulate crystallization, add an interfering agent — in this case, liquid glucose — to the syrup ingredients *(above)*.

2 **Dissolving sugar.** Stir the syrup over low heat until the sugar completely dissolves *(above)*. Imperfectly dissolved sugar will cause the mass to crystallize when it boils; if the mixture begins to boil before all of the sugar has dissolved, remove it from the heat. Continue to stir. When the syrup has cooled a little, return it to the heat.

3 **Removing stray crystals.** Stir the syrup gently so that it does not splash onto the pan sides and crystallize. To remove stray drops, wipe the sides of the pan with a pastry brush dipped in hot water *(above)*. Or briefly cover the pan after the sugar has dissolved so that any crystals are washed down the pan sides by condensing steam.

Caramel Made without Added Water

Melting sugar. Put sugar in a heavy pan set over low heat—on a heatproof mat if you cannot keep the stove heat very low. Add lemon juice for flavor. Stir continuously until the sugar is melted and golden brown. Add more sugar *(above, left)*; stir until all of the sugar has melted and the caramel is amber *(right)*. Still stirring, continue to add sugar in small amounts until you have the desired quantity of caramel.

Using a Candy Thermometer

Protecting against shock. If an unprepared candy thermometer is put into hot syrup, the thermometer may crack. Warm the thermometer in hot water beforehand. After using it, replace the thermometer in hot water to dissolve clinging sugar.

4 Boiling the syrup. When the syrup is completely clear, stop stirring. Place a warmed thermometer in the pan and bring the syrup to a boil *(above)*. Adjust the heat so that the syrup bubbles steadily and gently.

5 Arresting the cooking. Have a bowl of ice water ready. When the syrup has reached the temperature you require *(pages 10-11)*, take the thermometer out of the pan. Remove the pan from the heat, and dip it briefly in the ice water to cool it quickly and to prevent further cooking *(above)*.

6 Testing for hardness. With a spoon, take a small amount of syrup from the pan and submerge it in some ice water to cool it quickly *(above)*. By testing this small amount in your fingers *(pages 10-11)*, you can judge how the whole quantity of syrup will set. If the syrup is not hard enough, return the pan to the heat and continue cooking.

Forecasting a Syrup's Character

As a syrup cooks, it passes through distinct stages, each of which has a name in candymaking. The stage a syrup is allowed to reach determines the consistency the syrup will have when it cools and sets. Temperature can serve as a guide to these stages—but the addition of other ingredients to a syrup complicates the matter. Syrups that contain milk or butter, for instance, will reach each stage at lower temperatures than plain syrups; those that contain honey will reach each stage at slightly higher temperatures. For this reason, the chart below shows a range of temperatures for each stage.

Because combinations of different ingredients cause departures from even these ranges, you should test the consistency of a syrup as shown at right, instead of relying on temperature alone.

Using Temperature to Assess Consistency

The candy thermometer. This thermometer chart indicates temperatures for the main stages of a sugar syrup, and notes typical uses at each stage. Before making the candy, check your candy thermometer for accuracy by placing it in water and bringing the water to a boil. The thermometer should register 212° F. [100° C.]; if the reading is higher or lower, take the difference into account when testing the temperature of a syrup.

°F °C

400
180
350
340   170
Caramel
320-350° F. [160-177° C.]
Glazes, coating agent
330
320   160
310
Hard-crack
300-310° F. [149-154° C.]   150
Barley sugar   300
290
280   140
270
130
Hard-ball
250-266° F. [121-130° C.]   260
Marshmallow
250   120
Soft-ball
234-240° F. [112-116° C.]   240
Fondant, fudge
230   110
220
210   100

Soft-crack
270-290° F. [132-143° C.]
Taffy

Firm-ball
244-248° F. [118-120° C.]
Caramel candy

Thread
223-234° F. [106-112° C.]
Binding agent
for fruit pastes

Thread Stage

A thin filament. Take a teaspoonful of syrup and tip it out over a dish. If the syrup forms a fine, thin thread *(above)*, it has reached the thread stage. If the syrup is too liquid, return it to the heat and test it again when the temperature has increased by a few degrees.

Soft-Crack Stage

Pliable strands. Drop a little syrup into ice water, remove it, and stretch it gently between your fingers. If the syrup separates into strands that are hard but elastic *(above)*, then it has reached the soft-crack stage. The syrup will now feel only slightly sticky.

Soft-Ball Stage

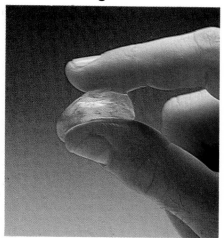

A rapidly flattening lump. Take a spoonful of syrup and submerge it in ice water. In the water, use your fingers to gather the cooled syrup into a ball. Remove the ball. If it immediately loses shape and flattens *(above)*, the syrup is at the soft-ball stage. At this stage, the syrup feels very sticky.

Firm-Ball Stage

A pliable globe. Drop a little syrup into ice water and mold it into a ball. Remove the ball. If the syrup has reached the firm-ball stage *(above)*, it will feel firm but pliable and still fairly sticky. The syrup will retain its shape longer than at the soft-ball stage, but it will soon lose its shape at room temperature.

Hard-Ball Stage

A rigid globe. Drop some syrup into ice water. If the syrup has reached the hard-ball stage, it should mold quite easily into a ball. Take the ball out of the water. It should hold its shape *(above)* and feel resistant to pressure. It will still be quite sticky.

Hard-Crack Stage

Brittle strands. Drop some syrup into ice water. It will solidify. Remove the syrup from the water and bend it. If it snaps easily *(above)*, it has reached the hard-crack stage. It will have a yellowish tinge and will not feel sticky.

Light-Caramel Stage

A honey-colored liquid. Take a spoonful of syrup from the pan and pour it onto a white plate. If the molten sugar is honey gold in color, it has become light caramel. If you require the slightly stronger flavor of dark caramel *(right)*, you can return the pan to the heat, but only briefly .

Dark-Caramel Stage

An amber liquid. As for light caramel, spoon a little liquid onto a plate. If it is a reddish amber color, it is dark caramel. Do not cook beyond this point, or the caramel will become bitter.

Tactics for Handling Nuts

Nuts of all sorts—almonds, hazelnuts, pecans, pistachios, walnuts, Brazil nuts, chestnuts and coconuts—are used in a variety of forms that give a distinctive texture and flavor to candies. A single whole nut dipped in chocolate *(pages 74-75)*, for instance, makes a simple treat; batches of whole nuts, mixed with caramelized sugar, produce brittles *(pages 34-35)*. Coarsely chopped nuts impart an interesting texture to fudge and nougat *(pages 38-39 and 42-43)*; finely chopped nuts can become an excellent coating for sticky balls of fondant or chocolate paste *(pages 32 and 66-67)*. Ground nuts, when mixed with sugar and egg, yield a wide range of nut pastes that can be molded into special shapes *(pages 56-63)*.

Preliminary shelling is necessary for all nuts, in whatever form they are to be used, and peeling is desirable to relieve nuts of their dark, bitter inner coat. Coconuts, which are exceptional in size and structure, need special treatment *(opposite, bottom)*, as do chestnuts *(pages 56-57)*. Most other nuts are easily shelled, by hand or with a nutcracker, but need to be parboiled or roasted before the skins can be removed.

Nuts with fairly loose skins—pistachio nuts and almonds, for instance—are easy to peel if they are first parboiled *(right, top)*. The boiling water penetrates the porous fibers of the skins, softening them and separating them from the kernels. However, when the nuts cool, the skins harden and cling again, so the peeling must be completed while the nuts are still warm. Nuts with tighter skins, such as Brazil nuts or hazelnuts, need to be roasted until their skins become parched and flaky *(opposite, top)*.

Once shelled and peeled, nuts can either be used plain, or toasted in an oven to darken their color and enhance their flavor. The nuts can be chopped with a heavy knife *(right)*, or ground with a pestle and mortar or in an electric food processor *(far right)*. A food processor transforms nuts into a fine and barely moist powder suitable for most candymaking purposes. Pounding in a mortar extracts more oil from the nuts and can produce a wet paste; if you use this method, it is essential to add a little egg white to help absorb excess oil.

Blanching Loose-skinned Nuts

1 **Parboiling nuts.** Put a small quantity of shelled nuts—in this case, almonds—into a pan of boiling water and parboil them for about one minute. Turn off the heat and retrieve the nuts with a skimmer *(above)* or with a perforated ladle; alternatively, remove the pan from the heat and drain the nuts in a colander.

2 **Removing the skins.** Let the nuts cool slightly. With your fingers, squeeze each nut lightly but firmly to pop it from its skin. To dry the nuts thoroughly so that they will keep longer, spread them on a baking sheet and place them in a preheated 325° F. [160° C.] oven for five minutes. Store the nuts in an airtight jar that is kept in a cool place.

Speedy Chopping

Chopping nuts. Put the nuts—pistachio nuts, here—on a work surface. Place the edge of a heavy, sharp knife blade across the nuts, and rest your free hand on the knife tip to hold it against the work surface. Slowly move the knife in an arc from side to side while rocking it up and down to chop the nuts.

Grinding in a Processor

Processing nuts. Put cooled, peeled nuts—almonds, in this case—in the bowl of a food processor. Operate the processor in short bursts to produce a coarse flour. (Continuous operation would heat the nuts and make them oily.) Between bursts, push down nuts that cling to the processor bowl.

Rubbing Off a Clinging Skin

1 **Roasting nuts.** Spread nuts—hazelnuts are shown here—on a baking sheet. Place the sheet in an oven preheated to 350° F. [180° C.] and roast the nuts for about 10 minutes. Lay a towel on a work surface and spill the roasted nuts onto one half of the towel.

2 **Peeling the nuts.** Fold the uncovered half of the towel over the nuts. Using the palms of your hands, roll the nuts in the towel; after one or two minutes, most nuts will have shed their skins.

3 **Removing stubborn skins.** Rub any partly peeled or unpeeled nuts between your fingers so that the skin flakes off. Nuts enclosed in their skins even after being rubbed should be reserved for purposes in which appearance is not important. Store the nuts in an airtight jar.

Cracking and Grating a Coconut

1 **Extracting liquid.** With a large knife, cut off the tuft of fibrous husk at the top of the coconut. Use a skewer or screwdriver to pierce through the three indentations—called eyes—that are exposed by the removal of the husk *(above)*. Invert the coconut over a bowl to drain off the milky liquid.

2 **Opening the coconut.** With a hammer or the back of a cleaver, briskly tap the coconut about one third of the way from the end opposite the eyes *(above)*. The coconut will fracture along a natural seam. Continue tapping until the nut cracks open along this line.

3 **Grating the coconut flesh.** Use a knife to divide the coconut flesh into portions that can be easily lifted from the shells. Lift out each portion and cut off the brown skin covering the flesh. Grate the flesh into crumbs *(above)* or chop it into fine pieces.

Additions for Flavor and Color

Some candies—chocolate fudge, for example—get their flavor and color from the ingredients that are used to make them. But many other candies are flavored and colored chiefly by small quantities of other ingredients.

Most of the flavorings added to candies are liquids and some of these, such as coffee and fruit juice, can be made at home (box, below). Many more flavorings are commercially manufactured. Among the liquids, the most concentrated are essential oils extracted from such sources as lemon and orange peels. Oils are sold at candymaking-supply stores and they are used to flavor a wide range of candies, including fondant and chocolates.

Slightly less concentrated and more widely available are liquid extracts produced by steeping peels, leaves, flowers, seeds, roots or bark in alcohol. Commonly used extracts include vanilla and almond; these flavor the same candies as essential oils.

Spirits, meaning rum, whiskeys, brandies and liqueurs, are somewhat milder than extracts, but they give sophisticated flavors to many candies, particularly to chocolate candies.

Flower waters, such as rose water and orange-flower water, are the lightest liquid flavorings of all. Sold at pharmacies, they are obtained by distilling the oil extracted from blossoms. These fragrant liquids are best suited to delicate candies such as marshmallows (pages 40-41).

The dry flavorings used in candies are readily available spices such as mace, cinnamon, nutmeg, cloves, allspice, anise and cardamom. Spices added to candy mixtures should be ground fine; for the freshest flavor, buy whole spices and grind them just before use.

Among the colorings used for candy, two can be made at home: Spinach leaves (box, opposite) yield a bright green liquid coloring; saffron (box, far right, top) gives candies a sunny yellow hue. Most colorings, however, must be purchased and come in two forms: highly concentrated pastes, which result in dark colors; and bottled liquids, which are less concentrated and produce pastel hues.

Most of the flavorings and colorings prepared at home should be used the day they are made. But homemade extracts and commercial oils, extracts, waters, spices and colorings may be stored in sealed jars, tubes or bottles in a dark, dry place. Spices will keep at least a year, liquid flavorings will last indefinitely, and colorings will last three to four years.

Most flavorings and colorings are very volatile; they should be added to a candy mixture just a moment before the end of cooking so that they dissolve in the liquid but do not have time to evaporate in the intense heat. The exception to the rule is spices: These should be added at the beginning of cooking so that heat can attenuate their strong flavors.

Use both flavorings and colorings in small quantities. More than a drop or two of an essential oil can give an entire batch of candy an overpowering taste.

Extracts, spirits, and flower waters may be used more generously, but recipe amounts should be followed closely: Excessive amounts could affect the concentration of sugar syrups and spoil the texture of the candy. The amount of coloring paste or liquid used determines how dark a candy is; start with only a tiny drop of coloring, then work more coloring into the candy to get the shade desired. Colorings are not fat-soluble and cannot be added to candy containing butter or oil.

Homemade Flavorings

Coffee

Freshly brewed coffee is a delicious flavoring for chocolate as well as for nut pastes (pages 56-59) and for boiled-sugar candies such as fudge (pages 38-39). To brew a coffee strong enough to use as a flavoring without diluting the candy, use three times the normal proportion of ground coffee to water.

Fruit

Peels. Lemon, orange and grapefruit peels can be used to add a tart citrus flavor to nut, fruit and chocolate pastes. To obtain the peel, rub the fruit against a grater, taking care to remove only the thin outer skin of the fruit, leaving the bitter, underlying pith behind. Candied peel (page 53) can also be used as a flavoring agent.
Juice. Intensely flavored citrus juices can be used in small quantities to give candies a tart edge. Or fruit juice can become an intrinsic part of the candy, flavoring and coloring it: The juices of berries, cherries, grapes and other fruits can be used in place of water in such candies as lollipops (pages 22-23) and jellies (pages 48-49).
Extracts. Flavorings similar to commercial extracts—and used in the same way— can be made from lemon, lime, orange or grapefruit peel. Peel the fruit in strips, leaving the pith behind. Place the strips in a jar and cover them with vodka, using half again as much vodka as fruit peel. Cover the jar tightly and let it stand at room temperature for two weeks, shaking the jar daily. Then discard the peel, replace it with fresh peel, and repeat the steeping process for two weeks more. Remove the peel and use the flavored vodka.

Vanilla

Beans. Whole vanilla beans can be added to boiling candy mixtures such as those used for caramels (pages 36-37); the beans should be removed at the end of cooking. Alternatively, the beans can be used to flavor sugar (box, far right, bottom); vanilla-flavored sugar can be used in place of the sugar and vanilla extract specified in many candy recipes.
Extract. A flavoring similar to commercial vanilla extract—and used in the same way—can be made with vanilla beans and vodka. Split vanilla beans lengthwise, cut them into pieces, and place them in a jar. Add about 2 tablespoons [30 ml.] of vodka for every bean and close the jar tightly. Let the beans steep at room temperature for four weeks, shaking the jar once a day. Remove the beans before using the flavoring.

Wintergreen and horehound

Liquids infused with mint-flavored wintergreen or astringent horehound can be used in place of water in sugar syrups. To make the liquids, use fresh wintergreen or horehound leaves. Rinse the leaves, then cover them with boiling water and let them steep for 15 minutes. Strain out the leaves before using the flavored water.

Extracting Color from Spinach

1 **Pounding spinach to a pulp.** Remove the stems from spinach leaves. Wash the leaves thoroughly and dry them. Put the leaves into a mortar and, with a wooden pestle, pound them *(above, left)* until they form a paste *(right)*.

2 **Preparing a sieve.** Fold a sheet of muslin or cheesecloth into a 12-inch [30-cm.] double-layered square. Drape it over a bowl and spoon the pulp into it. Fold the muslin to enclose the spinach.

3 **Wringing out the juices.** Grasp the ends of the muslin and twist the cloth to squeeze the spinach so that the spinach juice flows into the bowl *(above)*.

4 **Heating the juice.** Pour the juice into a small pan and set it over low heat. After a minute or two, stir the juice to see whether it has separated into solid matter and watery liquid *(above)*.

5 **Straining the solids.** Pour the juice through a fine strainer over a bowl. Use the solid matter that collects in the sieve to color cooked pastes such as fondant or marzipan; discard the liquid.

Dissolving Saffron

Dissolving the saffron. If you are using saffron threads, pound them into a powder, using a pestle and mortar. Put a pinch of powdered saffron into a small shallow dish. Add a teaspoon of cold water *(above)* and stir the mixture until the powder dissolves.

Making Vanilla Sugar

Distributing flavor evenly. Fill a jar about a quarter full with sugar—here, superfine sugar—and stand a vanilla bean upright in it. Add sugar *(above)* until the jar is full. Cover tightly. After a week or two, the sugar will be imbued with flavor. As the sugar is used up, pour more sugar into the jar. Replace the bean after three or four months.

Chocolate: A Sumptuous Resource

After sugar, chocolate is perhaps the most valuable ingredient in candymaking. In certain forms, it serves as the central element in a wide range of confections; other types of chocolate can be used as coatings or poured into molds to produce hollow candies.

The various chocolates used in candymaking all are made from a pastelike cacao-bean product called chocolate liquor—part cocoa butter and part cocoa solids. For chocolate used to form a candy rather than a coating, the paste may simply be molded into blocks and sold as unsweetened chocolate. Or the paste may be sweetened with sugar and sold as bittersweet, semisweet or sweet chocolate. It may also be enriched with cream or milk to produce milk chocolate.

All of these chocolates are handled the same way and may be interchanged —with adjustments of the sugar quantities—when making fudge *(pages 38-39)*, chocolate pastes and creams *(pages 64-65)*, and truffles *(pages 66-67)*.

Preparation of any of these chocolates is simple. Chocolate that will be used unmelted to flavor other ingredients can be reduced to fine shreds with a grater *(box, near right)* to ensure even blending. Chocolate that will be used melted can be grated or chopped into small pieces *(box, center right)* to facilitate melting.

The melting must be done very gently; chocolate may burn. Most chocolates can be melted in the top of a double boiler or in a bowl set over hot water. More sensitive milk chocolate should be melted over water that is only warm.

Any of the chocolates used to form candy will melt to a thick, soft mass that can be piped into individual candies or decorations *(below)*; the shaped chocolate will harden as it cools. More often, melted chocolate is blended with cream or butter to make rich, soft candies.

Two candymaking products are blended specifically for use as a coating—including the coating of a mold to yield a hollow confection. One—which demands special handling—is known as dipping chocolate. Available from candymaking-

supply stores, it contains a high proportion of cocoa butter, letting the chocolate melt into a thin fluid. Cocoa butter is composed of several different fats that melt and set at different temperatures, and as the chocolate-coated candy cools, some of these fats can rise to the surface and dull its finish. To prevent this, dipping chocolate must be tempered before use—carefully melted and cooled in a way that stabilizes the fats and ensures smooth, glossy candy *(pages 74-75)*.

The other product designed for these purposes is known as chocolate-flavored coating because it is technically not a chocolate. It consists of cocoa powder—made by extracting the cocoa butter from chocolate liquor and pulverizing the remaining chocolate solids—plus flavorings and stable vegetable fats. Also sold by candymaking-supply stores, it must be melted, but not tempered.

As a dry, chocolaty coating for sticky candies, you can use cocoa powder alone. It needs no preparation except sifting to remove lumps *(box, far right)*.

Creating a Miniature Piping Bag

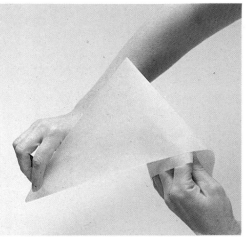

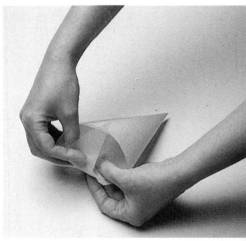

1 **Cutting out the paper.** Cut a parchment-paper rectangle 8 by 10 inches [20 by 25 cm.]. Cut the rectangle of paper in half diagonally: Only one triangle will be needed for the bag. Hold one oblique-angled corner of the triangle in each hand, leaving the right-angled corner free.

2 **Shaping a cone.** Bring your right hand over and then down behind your left hand so that the paper begins to make a cone *(above)*. The point of the cone should be about halfway down the longest side of the triangle.

3 **Securing the cone.** Continue to bring the corner held in your right hand all the way around until the cone is formed. The corner will protrude above the open end of the cone. Fold this tail into the cone to secure it and prevent the paper from unwinding.

Grating Shreds

Grating chocolate. Chill a bar of chocolate to firm it. Break the bar into large pieces and grate them over a tray placed to catch the shreds. Clean the surface of the grater frequently to prevent clogging. If your hands are warm, hold the chocolate with a piece of wax paper to keep it firm.

Chopping a Block

Cutting the chocolate. Place the chocolate on a wooden cutting board. With a sharp, heavy knife or cleaver, cut the chocolate into small pieces so that it can be evenly melted.

Sifting Cocoa Powder

Sifting the powder. Spoon cocoa powder into a fine-meshed metal sieve held over a bowl. Tap the sides of the sieve firmly *(above)* until all the powder has fallen through. For a sweeter powder, mix confectioners' sugar with the cocoa powder and sift them together.

4 **Fitting in a nozzle.** Choose a decorating nozzle—in this case, a star nozzle—available at kitchen-supply stores. Snip off the point of the cone so that there is just room for the tip of the nozzle to come through *(above)*. Insert the tip and make sure that it fits securely. If necessary, cut off more paper.

5 **Filling the bag.** Melt chocolate pieces in a bowl set over hot water. Stir occasionally until the chocolate is melted and smooth. To thicken it for piping, stir in a few drops of cold water. Spoon the chocolate into the piping bag *(above)* until the bag is no more than two thirds full.

6 **Piping the chocolate.** Bring the edges of the cone together at the top and fold them over to close the bag. Pipe the chocolate onto a cool surface; here, the bag is squeezed and moved forward to make oval, overlapping shapes that form a string of shells. Work quickly—the mixture sets rapidly.

Choosing and Preparing Molds

For candies that are set as slabs, you need molds. For most recipes, a straight-sided pan, 8 inches [20 cm.] square, will do. Larger batches may require a pan 9 by 13 inches [32 by 23 cm.].

If you make candy regularly, you can invest in metal confectioners' bars—also called slab bars—that can be arranged to enclose areas of various dimensions. Made from cast-iron or steel at least ½ inch [1 cm.] thick, the set should include two pairs of bars measuring about 20 inches [50 cm.] and 10 inches [25 cm.] respectively. The shorter bars are placed in between and at right angles to the longer ones to form a rectangle of the desired size. Portable bars made especially for candymaking are rarely available commercially, but you can order bars of the right dimensions from a foundry or sheet-metal shop. Or you can buy a section of iron or steel bar from a building-supply store and have it cut to size.

Because all candy mixtures are sticky, any container must be prepared for easy unmolding. The preparation depends on the container and on the candy.

There are several ways to prepare pans for molding. For soft candy mixtures that will be cut in the pan—fudge, for example (pages 38-39)—butter or oil the pan. Almond oil, mild and sweet, is best, but flavorless vegetable oil will do.

Firm types of candy such as caramels (pages 36-37) are turned out of their pans for cutting. To facilitate this, line the pans with oiled parchment or wax paper.

A pan used to mold fruit jelly (pages 48-49) need only be dampened with cold water (right). The water forms a film between the mold's surface and the jelly, allowing you to unmold the set candy.

Some candies, especially marshmallows, have damp surfaces after setting. Dust the pan with cornstarch and confectioners' sugar (opposite, bottom). The mixture forms a thin crust on the candy.

Confectioners' bars will not hold liquid jelly candies, but they can be used for any other kind. Always place the bars on parchment or wax paper to protect the work surface. Oil the paper and the inside edges of the bars for candies such as fudge or caramels; dust the paper and bars with cornstarch and confectioners' sugar for marshmallows.

A Paper Lining to Aid Unmolding

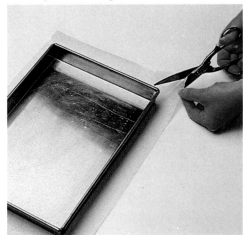

1 **Lining a pan.** Cut parchment or wax paper into a rectangle about 1 inch [2½ cm.] wider and longer than the pan. Center the pan on top of the rectangle of paper. With scissors, cut a diagonal slit from each corner of the paper to the corner of the pan.

2 **Folding the paper.** Place the paper inside the pan. Crease the paper along the inside edges of the pan; overlap the flaps at each slit corner (above). Brush the paper with almond oil or melted butter. Do not trim off any paper above the sides of the pan; it can be used to lift out the set candy.

A Water Film for Jellies

Dampening a pan. Choose a pan large enough for the quantity of jelly you have prepared. Fill a bowl with cold water. To speckle the pan lightly and evenly with water, dip the fingers of one hand into the water and flick drops of water all over the inside of the pan.

A Dusting of Cornstarch

1 **Oiling the pan.** With a pastry brush or a piece of paper towel, apply a light film of oil to the sides and bottom of a pan. Take care to coat all the corners and sides of the pan so that no portion of the candy can stick.

An Adjustable Frame of Metal Bars

1 **Positioning the bars.** Lay a rectangle of paper—in this case, parchment paper—on a cool work surface. Position the two long bars on top of the paper, parallel to each other. Between them, insert the two shorter bars; position the short bars to enclose an area that is appropriate for the volume of paste or syrup to be set and the final thickness desired.

2 **Oiling the bars.** With a pastry brush, apply a mild-flavored oil to the inside edges of the confectioners' bars. If you are unsure of where the shorter bars must be placed, oil the entire length of the longer bars. Brush the area of paper enclosed by the bars.

2 **Powdering the pan.** In a bowl, stir together equal quantities of cornstarch and confectioners' sugar. Fill a fine-meshed sieve with the mixture. Tap the sieve against the heel of your hand to sprinkle the mixture generously over the bottom of the pan.

3 **Tilting the pan.** Pick up the pan with both hands. Tilt and shake it in all directions so that the cornstarch-and-sugar mixture is evenly distributed over the bottom and sides of the pan.

4 **Tipping out excess.** Place a sheet of paper on the work surface. Invert the pan and tap the bottom to release excess cornstarch and confectioners' sugar. Form the sheet of paper into a funnel and tip the excess powder into a container for storage.

1
Boiled-Sugar Candies
A Dazzling Spectrum

Worked in a figure 8 to ensure even distribution of sugar crystals, a soft-ball sugar syrup begins to grain, becoming opaque and thick. After kneading and ripening, this syrup will be fondant, which can be flavored, colored and shaped in many ways, or used as an ingredient in other candies.

A plain syrup of sugar and water is the basis for an extraordinary variety of candies, ranging from glassy sticks of barley sugar to pillow-soft marshmallows. Some of this variety depends on differences in the degree to which the syrup is boiled *(pages 8-11)*: A syrup boiled to the crack stage acquires the brittle texture needed for lollipops and barley sugar, for example; a firm-ball syrup yields chewy caramels. But the temperature of the syrup is only one variable. The range of confections is further enlarged by handling the syrup in different ways as it sets, and by adding other ingredients to the syrup.

Manipulation of simple sugar syrups can effect remarkable changes in their characters. The traditional corkscrew shape of barley sugar *(pages 24-25)* results from nothing more than cutting and twisting a poured, hard-crack syrup at the crucial moment of pliability just before it sets. A syrup that is slightly softer—hence pliable for a longer period—can be repeatedly pulled and twisted so that it incorporates tiny air bubbles, becomes lighter in color and takes on the opaque satin sheen that distinguishes taffy *(pages 26-27)*.

Handling will cause a sugar syrup to crystallize or "grain" and acquire a soft, crumbly texture. For pulled candy such as taffy, graining is prevented by using a syrup that includes a generous amount of an interfering agent such as corn syrup. But the character of some confections, most notably fondant *(pages 30-31)*, depends on deliberately induced—and carefully controlled—graining: A sugar syrup that has been cooked to a relatively low temperature is stirred until it is suffused with minute sugar crystals.

Like fondant, fudge depends on crystallization for its texture. But fudge also is one of a group of sugar-syrup candies whose quality is determined by the inclusion of large amounts of other ingredients in the basic syrup. Among these candies are brittles, made crunchy by nuts, and cream-enriched caramels *(pages 34-37)*.

Soft, light marshmallows *(pages 40-41)* are produced by incorporating air, through the agency of beaten egg whites, into syrup and stiffening the confection with gelatin. Nougat *(pages 42-43)* is also aerated with beaten egg whites, but, unlike marshmallow, nougat is covered with heavy weights or bricks as it sets, to make a denser candy.

Bright-hued Disks of Hardened Syrup

The simplest boiled-sugar candies are made by cooking sugar syrup to the hard-crack stage *(pages 8-11)*, then dropping it in pools onto an oiled, cold surface—preferably, a marble slab. The syrup sets rapidly into hard, clear disks of candy *(box, below, right)*. The most popular of such candies are lollipops *(right; recipe, page 166)*. Sticks—sold at candymaking-supply stores—are set into the pools of syrup, providing handles.

To endow the candy with taste and color, you can use concentrated food coloring and flavoring *(pages 14-15)* in the syrup; add them just after you remove the finished syrup from the heat. For the freshest flavor, however, the syrup can be made with fruit juice rather than with water, eliminating the need for extra coloring and flavoring. Here, for example, juice is extracted from raspberries, then strained to remove any pulp that might cloud the candy. Finally, the juice is boiled with sugar to make the syrup.

Other fruits such as blueberries or cherries could supply flavor and color in the same way as the raspberries. However, highly acidic lemon or grapefruit juice would interfere with the setting of the candies if used full strength.

In every case, the syrup-making procedure follows the same rules as those for making plain sugar syrup. If you make the candies with fruit juice, do not add corn syrup: The acid in the juice will prevent crystallization. Remove the syrup from the heat when the temperature just approaches the hard-crack stage—290° to 300° F. [143° to 149° C.]: If the syrup's temperature exceeds 300° F., the juice may be discolored.

To ensure setting, make this candy on a dry day. A crack-stage syrup contains little water—2 per cent or less—and on a damp day the candies will absorb moisture from the atmosphere, which will make them sticky. Work quickly once the syrup is ready: It will soon become too stiff to pour. If it does stiffen, soften it by warming it gently over boiling water.

When the candies harden, they are ready to eat. To store them and to reveal their colors, wrap each one in transparent, nonporous material: cellophane—sold at art stores—or wax paper. Then pack the candies in airtight jars or cans.

1 Preparing the fruit juice. In a small, heavy pan, gently heat soft fruit—raspberries are shown—without stirring until the juice separates, about 20 minutes. To strain out the juice, set a fine-meshed sieve on top of a bowl and pour the fruit into it. Let the juice drain through without pressing the fruit.

2 Combining the ingredients. Put sugar in a heavy pan and add the strained juice. Put the pan over medium heat and stir until the sugar melts; to dissolve any crystals that form on the sides of the pan, cover the pan for a minute or two, or brush the sides with a dampened pastry brush.

Fruit Drops: A Gleaming Coinage

Lifting the set candies. Prepare a flavored hard-crack syrup *(Steps 1-3)*. With a teaspoon, pour out small pools of syrup—about 1 inch [2½ cm.] across—onto an oiled marble slab. Let the syrup cool and set. Then use a spatula to loosen the disks from the marble *(above)*; lift the candies one by one. If they are to be served at once, pile them on a plate *(inset)*. For storage, wrap each one in cellophane.

3 **Boiling the syrup.** When the sugar has dissolved, place a candy thermometer in the pan. Without stirring, boil the syrup until it reaches 290° to 300° F. [143° to 149° C.]—the hard-crack stage. To arrest the cooking, take the saucepan off the heat at once and dip the base in ice water.

4 **Forming lollipops.** Using a large spoon, pour four pools of syrup onto a marble slab that has been coated with flavorless vegetable oil. Make the circles large or small; in this case, they are about 2 inches [5 cm.] across (above, left). Quickly push a lollipop stick into each pool. Continue to pour four lollipops at a time, until only a little syrup is left. To make sure the sticks are secure, spoon a few drops of the remaining syrup over the embedded end of each stick (right). Let the lollipops cool and harden.

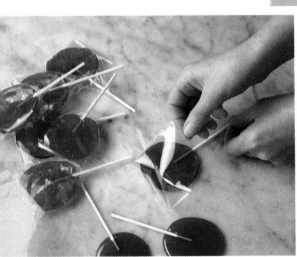

5 **Wrapping the lollipops.** Using a metal spatula, gently loosen the lollipops from the surface; lift them up by their sticks (above). To keep the lollipops from sticking, wrap each one in a rectangle of cellophane (right).

Twisted Sticks of Barley Sugar

When hard-crack syrup is poured out in one large pool, there is a brief period during its cooling when it is flexible enough to be folded, cut and twisted. The syrup will then set hard in whatever shape it has been given—be it simple sticks or complicated loops or twists. With a modicum of speed and dexterity, you can fashion the syrup into handsome confections such as the corkscrew-shaped barley sugar demonstrated at right.

Barley sugar is so called because the syrup is sometimes made with water in which pearl barley has been cooked—giving the twisted sticks a milky appearance and mellow flavor *(recipe, page 90)*. The barley sugar prepared here uses a simpler mixture of sugar and plain water, flavored with the juice and peel of a lemon *(recipe, page 90)*. For a brighter lemon color, the syrup may include a very small pinch of saffron. In place of the lemon and saffron, you could use any of the concentrated flavorings and colorings employed for lollipops *(pages 22-23)*.

The syrup begins to solidify as soon as it is poured onto a cold work surface. While it is still warm and soft enough to stick to itself, two opposite sides of the pool are gently lifted and folded to meet in the middle. The result is a double thickness for more substantial sticks.

The folded sheet of syrup must then be cut and shaped at once, before it becomes too brittle. For speed, it is advisable to have someone assisting you, to twist the strips as you cut them. Even if the sheet does solidify before you have finished cutting, it need not be wasted. Once hardened, it snaps easily and can be broken into irregular pieces instead of being shaped into sticks.

1 **Dissolving the sugar.** In a heavy pan, place sugar, corn syrup and water; for a more concentrated color, add powdered saffron dissolved in warm water *(page 15)*. Put the pan over medium heat and, with a wooden spoon, stir until the sugar has completely dissolved. Add thinly pared lemon peel.

2 **Adding lemon juice.** Put a candy thermometer in the syrup. Boil the syrup to 240° F. [116° C.]—the soft-ball stage *(pages 8-11)*. Add lemon juice. Boil the syrup to the hard-crack stage—300° to 310° F. [149° to 154° C.]. Dip the pan in ice water to arrest cooking. With a fork, lift out the peel.

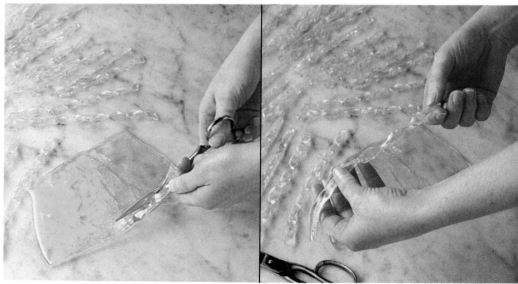

5 **Cutting and twisting.** As soon as the sheet is folded, use the oiled spatula to free the underside from the work surface. With oiled scissors, cut the sheet crosswise into strips about ½ inch [1 cm.] wide *(above, left)*. The unfolded edges will harden before the center does, so cut the strips alternately from opposite ends of the sheet. As each strip is cut, take its ends between your fingers and twist it into a corkscrew-shaped stick *(right)*.

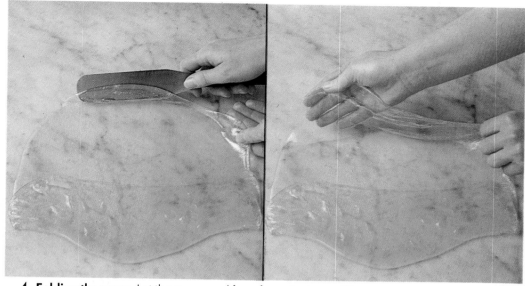

3 **Pouring the syrup.** Hold the pan of syrup low over a cool, oiled work surface and tip it slowly; the syrup will spread out into a shallow pool.

4 **Folding the syrup.** Let the syrup cool for a few minutes until it hardens around the edges and a slight skin forms on the surface. Oil a metal spatula to prevent the syrup from sticking, and use the spatula to ease up one edge of the sheet. With your hands, pull up the edge and fold it over to the middle of the sheet of syrup; take care to lay it down evenly to avoid wrinkling it. Immediately lift the opposite edge with the spatula *(above, left)* and fold it over to meet the first flap *(right)*.

6 **Serving the candies.** Let the sticks set hard—this takes about 15 minutes at room temperature. For immediate presentation, arrange them in a glass container that shows off their color and clarity *(right)*. To store them and prevent them from sticking together, put the candies in an airtight container, wrapped individually in cellophane or arranged in single layers between parchment or wax paper.

Pulling a Syrup to Make Taffy

If a sugar syrup is repeatedly pulled into a rope while it is still hot, it will incorporate many tiny air bubbles. As the pulled syrup cools and hardens, the air bubbles turn it into taffy—candy with an opaque, satiny sheen and a texture lighter than that of lollipops or barley sugar.

The basic syrup for pulled candies can incorporate any of the flavorings and colorings used for lollipops (pages 22-23), and preparatory steps can be altered to produce finished candies of different textures. The handling the syrup undergoes, for instance, makes it likely to crystallize and acquire a crumbly, chalky texture. For certain candies, such as Scotland's traditional Edinburgh rock (recipe, page 91), this is the intended result; but a hard, glossy finish—seen here—is more often the goal. Syrup for such glossy candies must include a large amount of corn syrup to avoid crystallization.

The syrup can be cooked to either the hard-ball or the soft-crack stage. A hard-ball syrup yields slightly soft, sticky candies; a denser soft-crack syrup—used in this demonstration—produces brittle confections. An even denser syrup—the hard-crack syrup used for lollipops—is recommended in some recipes for pulled candies, but it hardens so fast that only limited pulling is possible: Candies that are made from hard-crack syrup will not achieve the lightness of those that are formed from soft-crack syrup.

Once the syrup has reached the proper stage, it should be poured out immediately in a pool on a work surface and folded over on itself so that the edges of the pool do not cool before the center; this is an extra precaution against graining. Because the syrup cools quickly, you must begin to pull, fold and twist it (Step 3) as soon as it can be handled. But guard against burns: A syrup that is tolerably cool on the surface may be scorching hot underneath. Oil your hands well to keep the syrup from sticking to them, and pick it up with caution.

You can repeat the sequence of pulling, folding and twisting as often as you like until the syrup hardens. The twisting helps to keep the syrup in a cohesive mass, but it drives out some of the air incorporated during pulling. The less you twist, the more air bubbles will remain.

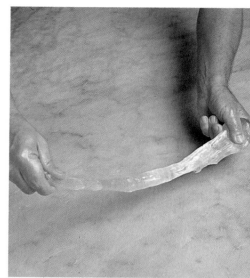

1 Turning the syrup. Cook a sugar syrup to the soft-crack stage (pages 8-11). Add peppermint extract. Using a spiral motion, pour the syrup onto a cold, oiled surface. Let the syrup cool until a skin forms—a minute or so. With an oiled metal scraper, fold the edges of the pool into the center.

2 The first stretching. Continue turning the syrup until it is just cool enough to handle. Oil your hands. Lift the syrup with the aid of the scraper, and push the syrup into a cylinder. Stretch it; it will be very soft and will sag in the middle when pulled.

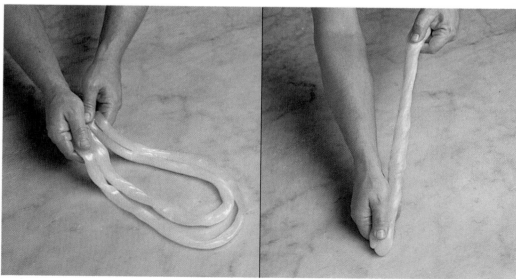

4 The final pulling. The syrup will change from yellowish and translucent to an opaque, creamy white. (If the syrup hardens before it has turned opaque, or crystallizes during pulling, you can rescue it by putting it in a pan with a few spoonfuls of water and corn syrup, dissolving it over low heat, then boiling it again to the same temperature as before.) To give the rope an even shape, fold it in two and then fold it again (above, left). Gently twist the four strands together. Pull the strands again, twisting them gently as you pull, to make a long, thin rope (right).

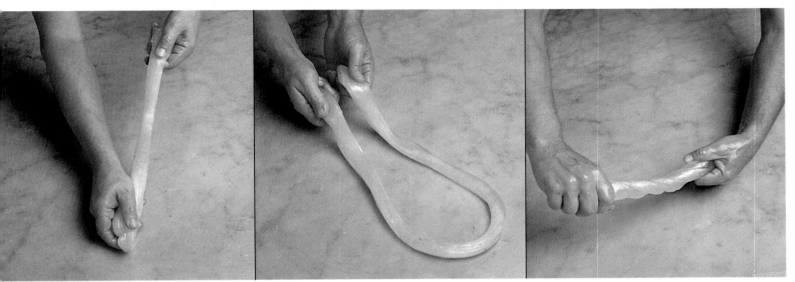

3 **Pulling and twisting.** Gather the syrup back together and pull it again; repeat these steps until the syrup begins to harden and holds its shape when stretched *(above, left)*. Fold the pulled syrup in two *(center)* and twist the two halves together. Pull the twisted syrup *(right)* to make a long, even rope about ½ inch [1 cm.] in diameter. Continue to fold, twist and pull the syrup for as long as it is supple—up to 20 minutes.

5 **Cutting and storing.** Using oiled scissors, cut the rope into short pieces of equal size *(above)*. The scissors flatten the rope where they cut, so cushion shapes result. To prevent the candies from becoming soft and sticky during storage, wrap them in wax paper or cellophane. If serving the candies the same day you make them, simply store them unwrapped in a jar *(right)*.

Two Ways to Create Patterned Taffies

The color of pulled candies depends on the ingredients used in the basic syrup and also on how much the syrup is manipulated: the longer the pulling, the lighter the color. Two-color candies can be produced by exploiting either of these factors *(recipes, pages 92, 93 and 97)*.

The confections shown at right start with a brown-sugar syrup. Half of the syrup is pulled and twisted into a light-colored rope. The other half is pulled just enough to make an even, dark rope. The ropes are twisted together and cut to make candies with swirling stripes.

For a stronger contrast, make two syrups—one colored and one plain. Pull the plain syrup until it is opaque but leave the colored syrup translucent. For the bull's-eyes shown below, a rope of raspberry syrup is enclosed within a sheet of plain syrup; the two are twisted, cut and rolled into spheres. Work quickly: Syrups harden fast. To keep the unused syrup malleable while you pull the rest, you can leave it in the pan and set it in a preheated 300° F. [150° C.] oven.

Stripes from a Single Syrup

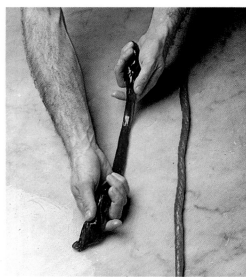

1 **Turning the syrup.** Cook a brown-sugar syrup to the soft-crack stage *(pages 8-11)*. Pour the syrup in two pools onto an oiled work surface. Turn up the edges of the pools with an oiled metal scraper and fold the edges into the center. Oil your hands well and push one pool of syrup into a sausage shape.

2 **Pulling the sugar syrup.** Quickly pull and twist the sausage until it is an opaque, creamy brown with a satin finish. Fold it over twice lengthwise to make four strands. Twist these together, pulling gently to make a long, even rope. Push the remaining syrup into a sausage and pull it into a dark rope the same size as the first.

Swirls from Contrasting Syrups

1 **Pulling white syrup.** Make two syrups, one with water and the other with fruit juice—here, raspberry juice. Cook them to the soft-crack stage *(pages 8-11)*. Pour them in separate pools onto an oiled work surface. Fold over the edges of each pool. Pull the plain syrup until it becomes white, satiny and opaque; then stretch it into an oblong.

2 **Adding the red syrup.** Roll the red syrup into a sausage shape. Pull the sausage gently until it is the same length as the sheet of white syrup *(above, left)*. Place the red sausage on one long edge of the white syrup sheet. Fold the edge over the sausage *(right)* and roll up the sheet to wrap the sausage inside.

3 **Combining the two ropes.** Lay the two ropes of contrasting colors side by side. Beginning at one end, loosely twist the two strands together. Then fold the rope over and twist again, to make a short, fat rope of alternating colors.

4 **Pulling and twisting.** Pull the rope gently but firmly, beginning at one end and working your way along its length; twist slightly as you pull. Work quickly but carefully until you have a long, thin rope of even thickness.

5 **Cutting the rope.** Using oiled scissors, cut a small piece off the end of the rope. Give the rope a half turn toward you, and cut the rope again to form a candy with triangular faces. Continue turning and cutting. Wrap the candies in cellophane or wax paper, and store them in an airtight container.

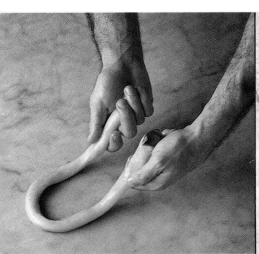

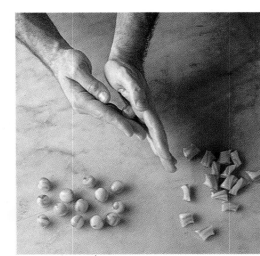

3 **Pulling and twisting.** Pull the wrapped cylinder into a rope and, holding the rope by either end, fold the rope in two *(above, left)*. Gently twist the two strands together. Pull the twisted rope gently but firmly *(right)* to make an even-sized rope of alternating red and white stripes.

4 **Rolling bull's-eyes.** Using oiled scissors, slice short, equal-sized pieces off the rope. Pinch down the sharp edges of each piece with your fingers, and then roll each piece into a ball. Each ball will have a swirling pattern of red and white. Wrap the bull's-eyes individually in wax paper or cellophane, and store them in an airtight jar.

Fondant: A Versatile Paste of Kneaded Syrup

When a sugar syrup is cooked to the soft-ball stage *(pages 8-11)*, cooled, and then worked in just the right way, tiny sugar crystals and air bubbles form in it and the syrup gradually turns into a firm, snow-white paste. The paste is known as fondant *(recipe, page 166)*—from the French *fondre,* "to melt"—and its name is fitting. Fondant has a rich, melting smoothness that makes it a classic confection in its own right, as well as an ingredient in a broad range of assemblies and dipped candies.

Concentrated food coloring and flavoring can be kneaded into a fondant paste *(Steps 5 and 6)* and the paste then can be shaped by hand into candies. Alternatively, the paste can be melted, then colored, flavored and poured into molds. Both of these candy-forming techniques are demonstrated on pages 32-33.

In assemblies, hand-molded fondant is often used as a stuffing for dried fruits *(pages 72-73)* or as a center for dipped candies *(pages 74-75)*. Melted fondant can be poured into molded chocolate cups *(page 86)* or can provide a coating for dipped confections *(pages 70-71)*.

Whatever its ultimate use, the way in which fondant is made does not vary. The first step is to add corn syrup to the sugar-syrup ingredients *(recipe, page 166)*. The corn syrup prevents large crystals from forming when the cooled syrup is manipulated; without it, the fondant's texture would be gritty.

As the pool of poured-out syrup cools, it should be folded inward so that the mass cools evenly. When the syrup becomes glossy and viscous, it can be stirred in a figure-8 pattern. Stirring causes minute sugar crystals to form; the figure-8 pattern helps the crystals to form evenly throughout the syrup. Next, the fondant is kneaded to make it smooth.

For fondant that will be melted, no further preparation is necessary. However, fondant intended for molding by hand must be allowed to rest for at least 12 hours to "ripen": Its crystalline structure changes, and the fondant becomes softer and more pliant. The ripened fondant need not be used at once. Although it dries with prolonged exposure to air, fondant keeps almost indefinitely if it is stored in a sealed jar in the refrigerator.

1 **Cooling the syrup.** Coat a marble slab or baking sheet with cold water. Cook a sugar syrup to 240° F. [116° C.]—the soft-ball stage *(pages 8-11)*; quickly dip the pan in ice water to stop the cooking and pour the syrup in a pool on the wet surface. Cool it for a few minutes. With a dampened metal scraper, fold the edges of the syrup into the center until the syrup is glossy and viscous.

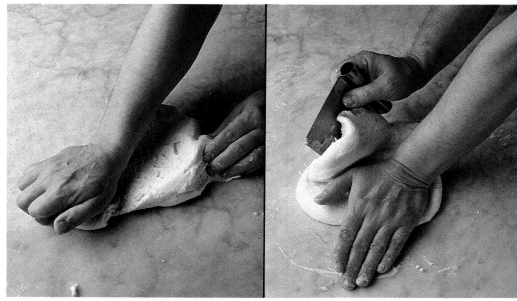

3 **Kneading the fondant.** Moisten your hands to prevent the fondant from sticking to them. Gather the fondant into a ball. Knead the fondant, pushing it out with the heel of one hand *(above, left)*, then gathering it back up and repeating the action. If the fondant sticks to the work surface, use a moistened metal scraper to lift it *(right)*. Continue to knead the fondant until it is free of lumps and feels moist and smooth—five to 10 minutes.

2 **Working the syrup.** Using a dampened wooden spatula, work the syrup continuously in a figure 8 *(above, left)* until the syrup becomes thick and opaque; as it stiffens, you will need to use both hands *(center)*. Work the syrup for five to 10 minutes, until it suddenly turns white, crumbly and too stiff to stir *(right)*.

4 **Ripening the fondant.** Lightly moisten a plate with water so that the fondant will not stick to it; with your hands, mold the fondant into a ball and put it on the plate. Cover the fondant with a damp cloth to prevent the surface from drying. Allow it to ripen in the refrigerator for at least 12 hours.

5 **Adding food coloring.** Dust the work surface with confectioners' sugar and put the fondant on top. Press the fondant flat. Using a knife or a metal scraper, cut slits along the surface of the fondant; then spoon a concentrated food coloring—here, spinach extract *(pages 14-15)*—into the slits.

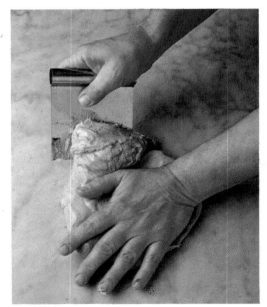

6 **Kneading in the food coloring.** Sprinkle a flavoring—peppermint extract is used here—over the fondant. Dust your hands with confectioners' sugar to prevent the fondant from sticking to them; knead the fondant, as shown in Step 3, until the coloring and flavoring are evenly distributed. ▶

7 **Rolling fondant balls.** Chop nuts fine *(pages 12-13)*—almonds and pistachio nuts are used here. Spread out the chopped nuts on the work surface. One at a time, pull off small pieces of colored and flavored fondant, and roll them between your fingers to shape them into neat balls *(above, left)*. As each ball is shaped, gently roll it in the chopped nuts to coat it evenly *(right)*.

8 **Serving the candy.** Let the fondant balls rest on the nuts for at least one hour to dry out slightly and firm up. Place each ball in a paper cup *(above)*. For serving, arrange the candies on a plate *(right)*. To store the fondant balls, place them in an airtight container, arranging them in single layers between sheets of wax paper.

Flavored Creams from Melted Fondant

1 **Melting the fondant.** Put already made fondant *(pages 30-31, Steps 1-3)* in a pan; the one used here has a spout to facilitate pouring. Place the pan in a larger pan filled with barely simmering water; the water should reach as high as the top of the fondant. With a wooden spatula, stir until the fondant melts.

2 **Coloring and flavoring.** Add a coloring—here dissolved saffron *(pages 14-15)*—to the fondant. Add flavoring—in this case, lemon extract—and stir well. If you use a more fluid flavoring such as fruit juice, it will dilute the fondant for pouring and you can omit the liquid used in Step 3.

3 **Adding liquid.** A little at a time, stir in liquid—water, as here, or sugar syrup that has been brought just to a boil. Stir until the mixture reaches 140° F. [60° C.], when the fondant will be fluid enough to pour and will set to a soft consistency; do not overheat the fondant or it will set too hard.

4 **Pouring fondant.** Pour the fondant from the pan into paper cups *(above)*: Take care to pour into the center of the cups so that they do not tip over. For decoration, press pecan halves into some of the warm candies. Let the candies cool before serving *(right)*; store in an airtight container.

Altering Texture with Added Ingredients

The texture of a basic sugar syrup *(pages 8-11)* can be changed without the aid of pulling or kneading: It may also be altered by the incorporation of lavish amounts of other ingredients. Adding generous quantities of butter to a syrup mixture and cooking it to the crack stage, for example, yields a smooth, opaque toffee *(right; recipes, pages 107-111)*. Nuts turn a caramel syrup into the crunchy confection known as nut brittle *(opposite, below; recipe, page 167)*.

The richness of a toffee is determined by the amount of butter you include. Among the richest mixtures is the aptly named butter toffee, or butterscotch, demonstrated here, best appreciated in small, bite-sized pieces. To make neat rectangles, the cooked syrup is poured into a buttered pan and scored with a knife when it has cooled but is still soft. As soon as the mixture has set completely, the toffee can be easily broken along the scored lines.

In a brittle, the nuts may make up more than half of the confection's total weight. You can select whatever nuts you like: whole, small nuts such as hazelnuts, almonds, cashew nuts or the peanuts used here; or chopped pieces of larger nuts such as Brazil nuts or walnuts. Whatever the choice, peel the nuts and warm them for about five minutes in the oven: If cold nuts are added to a hot syrup, the syrup may begin to congeal and set too quickly to be poured out.

To make the finished candy as transparent and brittle as possible, form the syrup-and-nut mixture into an extremely thin sheet. This is done by pouring the hot mixture straight out onto a cold surface, then—as soon as the edges of the pool of syrup are cool and firm enough to handle—stretching the sheet carefully from all sides. Once it has cooled, the brittle can easily be snapped into jagged serving pieces.

Melting In the Flavor of Butter

1 **Adding butter.** Pour cold water into a heavy pan. Add sugar—brown sugar is used here for its mellow flavor, but you could substitute white sugar. Cut butter into cubes and add them to the pan. Set the pan over medium heat.

2 **Stirring.** With a wooden spoon, stir the syrup constantly *(above)* until the butter melts and the sugar dissolves. Remove the spoon and place a candy thermometer in the saucepan; boil the syrup to 290° F. [143° C.]—the soft-crack stage. Take the pan off the heat and dip it in ice water to arrest cooking.

6 **Wrapping the toffees.** Run a sharp knife around the edges of the pan to loosen the toffee. Invert the pan and, if necessary, rap the bottom to release the toffee. Lift the pan *(inset)*. Snap the toffee into pieces along the scored lines. To keep the pieces from sticking together, fold each toffee in a square of wax paper and twist the ends *(above)*. Store the toffees in an airtight jar or can.

3 **Adding lemon juice.** If you like, add lemon juice *(above)* to flavor the toffee. The already frothy syrup will foam up with the addition of the liquid, but the foam will subside again after the syrup is poured.

4 **Pouring out the toffee.** Have ready a buttered or oiled pan *(pages 18-19)* large enough to contain the mixture in a thin layer. Pour the toffee into the pan *(above)*. It will be fluid enough to spread evenly in the pan.

5 **Scoring the toffee.** Let the toffee cool for about 15 minutes: It should be firm enough not to flow when the pan is tilted, but it should still feel warm. Score the toffee into 1-inch [2½-cm.] strips. Score across the strips to make rectangles. Let the toffee cool and set; this takes about 20 minutes.

Producing a Nut-packed Brittle

1 **Adding nuts.** Shell nuts—peanuts are shown. Peel the nuts *(pages 12-13)* and place them on a baking sheet in a preheated 350° F. [180° C.] oven to warm for five minutes. Cook a sugar syrup to a light caramel *(pages 8-11)*; pour the warmed nuts into the caramel. Stir gently to combine them.

2 **Stretching the brittle.** Pour the mixture onto a cold, oiled marble slab or baking sheet. Spread it evenly with an oiled spatula. Coat your hands with oil or butter; when the syrup is cool enough to handle, grasp one edge and pull it. Continue around the edges until the sheet is too thin to stretch further.

3 **Dividing the brittle.** Let the brittle set hard. Break it into pieces by lifting the sheet and sharply rapping it at intervals with the back of a spoon *(above)*. Store the brittle in an airtight container, packed in single layers between sheets of parchment or wax paper.

Caramels Enriched with Cream

Caramel candies are made by boiling a sugar syrup that has been enriched with cream. Their characteristic mellow flavor and brown color result from a reaction between milk protein and sugar, and also from the caramelization of lactose, a form of sugar naturally present in the cream. Lactose caramelizes at a lower temperature than ordinary sugar does—at the firm-ball stage *(pages 8-11)*—and the cooking of the syrup is therefore arrested at an earlier stage than with most boiled-sugar candies. For this reason, caramels remain relatively moist and set to a chewy consistency.

The moistness of the caramel will vary, however, depending on the temperature the syrup is allowed to reach. Soft caramels are produced by cooking the syrup only to the firm-ball stage; a firmer candy is produced by cooking the syrup to the hard-ball stage.

Because caramel candy is made with a high proportion of milk products, the syrup mixture must be gently stirred from time to time as it cooks, to prevent it from sticking to the bottom of the pan and burning. The thick, creamy syrup resists crystallization, but to make sure that none is caused by the stirring, you should include an interfering agent. At right, honey is used *(recipe, page 112)*.

Honey contributes its own flavor to the caramels. If you like, you can also heighten their flavor with a vanilla bean—used here—or, at the end of cooking, you can add a concentrated flavoring *(pages 14-15)* such as peppermint extract. A contrasting texture can be provided by chopped nuts or dried fruit, warmed in the oven and then stirred into the mixture at the end of cooking.

Once the caramel has been poured and set, it is easily cut into pieces. With hard caramel, the pieces should be bite-sized; softer, chewier caramels can be cut into larger pieces. Wrap the caramels immediately in cellophane or wax paper to prevent them from sticking together. Store the wrapped caramels in a cool place such as the refrigerator, where they will keep for up to two weeks.

1 **Melting syrup.** Pour heavy cream into a saucepan. Add sugar, butter and honey. For extra flavor, add half a vanilla bean, split lengthwise. Put the pan over medium heat. Using a wooden spoon, stir the mixture until the butter melts and the sugar dissolves. Place a candy thermometer in the pan.

2 **Testing the consistency.** Stirring occasionally, boil the mixture to 248° F. [120° C.]. Turn off the heat. Dip a spoonful of the syrup into a bowl of ice water, then pinch the cool syrup; it should be just firm enough to mold into a ball. For a firmer caramel, boil the mixture a little longer and test again.

5 **Cutting caramel pieces.** Peel the parchment or wax paper away from the caramel *(above, left)*. Soak a piece of paper towel with oil and use it to wipe the blade of a heavy knife. Pressing down firmly on the back of the blade, cut the sheet of caramel in half lengthwise. Cut across the sheet of caramel to make strips about 1 inch [2½ cm.] wide *(right)*, oiling the blade after each cut.

3 **Pouring the caramel.** Dip the bottom of the pan in the ice water to arrest cooking. With a fork, remove the piece of vanilla bean from the pan. Pour the caramel mixture onto oiled parchment or wax paper laid on a cool work surface, containing the candy with oiled confectioners' bars (pages 18-19). Or pour the mixture into an oiled, shallow pan.

4 **Unmolding the caramel.** Let the caramel candy cool and set—about two hours. Pull away the bars (above); if necessary, use a sharp knife to free any candy stuck to the bars. Oil another section of the work surface. Grasp two opposite sides of the paper underneath the set caramel and turn the caramel over onto the oiled section of the work surface.

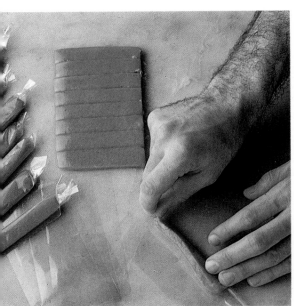

6 **Wrapping the caramels.** Cut cellophane into rectangles three times as wide as and 2 inches [5 cm.] longer than the pieces of caramel. Align each caramel along a long edge of a rectangle of cellophane (above) and roll up the confection to enclose it. Twist shut the free ends of the cellophane. Pile the caramels on a serving plate (right).

Two Techniques for Fudge

Like toffee and caramel candy, fudge is made from sugar syrup enriched with butter or cream; like fondant, fudge is cooked only to the soft-ball stage, then worked—in this case, beaten—so that air and minute sugar crystals disperse throughout the syrup.

The basic fudge mixture can be flavored with many sorts of ingredients, among them coffee, chocolate, vanilla and honey. And you can add both flavor and textural interest by folding nuts or candied fruits into the beaten syrup.

The diversity of fudges does not end with ingredients: By varying preparatory techniques, you can significantly alter the character of the candy. To make a firm, grainy fudge such as the chocolate fudge demonstrated at right *(recipe, page 114)*, beat the syrup while it is still hot: This encourages the formation of large crystals. For a smoother fudge *(below; recipe, page 116)*, let the cooked syrup cool before you beat it: It will become viscous and form small crystals.

Beating while Hot for a Grainy Result

1 **Adding chocolate.** Put sugar and milk into a heavy saucepan. Add butter and a flavoring—here, chopped semisweet chocolate *(pages 16-17)*. Put the saucepan over medium heat.

2 **Boiling the mixture.** Stir constantly with a wooden spoon until the sugar dissolves and the butter and chocolate are melted. Stop stirring and put a candy thermometer in the pan. Bring the mixture to a boil and cook it to 240° F. [116° C.], the soft-ball stage *(pages 8-11)*.

Cooling and Beating for a Fine Texture

1 **Heating the ingredients.** In a heavy pan, gently heat milk, butter and vanilla sugar *(page 15)*, stirring continuously with a wooden spoon until the butter has melted and the sugar has dissolved. Bring the mixture to a boil and cook it to 240° F. [116° C.], the soft-ball stage *(pages 8-11)*.

2 **Cooling and beating.** Remove the pan from the heat. To arrest cooking, dip the base of the pan in ice water. Let the mixture cool to 122° F. [50° C.], at which point it will be viscous and opaque. Using a wooden spoon and tilting the pan, beat the syrup *(above, left)* until it thickens and turns paler *(right)*.

3 **Beating the hot syrup.** To prevent further cooking, remove the pan from the heat and briefly dip its base into ice water. Using a wooden spoon, begin to beat the mixture immediately. To make the syrup deeper and thus easier to beat, tilt the pan slightly while you work.

4 **Pouring out the fudge.** Continue to beat the syrup for several minutes until it grains and thickens, becoming lighter in color and less shiny. Before it is too stiff to stir, pour and scrape the mixture into a buttered pan (above).

5 **Serving the fudge.** Let the fudge cool and set for one to two hours. Then use a greased knife to cut it into squares. With a narrow-bladed spatula, put the pieces on a plate for serving. To store the fudge for several weeks, place it between layers of parchment or wax paper in an airtight container.

3 **Serving the fudge.** Empty the fudge into a buttered pan. Let it set in a cool place—overnight if necessary. Cut the fudge into small squares, and use a narrow-bladed spatula to lift them from the pan. For immediate use, arrange the squares on a serving plate (right). Or store them as described in the top demonstration, Step 5.

Foamy Marshmallows from Whisked Egg Whites

A very small proportion of beaten egg whites and gelatin transforms a sugar syrup into light, springy marshmallows *(recipe, page 124)*. The syrup, cooked to the hard-ball stage, gives the marshmallows their sweetness. The air incorporated into the whites makes the mixture fluffy. Gelatin helps prevent the syrup from crystallizing when the ingredients are stirred together and, as the gelatin sets, it adds body to the marshmallows.

Prepare the gelatin while the syrup for the marshmallows is cooking. Dry, powdered gelatin does not combine well with other ingredients. It must first be soaked, to soften and swell its granules. At this stage, a little liquid flavoring is added; orange-flower water, used here, or rose water will add the delicate taste appropriate to such light confections. When the gelatin has been soaked, it is gently liquefied over boiling water so that it will mix easily with the sugar syrup.

While the sugar syrup finishes cooking, the egg whites are prepared. Beaten egg whites will be most stable if they are whisked in a copper bowl: A reaction with the metal gives extra strength to the walls of the egg whites' microscopic air bubbles. However, glass, porcelain and stainless-steel bowls are also suitable; to stabilize the egg whites when using these bowls, beat the whites to the foamy stage, then add ¼ teaspoon [1 ml.] of cream of tartar for every four whites.

As soon as the egg whites hold stiff peaks, the gelatin-and-syrup mixture is whisked in. The liquid must be poured in a thin, steady stream, and the whites must be beaten all the while; otherwise, the weight of the syrup would flatten the whites and the mixture would be heavy. You will need a helper to pour the liquid while you steady the bowl and whisk.

Further beating stiffens and thickens the marshmallow to the point at which it is ready for molding *(Steps 3 and 4)*. Once set and unmolded, the marshmallow can be cut into cubes with a knife and scissors, as shown here, or stamped with cookie cutters into whatever shape you choose. Serve the marshmallows plain, dusted with a mixture of confectioners' sugar and cornstarch to keep them from sticking; or dip them in melted fondant *(pages 70-71)* or chocolate *(pages 74-75)*.

1 **Adding gelatin.** Cook a sugar syrup that contains corn syrup to 260° F. [127° C.], the hard-ball stage *(pages 8-11)*. Steep powdered gelatin in cold water and orange-flower water. Stir the gelatin mixture over boiling water for about two minutes. Take the syrup off the heat and add the dissolved gelatin.

2 **Beating in the syrup.** Whisk egg whites until they form stiff peaks. While you continue to whisk, have someone pour the syrup-and-gelatin mixture in a thin stream at one side of the bowl into the egg whites.

6 **Cutting strips.** Lightly oil a large, heavy kitchen knife. Press down on the knife to cut the block of marshmallow into strips 1 inch [2½ cm.] wide *(above)*. To keep the marshmallow from sticking to the knife, clean and oil the knife after each cut.

7 **Cutting cubes.** With oiled scissors, cut each strip of marshmallow into cubes *(above)*. Sprinkle more of the sugar-and-cornstarch mixture over the cut surfaces of the marshmallow cubes to prevent them from sticking together.

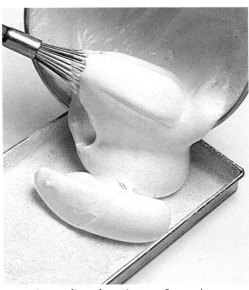

3 **Testing the consistency.** Continue to whisk the mixture until it is light and fluffy and just beginning to thicken and hold its shape *(above)*. But it should remain thin enough to flow easily from the bowl into the pan.

4 **Spreading the mixture.** Spread the marshmallow mixture immediately in a pan that has been oiled and dusted with confectioners' sugar and cornstarch *(pages 18-19)*. With a spatula, smooth out the marshmallow mixture evenly. Let it set for several hours.

5 **Unmolding.** Use a knife to loosen the mixture from the pan. Sift confectioners' sugar and cornstarch onto a work surface, and invert the pan to unmold the marshmallow *(above)*. Dust the top and sides of the marshmallow with more confectioners' sugar and cornstarch.

8 **Serving the candy.** Put the cubes of marshmallow on a wire rack *(above)* and let them dry for a few hours. The marshmallows will keep for about two weeks if they are stored in an airtight container lined with parchment or wax paper. To serve the marshmallows, pile them in a dish *(right)*.

Nougat: An Aerated Confection Compacted by Weighting

Like marshmallow *(pages 40-41)*, nougat is basically sugar syrup aerated with egg whites. Yet the dense texture of nougat could hardly be further from the foamy softness of marshmallows. Nougat owes its firmness to gentle cooking after the whites and syrup are combined; the cooking sets the whites. Weighting the nougat overnight then compacts it.

The choice of ingredients for the syrup helps determine the texture of the confection. A plain sugar-and-water syrup will crystallize when it is beaten with egg whites, resulting in a dry, crystalline nougat. For a chewy, noncrystalline candy, add an interfering agent such as corn syrup or honey—or a combination, as in this demonstration.

Corn syrup should be added before the syrup is cooked. Honey's flavor is altered by cooking; to minimize its cooking time, add it to the syrup for just the last few minutes of cooking. A plain syrup should be boiled until it reaches the hard-ball stage *(pages 8-11);* to counter the softening effect of corn syrup and honey, a syrup with these additions should cook a little longer—to the soft-crack stage.

Once the syrup has boiled to the right stage, it is combined with beaten egg whites: Either recruit a friend to pour the syrup while you whisk the whites, or use an electric mixer. The next step is whisking over hot water. If you want a chewy nougat, stop the moment the mixture thickens; the longer it is whisked, the more likely it is to crystallize.

When the right consistency is reached, nuts usually are folded in; almonds and pistachios are used here *(recipe, page 129)*. The nuts should be prepared in advance so that they can be added without delay. They also should be warmed in the oven to prevent them from cooling the syrup and setting it prematurely.

After the nuts are added, the nougat is ready to be pressed into thin slabs. For easy unmolding and handling, nougat is traditionally sandwiched between layers of edible rice paper—a thin, flavorless, gelatin-based material sold in sheets at candymaking-supply stores. If you have no rice paper, mold the nougat on a surface or in a pan sprinkled with cornstarch, and sprinkle the top of the candy with cornstarch before weighting it.

1 Adding honey. Prepare a sugar syrup with corn syrup *(pages 8-11)*. Put honey in a pan and set it in hot water so that the honey becomes runny. When the temperature of the syrup reaches 280° F. [138° C.], pour in the honey. Boil the syrup to a temperature of 290° F. [143° C.]. Remove the pan from the heat. Dip it in ice water to stop cooking.

2 Whisking egg whites. While the syrup is cooking, use a wire whisk to beat egg whites in a heatproof bowl until they form stiff peaks. As you continue to whisk, have a friend pour the finished syrup into the whites in a slow, thin stream at one side of the bowl.

6 Weighting the nougat. Cover both the mixture and the mold with another sheet of rice paper. Place a board over the nougat mixture. Place heavy weights *(above)* or bricks on top of the board. Let the nougat set overnight.

7 Trimming the nougat. The next day, remove the weights, the board and the mold from the nougat. With a sharp knife, trim off the excess rice paper and cut away any uneven edges from the set nougat. Slice the nougat in half.

3 **Firming the consistency.** When the syrup has been fully incorporated into the egg whites, put the bowl over a pan of barely simmering water. Continue to whisk the mixture while it thickens and firms. Stop whisking when the mixture clearly maintains its shape on the whisk *(above)* but is still pourable. Remove the bowl from the pan of water.

4 **Adding nuts.** If you like, add a little vanilla extract or other flavoring to the mixture. Then add halved or chopped almonds and chopped pistachio nuts— first warmed for five minutes in a 350° F. [180° C.] oven. Stir the nuts into the mixture gently but quickly.

5 **Shaping the mixture.** Transfer the nougat mixture to a pan that has been lined with edible rice paper, or, as here, pour it onto a work surface covered with the paper, molding the candy with prepared confectioners' bars *(pages 18-19)*. Using an oiled, narrow-bladed spatula to spread the mixture, fill the pan or mold.

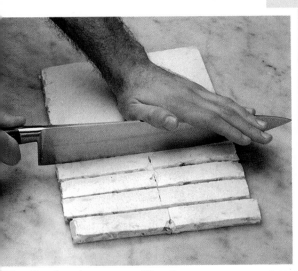

3 **Serving the nougat.** Slice the nougat again, lengthwise, to form quarters. Then cut each quarter into bars approximately ¾ inch [2 cm.] wide *(above)*. The bars may either be stacked on a plate and served *(right)* or they can be wrapped individually in cellophane and stored in an airtight container for several weeks.

Fruits are nature's own confections. With their sweetness and their bright colors, they need little artifice to transform them into beguiling candies. In fact, complicated flavorings or excessive cooking would distort the delicate natural flavors of most fruits. Preparation of fruit candies should be simple, and the list of ingredients often does not extend beyond the fruit itself and sugar. The main function of sugar is to intensify the flavor and sweetness of the fruit; but a sugar syrup also gives body to various fruit candies and, in sufficiently high concentration, it acts as a preservative.

Most fruit candies begin with chopped or puréed fruits or with fruit juices. Dried fruits such as dates and prunes are dense-textured and need only be chopped fine, then bound together with sugar syrup or honey; the mixtures will set to firm pastes that can be cut into small shapes to make individual pieces. Fresh fruits, which are softer in texture, are puréed and then cooked with sugar syrup to produce a similarly firm paste.

Fruit juices, carefully extracted to retain their clarity, have little body of their own. But you can use gelatin to set the juices to a solid slab; cut into small pieces, this candy jelly—firmer than the jellies of dessert cookery—makes a light and refreshing candy. Fruits left whole—or cut into relatively large pieces—provide some of the most appealing confections in the entire repertory of candymaking. Immersed in a sugar syrup of repeatedly increased concentration, the fruits slowly absorb the syrup. When the fruits dry, the sugar in their flesh hardens to give them a firm texture and a glittering surface (opposite). And the concentration of the sugar is so high that if the fruits are properly stored they will keep indefinitely.

While a particular fruit may be best suited to certain sorts of candies, almost all can be used in some way. Firm fruits that are able to withstand lengthy soaking in syrup are good for candying whole or in pieces and will also make the stiffest purées. Juicy fruits such as citrus fruits and berries will produce the most transparent jellies. Even the peels of oranges, grapefruits, lemons or limes will yield confections: A simple syrup coating (page 53) transforms them into crunchy, sugary morsels suitable for eating on their own or for decorating or flavoring other candies.

Wearing a decorative coating of uperfine sugar, candied apricots stand eady to be eaten whole or sliced. The uit was first soaked in syrup until it was aturated with sugar. After drying, the pricots retain much of their natural hape, color and flavor.

Turning Fruit into Moldable Pastes

Dried and fresh fruits both can be made into pastes with concentrated flavors. These pastes are easy to form and to shape into candies; however, different techniques are used for each type of fruit.

Dried fruits, low in moisture and firm in texture, need only be ground to a purée to become the basis for a paste *(recipes, pages 139-141)*. You can feature one fruit or grind several together *(top demonstration)*, and you can flavor the purée with spices or chopped nuts. The ground pulp is bound into a mass with any thick, sweet syrup—sugar syrup, molasses or the honey used here. Or you can omit the syrup and mix the ground fruit with lightly beaten egg white.

Pastes based on dried fruits are most simply shaped by hand into whatever forms you please—spheres or cylinders, for instance. The candies should be coated with sugar to keep them from sticking together. Before eating or storing them, allow them to dry out overnight.

Fresh-fruit pastes *(recipes, pages 134-138)*, like dried ones, can be produced with almost any puréed fruit, used alone or with other fruits and flavorings. (The exceptions are citrus fruits, which do not form stiff purées.) Most fresh fruits—including the apples used in the bottom demonstration—need preliminary cooking to make them soft enough to purée.

Once puréed, the fruit is cooked with a large amount of sugar—usually a quantity equal in volume to the puréed fruit. During cooking, the fruit's natural moisture partially evaporates and the purée thickens. At the same time, the sugar forms a dense syrup that hardens and helps the purée to set firm when the paste is spread out for cooling. Some cooks employ an alternative method of preparation in which a soft-crack or hard-crack syrup *(pages 8-11)* is combined with a thick, cooked purée; the resulting paste is then cooled until firm.

Once set, a fresh-fruit paste can be shaped by hand in the same way as a dried-fruit paste or it can be cut into flat individual pieces. Like pieces of dried-fruit paste, these can be stored between sheets of parchment or wax paper in an airtight container, where they will keep almost indefinitely.

Grinding a Mixture of Dried Fruits

1 **Pitting fruits.** To remove pits from dried fruits—in this case, dates and prunes—slit each piece with a small, sharp knife. Pull back the flesh *(above)* and pick out the pit.

2 **Grinding dried fruits.** Fit a food grinder with a medium or coarse disk. Push fruits—the pitted dates and prunes plus dried apricot halves *(above)*—through the food grinder to make a rough-textured purée.

Cooking to Concentrate Fresh Fruit

1 **Preparing the fruit.** Choose just-ripe fruit—in this instance, tart apples. Wash the fruit and slice it into a heavy nonreactive pan. The peel and cores are rich in pectin, a substance that helps the paste set. Add a little water to keep the slices from sticking. Cover the pan, and cook the fruit over low heat until just soft—apples take 20 to 40 minutes.

2 **Making a purée.** Remove the pan from the heat and let the fruit cool. Set a strainer over a large bowl. With a wooden spoon or pestle, press the fruit pulp through the strainer. Alternatively, press the pulp through a food mill. Discard the peel and seeds.

3 **Binding the mixture.** Transfer the purée to a bowl. Spoon in a binding ingredient—here, honey. Blend the ingredients with a spoon. If the paste feels too dry to cohere, work in more honey. If the paste is moist and very sticky, add a dry ingredient—sugar, finely ground nuts or more ground fruit.

4 **Shaping the candies.** Pick up one walnut-sized portion of the paste at a time, and roll it into a ball between the palms of your hands. As the balls are shaped, roll them in sugar and set them on a wire rack.

5 **Serving the candies.** Let the paste balls dry and firm overnight. Put each candy into a fluted paper cup, and pile the candies on small serving dishes.

3 **Cooking the purée.** Measure the purée and transfer it to a nonreactive pot. Stir in an equal amount of sugar. Stir over low heat for one hour—until the purée forms a paste so thick that the spoon leaves a trail on the bottom of the pan. During the last five minutes of cooking, flavor the paste, if desired, with ground spices and citrus peel.

4 **Firming the paste.** Remove the pan from the heat. Spoon the paste into a shallow, lightly buttered baking pan; tilt the pan to distribute the paste evenly. Let the paste cool several hours or overnight—until it has set firm.

5 **Cutting the candy.** With a sharp knife, cut the set paste into 1-inch [2½-cm.] squares. Sprinkle a tray or baking sheet with confectioners' sugar. With a spatula, set the squares of paste in the sugar. To coat the tops of the candies, sift more confectioners' sugar over them. Before serving, let the candies dry for about an hour.

Sparkling Jellies Based on Fresh Juice

Candy jellies, firm in texture, fresh in flavor and translucent as jewels, are produced by warming together fruit juice, sugar and gelatin, then letting the mixture cool and set. Fruits that easily yield the clear juice required for jellies include berries, such as strawberries, raspberries and blueberries, and citrus fruits—especially oranges and lemons.

To extract the juice from berries, heat them gently in a saucepan until their juice flows out; then drain the juice from the fruit through a fine-meshed sieve, discarding the pulp *(page 22, Step 1)*. Citrus juice, squeezed by hand or with a juice extractor, may be strained similarly to remove pulp; or it can be used as it is to make candies that are opaque and deeper in color.

Once the juice is ready, sugar and corn syrup are dissolved in it. The next step is to add the gelatin, which sets the confections and gives them a chewy texture. The gelatin must first be soaked in cold water to soften its granules so that they will dissolve easily in the sugared juice.

By following this procedure, you can make either simple jellies in single flavors or—with a little extra effort—layered combinations of two or more flavors, exemplified by the orange and raspberry jellies demonstrated here *(recipe, page 130)*. For layered creations, one jelly is allowed to set and then another, warm jelly is poured on top; the warmth of the second jelly melts the top of the first, binding the layers together.

Either type of jelly can be molded in a pan to form a single slab that can be cut up once it is set. Or the liquid can be poured into small, individual molds. As the jelly sets, a slight skin forms on its surface; this skin prevents it from absorbing moisture from the air and thus keeps it firm and intact.

Once they are set and unmolded, the jellies should be kept in a cool, dry place —not the refrigerator—and served as soon as possible. The skin on the jellies will begin to toughen after about 24 hours; however, a light coating of sugar will help keep them a few days longer.

1 Sweetening juices. Extract and measure separately the juice of oranges and raspberries. Soften powdered gelatin— 4 tablespoons [60 ml.] for every ⅔ cup [150 ml.] of juice. Put sugar and corn syrup—6 tablespoons [90 ml.] each for every ⅔ cup of juice—in a nonreactive pan. Add the raspberry juice.

2 Adding the gelatin. Set the pan over low heat; stir frequently with a wooden spoon until the sugar has dissolved completely. With the pan still on the heat, add half of the soaked gelatin *(above)*.

5 Adding the second layer. Take the pan from the heat; let the orange mixture cool for 10 minutes. Touch the jelly in the baking pan to make sure it can support another layer. Then pour in the orange mixture in a thin, even stream. Let the layered jelly rest for at least six hours in a cool place to set.

6 Unmolding the jelly. To loosen the jelly from the pan, run the tip of a small knife along the inside edges. Invert the pan over a cool, level cutting surface. The jelly should slip out easily, but if it sticks, flex the pan slightly to release it, or quickly wipe the bottom of the pan with a hot, damp towel.

3 **Pouring the first layer.** Stir the contents of the pan until the gelatin dissolves and the liquid is clear. A little scum may form on the surface; the scum should be removed with a skimmer. Dampen a baking pan *(page 18)* and set it on a cool surface. Pour the hot raspberry mixture into the prepared pan. Let the jelly rest undisturbed for a few hours at room temperature until it has set.

4 **Making the second jelly.** In a small saucepan, put sugar, corn syrup and the orange juice. Set the pan over low heat and stir the mixture often until the sugar has dissolved. Add the remaining gelatin and stir until the gelatin dissolves and the liquid is clear.

7 **Cutting cubes.** With a heavy, sharp knife, cut the jelly into strips about ¾ inch [2 cm.] wide; then cut across the strips to form squares *(above)*. Serve the jellies plain *(right)* or coat them with sugar.

Impregnating Fruit with Sugar

When fruits are saturated with syrup, sugar replaces their moisture and gives them a firm texture, intense sweetness and excellent keeping properties (recipes, pages 132-133). This transformation must be brought about gradually. A sudden exposure to high concentrations of sugar would dry and shrivel the fruits. To ensure that they retain their shape and tenderness, they are left for two weeks in a syrup whose concentration of sugar is increased periodically. After the fruits are impregnated with sugar, they are dried out so that they will keep.

Fruits to be candied should be firm-fleshed ones such as the pineapple in the demonstration at right; plums, apricots, peaches, cherries, apples and pears can be treated in the same way. Strawberries, raspberries and other delicate fruits would disintegrate during the prolonged soaking. Any fruits used should be ripe but not yet turning soft.

Large fruits such as pears or pineapple are peeled and sectioned into sizes easy to eat with the fingers; smaller ones are often candied whole. Any fruits left intact should be pricked all over to help the sugar penetrate.

All fruits should first be poached in water to soften them so that they absorb the sugar readily. Large fruits need about 15 minutes of cooking; smaller fruits such as cherries require four minutes at most. The cooking water is then combined with sugar to make the syrup used for steeping the fruit. Part of the sugar in the syrup may be replaced by corn syrup, which is absorbed more easily than sugar and thus helps to prevent wrinkling.

Almost every day for 10 days, the syrup is concentrated, either by the addition of more sugar—as here—or by reduction, and poured back over the fruit. After four more days of immersion, the fruit is lifted out and dried. It is important not to hurry the drying process, lest the fruit shrivel. Dry the fruit in a gas oven heated only by its pilot light, or place it near a radiator or sunny window.

Once dried, the fruit is ready to eat. Or you can alter its appearance by dipping it in hot water to make its surfaces sticky, then rolling it in sugar or glazing it with syrup (page 52).

1 **Preparing the pineapple.** With a sharp knife, cut off the top and base of a pineapple. Slice off the hard skin and cut out any bits of skin embedded in the flesh. Slice the pineapple crosswise into disks about ½ inch [1 cm.] thick. Using a small cookie cutter or a small, sharp knife, remove the tough core of each disk (above).

2 **Cooking the fruit.** Weigh the fruit and place it in a large pan. For every pound [½ kg.] of fruit, add 1¼ cups [30 ml.] of water. Cook the pineapple over medium heat until it is just tender—about 15 minutes. Set a stainless-steel rack over a tray. With a slotted spatula, transfer the fruit to the rack to drain. Reserve the cooking liquid.

6 **Concentrating the syrup.** For every 1¼ cups [300 ml.] of syrup, add ¼ cup [50 ml.] of sugar. Set the pan over medium heat and bring the syrup to a boil. Transfer the drained fruit from the rack to the steeping dish. Pour the syrup over the fruit. Cover with parchment or wax paper and let the fruit steep for another 24 hours.

7 **Increasing concentration.** On each of the next five days, repeat Steps 5 and 6. Repeat the steps on the eighth day, but add ⅓ cup [75 ml.] of sugar for every 1¼ cups [300 ml.] of syrup. Then let the fruit steep for 48 hours. On the tenth day, again add ⅓ cup of sugar for every 1¼ cups of syrup. Bring the syrup to a boil and pour it over the fruit.

3 **Making the syrup.** For every 1¼ cups [300 ml.] of the reserved cooking liquid, measure ¾ cup [175 ml.] of sugar or use ½ cup [125 ml.] of corn syrup and ¼ cup [50 ml.] of sugar. Put the sugar in the pan with the cooking liquid; add the corn syrup, if using. Set the pan over medium heat. Stir continuously until the sugar dissolves.

4 **Immersing the fruit.** Place the fruit in a large, shallow, nonreactive dish. Bring the syrup to a boil and then remove the pan from the heat. Pour the hot syrup over the fruit, submerging it. Press a sheet of parchment or wax paper on top of the syrup to keep the fruit submerged. Let the fruit steep undisturbed for 24 hours.

5 **Draining excess syrup.** The next day, remove the paper from the syrup. With a slotted spatula, lift the fruit from the syrup and drain it on a stainless-steel rack set over a tray. Measure the syrup in the steeping dish and the tray and pour it into a heavy pan.

8 **Drying the fruit.** Cover the fruit with parchment or wax paper and steep it for four more days. Then use a slotted spatula to transfer the fruit from the syrup to a stainless-steel rack set over a tray. Put the tray in an oven heated only by a pilot light for at least four hours—or in a warm, dry room for about three days—to dry the fruit.

9 **Serving candied fruit.** Cut the slices of dried pineapple into segments and serve them in a clear dish that will display their color. Or coat the fruit as demonstrated overleaf. To store candied fruit, place it in layers between sheets of parchment or wax paper in an airtight container. The fruit will keep indefinitely.

A Dry, Glittering Coat

1 **Softening candied fruit.** Bring water to a boil in a pan. Remove the pan from the heat. A few pieces at a time, place the candied fruit—here, pineapple segments—on a perforated spoon, and lower it into the hot water for a second to melt its surfaces. Hold the fruit over the pan to drain excess water.

2 **Coating the fruit.** Put superfine sugar in a shallow bowl. A few pieces at a time, roll the moistened fruit segments in the sugar until they are evenly coated. Cover a tray with parchment or wax paper and place the coated fruit pieces on the tray.

3 **Serving sugared fruit.** Let the fruit pieces dry overnight at room temperature until the sugar coating is firm. Transfer the pieces of fruit to a plate for serving.

A Smooth Glacé Finish

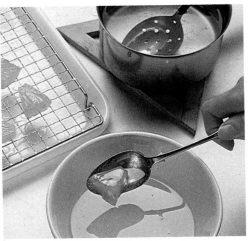

1 **Moistening candied fruit.** Make a syrup by bringing to a boil ⅔ cup [150 ml.] of water and 2 cups [½ liter] of sugar. Pour some of the syrup into a bowl; reserve the rest. Dip the candied fruit in hot water to soften the surfaces, then drain it over the pan.

2 **Dipping the fruit in syrup.** One piece at a time, quickly dip the drained fruit pieces in the syrup, then place the fruit on a stainless-steel rack set over a tray to drain. When the syrup in the bowl becomes cloudy, replace it with a fresh supply from the pan of reserved syrup.

3 **Serving the fruit.** Allow the segments of fruit to drain until their surfaces have dried; this will take about 24 hours at room temperature. They are then ready to be served.

Citrus Peels Simmered in Syrup

The flesh of citrus fruits such as grapefruit, oranges, lemons and limes is too fragile to be successfully candied in sugar syrup, but the peels can be candied (recipe, page 132) to make bright-colored garnishes for other confections or flavorings for nut or chocolate pastes. The candied peels also can be served in their own right, either as they are or coated with chocolate (recipe, page 161).

Few preliminaries are necessary for candying peel. To slice it from the fruit, use a vegetable peeler or a very sharp knife, making shallow cuts that remove the peel but leave behind the bitter white pith. The peel itself often contains bitter flavors, and these must be drawn out by brief simmering in water (Step 2, right), which also softens the peel.

After these steps, you can, if you wish, candy the peel by the method used for whole fruit (pages 50-51), but citrus peel is so sturdy that this scrupulous time-consuming process is unnecessary. Instead, you can simply simmer the peel in sugar syrup for three hours, then dry it.

1 Peeling fruit. Slice off the top and the bottom of the fruit—oranges are shown here. Cut the peel from the fruit in spirals, using a sharp knife to obtain thin slices of peel with no pith attached.

2 Softening the peel. Bring water to a boil in a pan, add the peel and simmer it for about three minutes, until soft. Use a skimmer to transfer the peel to a bowl of cold water to rinse it (above). Repeat this process twice, changing the water in both the pan and the bowl each time. Drain the peel well.

3 Candying the peel. Prepare a syrup from sugar, corn syrup and water (pages 8-11). Bring the syrup to a boil, add the drained peel and cook at a bare simmer for three hours. Using a fork, transfer the peel to a rack set over a plate (above). Place the rack in a gas oven heated only by its pilot light; the peel will be dry enough to serve (right) in approximately three hours.

3
Nut and Chocolate Pastes
Binding Diverse Ingredients

Among the least difficult and most rewarding candies to make at home are those based on nut or chocolate pastes. The preparation of the pastes requires nothing more than binding ground nuts or melted chocolate with liquid or fat. Such amalgams are valued both for their luxurious texture and because they can be readily molded into different shapes.

For nut pastes, egg is the essential binding and moistening element; egg white serves most often, but egg yolks or whole eggs are also used. The simplest nut pastes are made by kneading ground nuts with sugar and egg. A smoother, more pliable paste is made by cooking the mixture. One method is to cook the nuts with the sugar until the sugar melts; when this mixture has set, it is ground up and bound with egg white. Alternatively, you can use a soft-ball syrup in place of sugar and briefly cook the syrup, nuts and egg together *(pages 58-59)*. Cooked pastes made from ground almonds are known as marzipan.

Nut pastes are an excellent modeling material. Uncooked pastes can be rolled out and cut or stamped into simple shapes. Cooked pastes, with their greater cohesiveness, offer further possibilities. Differently colored and flavored sheets of paste may be stacked, bound with egg white and sliced into gaily striped bricks *(opposite)*. If the bound sheets are cut and restacked, checkered designs result; if they are rolled into a cylinder, bull's-eyes are produced *(page 60)*. Miniature fruits, vegetables and animals can be fashioned from differently colored cooked pastes and decorated with chopped pistachios or slivered almonds. For a different texture and appearance, you can coat any nut-paste confection with a sparkling film of sugar crystals or bake it to make it crisp *(pages 62-63)*, then glaze it with icing.

For a chocolate paste, butter, cream or milk is incorporated into the melted chocolate. Chocolate pastes are too soft and too easily melted to be handled much, and they cannot be formed into such elaborate designs as nut pastes. But you can make spheres or logs by rolling the paste between your palms, or you can create a variety of swirled shapes by piping the mixture from a pastry bag fitted with a plain or decorative tip. For added variety, the candies can be finished in different ways—dusted with confectioners' sugar or cocoa powder, for example, coated with chopped nuts or enclosed in a nut paste.

long block of pastel-striped
arzipan is sliced to make individual
andies *(pages 58-59)*. Rolled-out
heets of marzipan, two left uncolored,
vo colored pink, have been stacked,
ound with egg white and cut into strips
o make this patterned confection.

A Simple Nut Mixture That Needs No Cooking

The simplest nut pastes are uncooked mixtures of ground nuts, sugar and egg. These ingredients can be varied to yield pastes with different tastes and textures, and the pastes can be flavored.

Pastes may be formed from any type of nuts, used alone or in combination with another type. The paste shown here, for example, contains almonds and hazelnuts *(recipe, page 166)*. The nuts must be peeled *(pages 12-13)*, and chestnuts must be cooked, first briefly to loosen their shells and skins, then at greater length to soften their flesh. Before the first cooking, slit a cross in the flat surface of each chestnut. Boil the nuts for 10 minutes, drain them and peel off the tough shell and the bitter skin. Simmer the nuts for 40 minutes more, until tender.

The prepared nuts are ground fine— or, in the case of chestnuts, puréed. They are then mixed with sugar—at least an equal volume or, for a sweeter paste, up to twice that. The sugar affects the texture of the paste. Confectioners' sugar, used here, yields a smooth paste; granulated sugars make a grainier product. Brown sugar produces a dark, rich paste, but its taste will mask the flavors of most nuts; use it only with strong-flavored nuts such as walnuts or chestnuts.

Once the nuts and sugar are combined, they are bound with egg. Egg whites alone produce a light, mild paste; yolks alone yield a denser, richer paste; whole eggs balance the extremes.

The paste is kneaded to make it smooth and homogeneous. At this point, it can be used as is or it can be enclosed in plastic wrap or foil and stored for later use; if made with egg whites it will keep for three weeks in the refrigerator or for six months in the freezer. If it includes yolks, the storage times are one week and two months, respectively.

Before you shape the paste into candies you can knead flavorings into it. Here, candied orange peel and orange liqueur are used; grated fresh lemon peel, brandy, cocoa powder and coffee all are suitable. Any flavoring should be used in small amounts: The subtle taste of the nuts can easily be overshadowed.

To form the candies, shape the paste into small balls or roll it out and cut it.

1 **Mixing nuts and sugar.** Blanch and peel almonds and grind them to a fine meal in a food processor *(page 12)*. Lightly toast an equal quantity of hazelnuts and rub off their skins; grind the nuts. In a large bowl, mix together the ground almonds and hazelnuts with a quantity of sifted confectioners' sugar equal to their combined volume *(above)*.

2 **Adding egg white.** In a small bowl, lightly beat egg whites until they begin to foam. A little at a time, stir the whites into the nuts and sugar, using just enough to make them cohere.

6 **Rolling out the paste.** With your hands, mix in the candied peel and liqueur and knead the paste lightly. If the liqueur has made the paste wet and sticky, work in a little additional confectioners' sugar. Dust a rolling pin with confectioners' sugar to prevent it from sticking, and roll out the paste to a thickness of about ¼ inch [6 mm.].

7 **Cutting out shapes.** Dip a small cutter—an aspic or truffle cutter, for instance—into confectioners' sugar to coat its cutting edge. Cut the paste into individual candies, leaving them on the marble surface. After each cut, dip the cutter into confectioners' sugar to prevent sticking and to ensure that the finished confections have neat edges.

3 **Combining ingredients.** With one hand, gently work the mixture together. If it feels dry and mealy, add a little more egg white to moisten it—the amount of egg white needed will vary with the moistness of the nuts. Continue to work the mixture until it forms a thick paste.

4 **Gathering up the paste.** Knead the paste lightly *(page 30, Step 3)* until it pulls away from the bowl in a mass, leaving the sides clean. Do not overwork the paste; you might draw out too much oil from the nuts and make the paste greasy. With your hands, gather up the paste.

5 **Adding flavoring.** Lightly dust a cool work surface—here, marble—with confectioners' sugar and set the paste on it. Flatten the paste slightly with your hands and sprinkle it with a little orange-flavored liqueur. Chop candied orange peel *(page 53)* and scatter it over the flattened paste.

8 **Serving.** Cut candied orange peel into small wedges and lightly press one into the center of each piece of paste *(above)*. Put the candies on a rack and let them stand at room temperature for about one hour to firm slightly. Serve the candies the same day *(right)* or store them in an airtight container.

Marzipan: A Cooked Almond Paste

Cooked nut pastes—the most famous being almond-based marzipan *(right; recipe, page 148)*—are made, like uncooked ones *(pages 56-57)*, from ground nuts, sugar and eggs. Heat, however, gives these pastes a distinctive texture—satiny, firm and very pliable. Sugar receives the first application of heat: It is boiled with water to form a syrup. Next, ground nuts and egg are cooked briefly in the syrup. During this time, the egg whites coagulate, firming the paste. The mixture will become even firmer as it cools and the syrup in it hardens.

The cooled paste is kneaded to make it smooth. It then may be enclosed in plastic wrap or foil and refrigerated for as long as six weeks or frozen for as long as six months. Or you can make candy immediately by coloring, flavoring and shaping the paste.

Any of the colorings or flavorings described on pages 56-57 will serve. If you wish, divide a batch of paste into portions and knead different colorings and flavorings into each portion. Confections may combine two, three or even four different-colored portions of the paste, but to avoid a confusion of tastes, use no more than two flavorings in any one confection.

Because of their cohesiveness and pliability, cooked nut pastes are the best mediums in candymaking for fanciful shaping. Miniature fruits or vegetables can be formed from them, or differently colored batches of paste can be rolled into sheets, which are stuck together with egg white, then cut to yield simple confections such as the small striped sandwiches shown here.

On pages 60-61, two designs of greater complexity are shown. In the top demonstration, different-colored sheets of marzipan are stacked, cut, then restacked and recut to yield checkerboard patterns. In the bottom demonstration, two sheets of marzipan are rolled around a colored cylinder so that when the roll is sliced bull's-eye patterns are revealed.

If you plan to eat any cooked nut-paste candy the same day, let it dry and firm at room temperature for at least an hour. It should be dried overnight if you plan to coat it as described on pages 62-63. To store the candies, put them in an airtight container between layers of wax paper.

1 **Cooking the syrup.** Blanch and peel almonds and grind them fine *(page 12)*. Cook a sugar syrup to the soft-ball stage *(pages 10-11)*, then dip the pan in ice water to arrest cooking. Stir the syrup for a moment until it clouds; the crystallization thus induced makes the candy mildly chewy. Add the almonds.

2 **Blending the ingredients.** With a wooden spoon, stir the almonds into the syrup until they are well blended and the mixture forms a loose paste. Stir in lightly beaten egg whites.

6 **Rolling the marzipan.** Color the remaining portions. Here, one ball has been colored green with spinach extract, one yellow with saffron and one has been left uncolored. Dust a rolling pin with confectioners' sugar and roll out the balls of marzipan into rectangles about ¼ inch [6 mm.] thick.

7 **Stacking.** Brush the coffee-colored sheet with beaten egg white. Lay the green sheet on top *(above)* and brush it, too, with egg white. Do the same with the uncolored sheet. Add the yellow sheet but do not brush it. With a rolling pin, lightly roll over the stack to press the layers together.

3 **Cooking the marzipan.** Set the pan over low heat and, with the spoon, blend the egg whites thoroughly into the paste. Continue to stir for several minutes, until the paste thickens. Remove the pan from the heat. Lightly sprinkle a cold work surface with confectioners' sugar.

4 **Kneading.** Spoon the marzipan onto the work surface; spread it with your hands and turn it over a few times. When it is cold and firm, dust your hands with confectioners' sugar and gather the marzipan into a ball. Knead it gently *(page 30, Step 3)* until it is smooth— about five minutes.

5 **Coloring.** Prepare flavorings and colorings. Separate the marzipan into as many portions as you have colors. Flatten a portion and spoon a coloring or flavoring—such as the strong black coffee used here—into it. Knead the marzipan until it is evenly colored, then shape it into a ball.

8 **Cutting.** To make a neat shape, cut away the uneven edges of the marzipan. If you like, divide the trimmings into small pieces and roll them between your palms to make balls. With a long, sharp knife, cut the rectangle lengthwise into equal-sized strips *(above)*.

9 **Finishing the candies.** Slice across the strips at ½-inch [1-cm.] intervals *(inset)*. Line a tray with wax paper; put the candies on it. Brush off any clinging confectioners' sugar. Let the candies dry, uncovered, for at least an hour. Serve them piled in a dish.

A Complex Checkerboard Design

1 **Coloring marzipan.** Make marzipan (*pages 58-59*) and halve it. Color one half—in this case, with spinach extract (*pages 14-15*). Sprinkle a work surface with confectioners' sugar; roll each half into a rectangle about ¼ inch [6 mm.] thick. Brush one rectangle with beaten egg white; lay the second on top.

2 **Cutting wide strips.** Dust a rolling pin with confectioners' sugar and roll it over the marzipan. Trim off the uneven edges. With a long, sharp knife, cut the layered rectangle lengthwise into three strips of equal width.

3 **Stacking the strips.** Brush the top of one strip with lightly beaten egg white. Place another strip on top, aligning the edges carefully. Brush its upper surface with egg white and add the third strip to the stack.

Concentric Circles of Color

1 **Rolling a center.** Make marzipan (*pages 58-59*) and divide it into two portions, one twice the size of the other. Dust a work surface with confectioners' sugar. Knead coloring—red food coloring was used here—into the larger portion and divide it in half. With your palms, roll out one pink portion into a long cylinder.

2 **Enclosing the center.** Roll the other portions into narrow rectangles the length of the pink cylinder; roll the pink sheet slightly thinner and wider than the uncolored sheet. Brush the uncolored sheet with egg white and place the pink cylinder at one long edge. Roll the uncolored sheet around the pink cylinder and trim off any overlap.

3 **Cutting the roll.** In the same way, roll the pink sheet around the cylinder; cut off any overlap. Trim the ends, then slice across the cylinder at ½-inch [1-cm.] intervals. Line a tray with wax paper and put the slices on the tray. When the marzipan has hardened and dried slightly—after at least an hour—the candies are ready to eat.

4 **Cutting narrow strips.** Roll the sugar-dusted rolling pin over the stack. Then cut the long marzipan sandwich lengthwise into four narrow strips.

5 **Alternating the colors.** Lay one strip flat and brush it with egg white. Turn another strip over so that its uncolored stripes will be aligned with the green stripes of the lower strip, and set it in place. Brush the upper strip with egg white. Stack the remaining strips in the same way, alternating colors.

6 **Cutting the checkerboards.** Roll over the top of the stack lightly with the sugar-dusted rolling pin. To make checkerboards, cut across the block of marzipan at ¼-inch [6-mm.] intervals.

7 **Serving the marzipan.** Line a tray with wax paper. Put the checkerboards on the tray and let them dry for at least an hour. To serve the candies, arrange them on a dish to show off their checkerboard design *(left)*.

Appealing Finishes for Nut Pastes

By applying different finishes, you can give any sort of nut-paste candies decorative guises and quite unexpected textures. If you steep pieces of paste in a sugar syrup, they will acquire a fine, sparkling coat *(right)* and remain moist inside. For a drier texture and delicately browned edges, you can bake the candies *(below; recipes, pages 147 and 148)*.

Candies that are to be submerged in syrup should be made a day in advance; they will then be dry and firm enough to keep their shape in the syrup. You can steep the candies for as long a time as you wish; the usual period is eight to 10 hours. The longer you leave them in the syrup, the thicker the coating will be.

The texture of baked nut paste will vary according to oven temperature and baking time. Brief baking in a hot oven will crisp the outside and leave the inside moist and chewy. Longer baking in a cooler oven will crisp the candies' interiors as well. For a crunchy surface, brush them with confectioners' sugar halfway through baking.

A Fine Coating of Sugar Crystals

1 Preparing the syrup. Boil sugar syrup *(pages 8-11)* to a temperature of 222° F. [105° C.], then dip the bottom of the pan in ice water to arrest cooking. Cover the pan to prevent the syrup from thickening because of evaporation. Let the syrup cool completely; this will take about six hours.

2 Pouring the syrup. Arrange the candies—here, two-tone marzipan sandwiches *(pages 58-59)*—in one l... in a shallow pan. Cover them with th... cold syrup, keeping them separate. P... a sheet of parchment or wax paper ... them to keep them submerged. Let th... steep for about eight hours.

A Crisp Surface from Baking

1 Cutting shapes. Make a nut paste—marzipan *(pages 58-59)* is shown. Line a baking sheet with parchment paper. Roll out the paste ¼ inch [6 mm.] thick. With a knife or cookie cutter dipped in confectioners' sugar, cut out shapes; place them on the baking sheet. Gather any scraps into a ball, and roll and cut it.

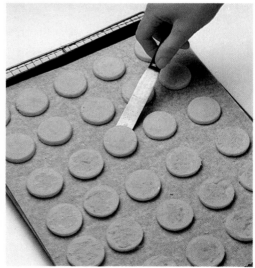

2 Baking the candies. Put the candies in an oven preheated to 400° F. [200° C.]. After five minutes, remove them from the oven; let them cool for two to three minutes, until the upper surfaces are no longer sticky. Using a small spatula, turn the candies over.

3 Decorating the tops. Holding each candy steady with one hand, ... holes all over its surface with a fork' tines or, as here, gently drag the tin... across the surface to score lines.

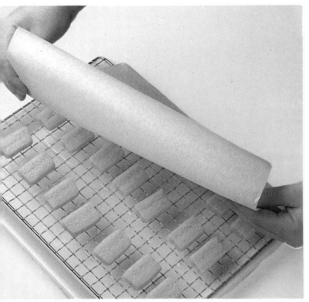

3 **Draining.** Place a wire rack on a tray lined with parchment paper. Put the candies on the rack; cover them with paper *(above)*. Let them dry for a few hours, turning them occasionally. When they are dry, serve them *(right)* or store them in an airtight container between layers of wax paper.

4 **Glazing the candies.** Combine confectioners' sugar with enough cold water to form a liquid glaze that is thin enough to drip easily from a spoon. Use a pastry brush to coat the surface of each candy. Return the candies to the oven for five to 10 minutes, until they are golden brown around the edges.

5 **Cooling and serving.** Remove the candies from the oven and let them cool for 10 minutes on the baking sheet to firm them. With a spatula, transfer the candies to a wire rack to cool completely. Serve the candies as soon as they are cool, or store them in an airtight container between layers of wax paper.

A Chocolate Mixture Softened with Butter

Combining melted chocolate with butter and sugar produces a thick paste that can be shaped into delectable confections *(recipes, pages 150-155)*. The first step in making the paste is to soften the butter and mix it with the sweetener and a flavoring. In addition to sweetening the paste, the sugar component can alter its flavor or texture. Honey and brown sugar add their own particular tastes; superfine sugar, confectioners' sugar, fondant and sugar syrup provide only sweetness. Syrups give the paste smoothness; uncooked sugars contribute a grainy edge.

The flavorings used in chocolate pastes should be strong-tasting ingredients that can hold their own with the richness of the chocolate and fat. Concentrated extracts and oils such as vanilla and peppermint are good flavorings, as are strong black coffee, brandy, sherry, whiskey and flavored liqueurs. Liquid flavorings must be added in small quantities that will not overdilute the paste.

Any chocolate can be used in these pastes. Whatever type you choose, melt the chocolate with care. Chocolate melted over direct heat—even at the gentlest setting—may scorch. It is safest to melt chocolate slowly, in a bowl or pan set over hot water. Once melted, the chocolate should be cooled to room temperature before you combine it with the remaining ingredients: Hot chocolate would melt the flavored-and-sweetened butter.

While the paste is still fairly soft, you can use a pastry bag to pipe it in swirls into foil cases *(Steps 6 and 7)* or in small free-form shapes on a lightly oiled baking sheet. Alternatively, you can chill the paste to firm it, then mold it into balls by hand, as shown on pages 66-67, or shape it into a cylinder and slice it into disks. Once the candies have set, they should be covered and stored in the refrigerator, where they will keep safely for as long as two weeks.

1 **Mixing butter and sugar.** Put chilled butter in a bowl. Using a wooden spoon, mash the butter against the bowl; when it becomes supple, beat it until it is creamy. Gradually stir in sugar—confectioners' sugar is shown. Beat the ingredients together.

2 **Adding flavorings.** Add the liquid flavorings to the butter-and-sugar mixture. In this case, strong black coffee and rum are used. Stir the mixture thoroughly to incorporate the flavorings

5 **Stirring the paste.** Vigorously stir the melted chocolate into the butter-and-sugar mixture until the ingredients are thoroughly blended. Continue to stir the paste until it is thick and firm.

6 **Filling a piping bag.** Fit a pastry bag with a decorative tube—here, a star tube—and fold down the top of the bag. Hold the bag over the bowl. Spoon the paste into the bag, squeezing each addition toward the tube, until the bag is filled up to the fold. Unfold the bag and twist it closed.

3 **Melting chocolate.** Put chocolate pieces—semisweet chocolate is used here—into a small pan. In a larger pan, bring water to a boil; take the pan off the heat. Place the small pan in the larger—its base should not touch the water. Stir the chocolate until it melts.

4 **Incorporating the chocolate.** Remove the smaller pan and let the melted chocolate cool and thicken for about five minutes. Stir the chocolate occasionally so that it cools evenly. Pour and scrape the chocolate into the bowl of butter and sugar.

7 **Piping the paste.** Pipe the paste into small foil cases until each is about two thirds full. Swirl more paste on top to finish each chocolate in a spiral. Let the candies cool at room temperature for a few hours or in the refrigerator for about 30 minutes. Serve the chocolates at room temperature.

Truffles: Chocolate-and-Cream Confections

The lightest, freshest-tasting chocolate pastes are made with cream and melted chocolate *(recipes, pages 152, 154-155)*. Such pastes may be formed by stirring warmed cream into melted chocolate or by melting grated chocolate in cream. When the ingredients blend and cool, you can add a flavoring *(pages 64-65)*. Then whisk the paste to make it fluffy.

These pastes may be piped from a pastry bag to produce fancy shapes *(pages 64-65)* or molded by hand into balls—called truffles because of their resemblance to the prized fungi. If you choose the latter approach, chill the paste until it becomes firm. A protective coating of cocoa powder will help prevent melting of the paste during molding: Spoon the chilled paste onto the powder, then roll the truffles with your fingers.

If you like, add a further coating of grated chocolate, confectioners' sugar or chopped nuts, or dip the truffles in melted chocolate *(pages 74-75)*. Store them in the refrigerator and eat them within a few days, while they are fresh.

1 **Melting chocolate.** Break chocolate—semisweet chocolate is shown—into a heatproof bowl. Set the bowl over a pan filled with hot—not boiling—water. With a wooden spoon, stir occasionally as the chocolate melts. When the chocolate is smooth, lift the bowl out of the pan.

2 **Adding cream.** Warm heavy cream over low heat until it is tepid. Trickle the cream into the melted chocolate, stirring constantly to incorporate the cream smoothly. Let the mixture cool to room temperature.

5 **Forming truffles.** Sift a generous layer of cocoa powder onto a tray or baking sheet. Using a small spoon, scoop up walnut-sized pieces of the chilled paste and, with another spoon, push the lumps of paste onto the cocoa powder *(above, left)*. Dust your finger tips with some of the cocoa powder and quickly roll each lump between your fingers to form a ball *(right)*.

3 **Flavoring the mixture.** Add a little flavoring to the paste. Here, a spoonful of brandy is used, but you could substitute rum or a liqueur. With the wooden spoon, stir in the flavoring.

4 **Whisking the paste.** Steady the bowl with one hand and vigorously whisk the paste *(above, left)*. Continue whisking until the paste becomes fluffy, lightens in color and holds soft peaks when the whisk is lifted above the bowl *(right)*—the paste should reach this stage after about five minutes of whisking. Remove any paste that clings to the whisk. Place the bowl in the refrigerator and chill the paste until it thickens and is firm enough to shape by hand—approximately five to 10 minutes.

5 **Coating the truffles.** Fill separate bowls with grated chocolate, finely chopped nuts—walnuts, in this case—and confectioners' sugar. Hold each truffle in one hand and, with your free hand, apply a coating of chocolate, nuts or sugar *(above)*. Put the truffle in a paper case. Arrange the coated candies on a dish and serve *(right)*.

4
Dipping and Molding
A Choice of Splendid Finishes

Molded in two pieces that have been joined, a chocolate Easter egg (pages 84-85) is carefully balanced on finger tips and thumb to be decorated. The decoration (pages 16-17) will cover the seam between the two halves, leaving the rest of the glossy surface of the egg untouched.

Confectionery's sweetest rewards await the cook who acquires skill in handling a bath of molten sugar or chocolate. Dipped into the warm liquid, fruits, nuts or ready-made confections emerge with a thin, smooth coating that—once set—becomes an integral part of the candy. The chief gains from dipping are contrasts of texture and flavor, but the coating also serves to protect the candy. A chocolate coating, for example, keeps caramels from being damaged by humidity (pages 36-37), and provides a strong encasement for the fragile sugar walls and liquid center of a liqueur chocolate (pages 80-83). Furthermore, a coating will help unify a confection whose center is made up of different elements.

For dipping, you can use hard-crack syrup, caramel, fondant, or either of two types of chocolate coating. Whatever dipping medium you choose, the principles of dipping are the same. The medium should be melted to a completely smooth fluid and, if necessary, kept over a water bath so that it does not solidify during the dipping process. The confections should be dry and firm enough not to disintegrate in the warm liquid: Make soft confections a day ahead so that they can harden.

Use your hands to dip the candy centers if you want to immerse only part of a confection or fruit (pages 70-71) or if you want a rough-textured finish (pages 78-79). Otherwise, dip centers with a table fork or, for greater precision, a dipping fork, which is sold at candymaking-supply stores. Dipping forks come in several styles. The most versatile is the straight-tined variety, which can be used to dip any center and to decorate the tops of the dipped candies. Loop-tipped forks—either round or teardrop-shaped—are designed specifically for dipping round centers.

While molten syrup and fondant rival chocolate as a dipping medium, dipping chocolate and chocolate-flavored coating share a property that makes them uniquely suitable for molding. Poured to coat the inside of a mold, the coatings will shrink as they dry and, once set, can be easily detached from the mold. Separately molded shapes can be welded together with more melted chocolate; two half ovals, for example, were joined to make the Easter egg opposite. On a miniature scale, a foil cup can serve as a mold for chocolate (page 86). The chocolate container formed against the cup's base and sides can be filled with whatever soft center you like, and sealed with a lid of chocolate.

Applying a Lustrous Coat of Fondant

Fondant is not only a delicious candy in its own right *(pages 32-33)*, but may also be melted and used to coat almost any firm candy, including marzipan, caramel and candied fruits. You can even, as in the demonstration at right, coat balls of fondant with additional fondant, using a contrasting color and flavor for the outer layer. Or, as shown below, you can dip fresh fruit into fondant, then coat it with sugar for a frosted effect. Any center you choose should be thoroughly dry before it is dipped: Surface moisture would keep the coating from adhering evenly, spoiling the appearance of the candy.

To melt fondant to coating consistency, warm it slowly over hot—not boiling—water, stirring it constantly. The fondant should have the proper consistency for dipping when its temperature measures about 140° F. [60° C.]. If it is too thick at that point to form an even coat, add a little hot water or other liquid *(page 33)*. Take care not to heat the fondant above 150° F. [66° C.], or it will become brittle rather than pleasantly firm when it sets.

You can coat the entire surface of a candy or fruit center or just part of it. For partial dipping, simply hold the candy or fruit center in your fingers at one end—or hold such fruits as cherries and strawberries by their stems.

Confections that are to be completely coated must be carefully turned in the fondant. To avoid marking the surface, use a table fork or, better still, a straight-tined dipping fork to turn the confection and to lift it out. Do not pierce the center; instead, slide the tip of the fork under it, keeping the tines parallel to the surface of the liquid so that you do not drop the candy. When working with a small quantity of fondant, tilt the bowl to keep its rim out of the way. Let the dipped candy slip from the fork onto wax paper, nudging it with a knife tip if necessary.

The candy can be served as soon as the fondant coating is firm. Stored between sheets of wax paper in a box, fondant balls will keep almost indefinitely; fresh fruit dipped in fondant, however, should be eaten on the day it is dipped.

Covering Fondant Centers

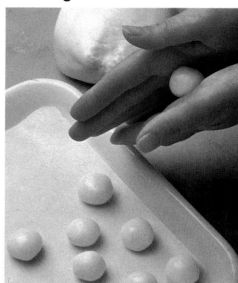

Making fondant balls. Pull small pieces off a slab of fondant *(pages 30-31)* and roll each piece between your hands to form smooth balls. Put the balls on a tray lined with wax paper, and let them rest overnight at room temperature to firm and dry. If the balls flatten, reshape them before dipping.

Partly Dipped Fruits with a Frosted Finish

Dipping fruits. Wash grapes, cherries and strawberries; leave the stems on. Pat the fruits dry. Segment peeled tangerines; do not puncture the surface membranes. Melt fondant. Holding each piece of fruit by its stem or by one end, dip it into the fondant; let the excess fondant drain *(left)*. Dip the fondant-coated area in sugar *(inset)*.

Dipping. Color and flavor melted fondant—here, red food coloring and vanilla extract have been added. Tilt the bowl by bracing it with a towel in its pan of hot water. Drop one fondant ball at a time into the bowl; turn it over with a dipping fork and lift it up *(above)*. Wipe the underside of the fork on the bowl rim, then slip the ball onto wax paper. When the coating is firm—after five to 10 minutes—serve the candies in paper cups *(right)*.

Presenting the fruits. Place the sugar-dipped fruits on a tray lined with wax paper and allow the fondant coating to set and harden completely— five to 10 minutes. Arrange the pieces of dipped fruit—tilted slightly to display their sugared tips—in individual paper cups and serve.

Glossing Confections with Sugar Syrup

Among the various roles sugar syrup *(pages 8-11)* plays in candymaking, one of the prettiest is that of a coating: The syrup, properly handled, endows the candy with a glittering sheen.

With the exceptions of fudge or caramels, whose soft surfaces would melt in the extreme heat of a liquid syrup, any candy can be given a sugar-syrup coating. Nuts or dried fruits frequently are used, alone or in combination with sweet pastes such as marzipan *(pages 56-59)* or fondant *(pages 30-31)*. Two such assemblies are shown on these pages. In the top demonstration, pitted prunes and dates are stuffed with a mixture of fondant and grated coconut *(recipe, page 157)*. At bottom, walnut halves are sandwiched around a flavored and colored marzipan *(recipe, page 164)*.

The combinations of nuts, fruits and fillings can be extensively varied. Dried fruits such as apricots, figs and candied cherries could replace the fruits selected here; flat nut halves such as pecans or split almonds could be substituted for the walnuts. The marzipan is flavored with orange liqueur, but other liqueurs or spirits such as rum or brandy could be chosen instead. If you use liquid flavorings, you may need to add a little confectioners' sugar or other dry ingredient to firm the paste. You may also need to add sugar when using moist, freshly grated coconut to flavor a paste. Dried coconut might make the paste too stiff; in that case, add some water or other liquid.

The sugar syrup used for the coating may be cooked to the hard-crack stage to provide a crystal-clear surface, or to a caramel to form a golden one. In either case, you should guard against the crystallization that occurs as the syrup cools: Make only small batches of syrup at a time and avoid agitation of the syrup.

Sugar syrup is sticky and tends to adhere to dipping implements. To minimize sticking, coat the dipping fork with a clear, mild-flavored oil such as almond oil. When syrup hardens on the fork, wash it in hot water and oil it again before continuing.

A hardened syrup coating will rapidly absorb moisture from the air and become sticky. Syrup-dipped candies should thus be eaten on the day they are made.

A Natural Pocket Filled with Fondant

1 **Preparing a filling.** Place fondant in a mixing bowl. Add freshly grated coconut and knead the mixture until the coconut is fully incorporated. Gather the mixture into a ball.

2 **Filling the fruits.** Pit prunes and dates *(page 46, Step 1)*. For each fruit, pull off a piece of fondant slightly larger than the fruit's pit and roll it into a oval. Pinch open the fruit and insert the fondant into the cavity. Press the fru around the filling.

Walnuts Sandwiched with Marzipan

1 **Preparing a filling.** Select perfect walnut halves. Color marzipan. Make a hollow in the paste and add a flavoring—in this case, a spoonful of orange liqueur. Knead the paste until the flavoring is thoroughly incorporated.

2 **Filling the walnuts.** Pull off small pieces of the marzipan and roll them between your palms to form balls. Take two walnut halves and press a marzipan ball firmly between their flat sides. Continue sandwiching marzipan balls until you have used all the walnuts.

3 **Dipping.** Oil a baking sheet. Cook sugar syrup to the hard-crack stage, then briefly dip the bottom of the pan in ice water to stop the syrup from cooking further. Place the pan on a trivet on a work surface. Drop one filled fruit at a time into the hot syrup; with an oiled fork, gently turn the fruit over to coat it. Lift the fruit on the fork, wiping the underside of the fork on the pan rim to remove drips. Ease the fruit from the fork onto the baking sheet.

4 **Serving.** Let the dipped fruits cool until the syrup coating has hardened—about two hours. Place the fruits in individual paper cups. You can serve the dipped fruits at once or store them for up to eight hours in a cool, dry place.

3 **Dipping and serving.** Cook sugar syrup to a light caramel; dip the pan in ice water and place it on a trivet. Drop the balls one at a time into the syrup, then transfer them with an oiled fork to an oiled baking sheet *(inset)*. Let the balls cool until the syrup hardens—about two hours. Arrange them in paper cups *(right)* and serve.

The Special Demands of Chocolate

Sheathing nuts and candies in chocolate is a classic candymaking procedure. The actual coating technique is the same as for fondant *(pages 70-71)*, but extra care must be taken to ensure that the chocolate coating sets to a firm, glossy finish.

Two products—both are sold in blocks at candymaking-supply stores, and both are available in either semisweet- or milk-chocolate flavors—are specifically manufactured to melt to the thin consistency required for dipping. Chocolate-flavored coating, made from cocoa powder and vegetable fats, is one; the other is dipping chocolate, composed of chocolate liquor enriched with extra cocoa butter.

In some respects, the handling of the two products is identical. Like any chocolate, both coatings must be melted slowly over hot water to prevent burning. During the melting period, the temperatures of the coatings must not exceed 115° F. [46° C.]: A higher temperature would cause the fats in them to set improperly. Similarly, either type of coating can be ruined by moisture: Even a drop of water can thicken an entire batch. To prevent

this, keep dipping utensils absolutely dry; be sure the candies to be dipped are also dry. Nuts should be prepared as shown on pages 12-13. Candy centers such as the marzipan, caramel and fondant used below should be made at least a day in advance so that they can dry out.

In certain other respects, the two coatings are handled differently. To prepare chocolate-flavored coating, simply chop and melt it. When the chocolate passes the pinch test shown in Step 2 at right, it is ready for use. Keep the bowl of coating over warm water to maintain the proper dipping temperature and consistency—90° to 110° F. [32° to 44° C.].

The use of dipping chocolate requires more painstaking preparation because of the cocoa butter it contains. This cocoa butter is made up of stable fat crystals of a type known as beta. When dipping chocolate melts, these microscopic crystals dissolve and, if the melted chocolate is allowed to cool without interference, the fat will recrystallize in two forms— the original beta type and an unstable variety known as alpha. Alpha crystals

will rise to the surface of the chocola[te] when it cools, making unsightly gra[y] streaks. To prevent this, the cocoa butt[er] must be allowed to form only stable be[ta] crystals—a process called tempering.

The first step in tempering is to remo[ve] the dipping chocolate from the heat a[s] soon as it has melted. As the liquid b[e-] gins to cool, the cocoa butter will initial[ly] form stable beta crystals. To ensure tha[t] it continues to do so, stir in more dippin[g] chocolate—unmelted and finely grate[d] *(box, opposite)*. The beta fat crystals i[n] this solid chocolate act as seeds, promp[t-] ing the creation of more beta crystals.

Once dipping chocolate cools to a tem[-] perature between 86° and 90° F. [30° an[d] 32° C.] for semisweet chocolate, or 8[4°] and 88° F. [29° and 31° C.] for milk choco[-] late, the tempering is complete and th[e] chocolate ready to be used. Keep th[e] chocolate over warm water to maintai[n] the proper temperature: If the chocolat[e] cools below 83° F., it will be too thick t[o] form a smooth coating; if the tempera[-] ture rises above 90° F., you will have t[o] retemper the chocolate.

3 **Dipping the centers.** Place a tray of cool, dry candy centers on one side of the bowl of coating; line a second tray with wax paper and place it on the other side of the bowl. Drop one center at a time into the coating; here, a peeled Brazil nut is being dipped. Touch the center lightly with a dry dipping fork to submerge it *(above, left)* and turn it over in the coating. Lift out the coated center, tapping the fork on the bowl's edge *(above, center)* to shake off the excess coating. To remove any last drips, wipe the bottom of the fork on the rim of the bowl *(right)*.

Melting Dipping Chocolate

Tempering. Chop dipping chocolate. Grate a quarter as much dipping chocolate as chopped dipping chocolate. Stir the chopped chocolate in a bowl set over hot water. When the chocolate has melted, set the bowl on a towel to steady it. Add a spoonful of grated chocolate and stir until it melts. Repeat until the chocolate in the bowl cools to dipping temperature.

Melting coating. Place chopped chocolate-flavored coating in a bowl. Then set the bowl over—but not touching—hot water. As the coating begins to melt, stir it frequently with a dry wooden spoon. When it has melted—after about 20 minutes—monitor its temperature periodically with a rapid-response thermometer.

2 **Testing the consistency.** When the coating is completely liquid, pick up a small blob of it between your thumb and forefinger. If it tightens and shrinks away from your finger tips almost immediately, it is ready. If the coating remains liquid for several seconds, take it off the water, let it cool for a few minutes, and repeat the test.

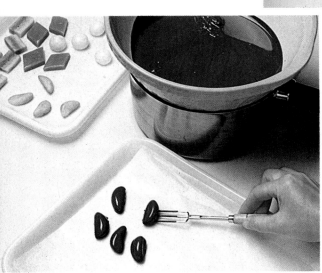

4 **Drying the candy.** Hold the fork over the paper-lined tray and angle it slightly so that the coated candy slides off the fork's tines *(inset)*. Let the candies set—this takes just a few minutes. Then arrange them for serving *(right)*, or place them in individual paper cups and store them in a cool place.

Embellishments for a Chocolate Coating

Surface decoration gives dipped chocolates a professional finish. The decoration could be a nut or a twist of candied citrus peel *(page 53)* pressed into the coating before it dries. You can also make designs in the coating itself while it is still liquid, or add a design of extra chocolate when the coating has dried.

Some of the most elegant decorations are done with the fork used to dip the confection. Lightly touching the newly dipped chocolate with the fork's tines can create parallel ridges *(below, left)* or peaked designs *(opposite)* that neatly finish off straight-sided candies. For rounded candies *(below, right)*, you can use the round or teardrop-shaped ring of a looped dipping fork—or a circle of wire—to make designs that complement the candies' domed shapes.

Instead of impressing a design in a candy you can trail coating over it to form raised patterns. A simple technique suitable to uneven shapes such as Brazil nuts is to apply the additional coating with your finger tip *(bottom, left)*. For a more striking decoration, use a chocolate-flavored coating or dipping chocolate of a contrasting color and pipe it onto the candy. Snip a tiny hole in a small paper piping bag to make fine lines *(bottom, right)*, or thicken the chocolate and attach a nozzle to pipe shells *(pages 16-17)*.

Decorating a straight-sided shape. Using a straight-tined dipping fork, dip three candies *(pages 74-75)*. Wipe the fork and lay the tines on top of the first-dipped candy. Lift the fork slightly and pause so that coating adhering to the tines creates ridges. Draw the fork away, following the ridges. Decorate the other candies, then dip and decorate another batch.

Decorating a round shape. Dip three candies. Lay the ring of a loop-tipped dipping fork on the wet surface of the first-dipped chocolate and raise the ring slightly so that the chocolate forms a circular ridge. Lift the fork off vertically. Decorate the second- and third-dipped candies in turn, then proceed with another batch of three.

Decorating an irregular shape. Dip three candies. To decorate them, dip the tip of a forefinger into the chocolate-flavored coating or dipping chocolate and draw your finger tip along the length of each one; the liquid coating will trail along the surface to form a raised ridge.

Decorating with piped lines. Set dipped candies on wax paper and let the coatings dry. Make a paper piping bag. Spoon prepared chocolate-flavored coating or dipping chocolate of a color that contrasts with the candies into the bag and snip off the end. Pipe lines back and forth over each candy, piping a little beyond the edges with each pass.

Dipping to Unify a Three-Layer Sandwich

Candies constructed of layers of pastes and creams can be given unity and extra visual appeal by a rich coat of chocolate. To form the base for these candies, use mixtures that are firm enough to roll out. Plain marzipan *(pages 58-59)* is the choice in this demonstration, but you could use fondant *(pages 30-31)* or a flavored nut paste *(pages 56-57)*. Confections that are too soft to be rolled out, for example, chocolate-and-cream pastes *(pages 66-67)*, can then be spread on the solid base to form a thick, even layer.

For variety of texture, you can sandwich between the layers a more solid ingredient—such as chopped nuts *(pages 12-13)* or the candied fruit *(pages 50-51)* used here. Once the slab is formed, it can be cut into small shapes and dipped.

To decorate the coated candies, use a dipping fork *(below, right)*, or sprinkle a dry ingredient such as finely chopped nuts or grated chocolate *(pages 16-17)* into the coating before it sets.

1 Pressing in pineapple. Cut candied pineapple into small slivers. Flavor the pineapple with a few drops of liqueur. Dust a marble slab and a rolling pin with confectioners' sugar; roll marzipan into a rectangular shape ¼ inch [6 mm.] thick. Press the slivers of pineapple firmly into the marzipan.

2 Spreading chocolate paste. Make a chocolate paste. This one is prepared from chocolate and fresh cream. With a spatula, spread the paste firmly over the pineapple-studded marzipan to form an even layer. Allow the chocolate paste to harden until it is firm to the touch—about one hour.

3 Cutting into pieces. With a sharp knife, cut the layered sheet into even-sized pieces; square, triangular or diamond shapes are all suitable. Separate the pieces and put them on a tray to allow the cut surfaces to harden.

4 Dipping and decorating. Dip the centers *(pages 74-75)* and decorate them as shown opposite. Or, as here, lay the tines of a dipping fork across the wet surface of the chocolate *(above)*, then move the fork sideways as you lift it from the surface to form peaked ridges. You can serve the confections as soon as the coating has set; the inner layers will remain distinct *(inset)*.

Different Routes to a Rough Finish

Because any chocolate coating closely follows the contours of the surface beneath it, you can produce textured chocolates simply by using rough-surfaced centers. Such candies offer a contrast to smooth cubes or spheres, and are especially welcome in a mixed presentation.

Centers for these confections can be shaped in several ways. Smooth-surfaced centers such as chocolate-cream or fondant balls can be roughened with coatings of chopped nuts or crushed nut brittle *(right)*. Or you can make a center by binding ingredients into clusters with sugar syrup, caramel or chocolate; below, nuts and dried and candied fruits are bound with chocolate.

The textured centers can be dipped in chocolate-flavored coating or in dipping chocolate with a fork in the usual manner *(pages 74-75)*. Or the centers can be dipped into a coating medium that has been allowed to cool and thicken. The coating will set unevenly, thus emphasizing the undulating shape of the center.

Hand-dipping in Extra-thick Chocolate

1 Crushing brittle. Prepare brittle *(pages 34-35)*, using one kind of nut or a combination; here, hazelnuts are chosen. Put a few pieces of brittle at a time into a plastic bag. With a rolling pin, crush the brittle to a coarse powder. Pour the crushed brittle onto a shallow tray and spread it out in an even layer.

2 Shaping truffles. Sift cocoa powder onto a second tray. Take teaspoonfuls of chocolate paste *(pages 64-67)* and, with another spoon, push the paste onto the cocoa. Dust your fingers with cocoa, roll each portion of paste into a ball, pat cocoa on it and place it on the crushed brittle.

Following the Contours of an Uneven Center

1 Assembling ingredients. Melt semisweet chocolate until it is smooth *(pages 16-17)* and remove it from the heat. Put equal quantities of nuts and raisins into a bowl. Finely chop candied orange peel *(page 53)* and add the bits to the nut mixture.

2 Binding with chocolate. Pour the melted chocolate into the nut-and-fruit mixture. Stir the mixture with a wooden spoon to blend the chocolate thoroughly with the rest of the ingredients.

3 Shaping the confections. Line a tray with wax paper. Take teaspoonfuls of the chocolate mixture and, with another teaspoon, push the spoonfuls of mixture onto the wax paper. Place the tray in a cool place until the clusters have completely set—about one hour.

3 **Rolling in brittle.** Pick up some of the crushed brittle. Roll each ball between your fingers, gently patting in brittle. Replace the truffles on the tray of brittle; chill them to firm them but remove the truffles from the refrigerator about 10 minutes before dipping to let their surfaces warm slightly.

4 **Dipping.** Line a tray with wax paper. Melt chocolate-flavored coating and let it cool until it just begins to thicken. Using your fingers, submerge the truffles one at a time in the coating. As you lift out each coated truffle *(above),* trail your finger tips over the surface of the coating to form irregular swirls. Place the truffles on the prepared tray. When the coating has set, place the candies in paper cups *(inset)* and serve.

4 **Dipping and serving.** Line another tray with wax paper. Melt chocolate-flavored coating and use a dipping fork to dip the clusters *(inset).* Slip the candies onto the wax paper to dry, then serve them in paper cups *(right).*

Inducing a Liquid to Form Its Own Container

Encasing a sweet, syrupy liquid in chocolate is one of the most dazzling accomplishments of the confectioner. As demonstrated here and on the next two pages, it is achieved by molding the syrup in such a way that only its surfaces crystallize, forming a thin shell with a liquid core. This delicate parcel can be dipped like any other center.

The molding is done in cornstarch—which has limited absorbency, does not affect taste and permits easy handling of the shells. The starch is placed in a tray and uniform depressions are formed in it with a homemade modeling block made from wood and a modeling compound—oven-firing or self-hardening clay—purchased at an art-supply store (box, below). These hollows are filled with syrup, which is covered with more cornstarch.

The cornstarch, having been dried out in a slow oven, draws a little moisture out of the syrup, concentrating so that it crystallizes readily. But the crystallization process is self-stopping: As the wall of sugar crystals thickens, it eventually

prevents moisture from being drawn out of the syrup, so the interior of the candy center remains liquid.

The syrup for these confections must be prepared with great care. Only a fairly light syrup, cooked to a temperature of 227° F. [108° C.], will produce a fine, even shell. A thick, lumpy shell would result from too concentrated a syrup. Traditionally, the syrup is flavored with a liqueur or, as in the demonstration on these pages, with brandy (recipe, page 160). It is cooled to 120° F. [49° C.] before molding so that it becomes supersaturated (page 8) and ready to crystallize.

When molded syrup begins to form a shell, the top is thinner than the walls and base. To promote even thickening, the centers should be turned. Crystallization is slow: The syrup takes at least 12 hours to develop a shell of an even thickness that can be dipped without cracking. Once they are formed, the finished centers can be given a single coating of chocolate, or dipped two or three times to build up a more protective surface.

1 **Preparing the cornstarch.** Spread thin layers of cornstarch on baking sheets and put the sheets in an oven at its lowest setting; let the cornstarch dry for about an hour. Sift the cornstarch through a fine sieve into a baking pan until it mounds above the pan rim.

A Homemade Modeling Block

1 **Cutting out shapes.** Roll clay into a rectangle ½ inch [1 cm.] thick. Choose an aspic, truffle or cookie cutter slightly larger than you want the finished candies to be, to allow for the clay's shrinkage as it dries. Use the cutter to stamp shapes out of the damp clay.

2 **Smoothing the shapes.** Pick the shapes out of the excess clay and dry them according to the manufacturer's instructions. To smooth the surfaces of the dried clay shapes, rub them lightly on fine-grained sandpaper.

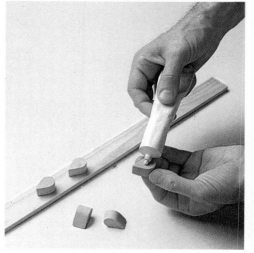

3 **Assembling the block.** Cut a strip of wood 1 inch [2½ cm.] wider than the shapes and 4 inches [10 cm.] longer than the length of your baking pan. Glue the shapes to the wood. Space the shapes about ¾ inch [2 cm.] apart, leaving about 2 inches [5 cm.] clear at each end of the strip of wood.

2 **Leveling the surface.** Make a modeling block (box, opposite). To smooth the cornstarch, push a straight side of the block across the rim of the pan, sweeping the excess over the far edge and creating an absolutely level surface.

3 **Shaping molds.** Press the molded shapes of the modeling block straight down into the cornstarch. Smoothly lift the block up and out of the cornstarch. With a dry pastry brush, dust off any cornstarch that clings to the block. Continue to make rows of molds, leaving a 1½-inch [4-cm.] space between the rows. Very gently, transfer the tray to an oven at its lowest setting. Pile the excess cornstarch into a bowl and put it in the oven, too.

4 **Making a flavored syrup.** In a heavy pan, dissolve sugar and water over medium heat, stirring occasionally. When the sugar has dissolved, put a candy thermometer into the pan, turn up the heat and boil the syrup to a temperature of 227° F. [108° C.]. Dip the pan in ice water and let the syrup cool for five minutes. Add brandy (above) or a liqueur; blend the mixture by pouring it into a clean pan and then back into the first pan. Do not stir the syrup.

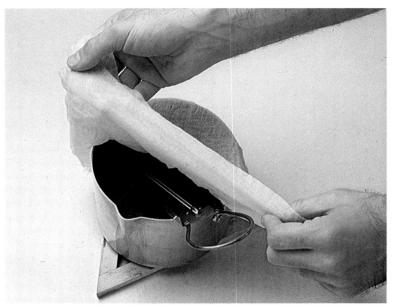

5 **Cooling the syrup.** Return the candy thermometer to the pan. To encourage recondensation of the alcohol that escapes during cooling, drape a damp cloth over the pan. Let the flavored syrup cool until its temperature falls to 120° F. [49° C.]. Lift the cloth every few minutes to check the falling temperature. ▶

6 **Filling a funnel.** Select a funnel with a tube that is narrower at its tip than the molds in the cornstarch. Insert the handle of a wooden spoon into the tube to serve as a stopper. Fill the funnel about half-full with the cooled syrup. Leave any excess syrup in the pan, covered with the cloth, until you need to refill the funnel.

7 **Dispensing the syrup.** Remove the pan of cornstarch from the oven and set it on a work surface. Center the tube of the funnel over a mold and raise the spoon slightly so that the syrup drips slowly into the mold. When the mold is full, push the spoon back into the tube to stop the flow. Fill the other molds.

10 **Removing the centers.** After the centers have set, carefully lift them one by one from the cornstarch with your fingers. Gently dust away any excess cornstarch with a soft pastry brush and put the centers on a plate. If you intend to re-use the cornstarch, sift it, bake it, and sift it again to remove any stray bits of hardened syrup.

11 **Coating with chocolate.** Line a tray with wax paper. Melt chocolate-flavored coating in a bowl set over hot water (pages 74-75). Put a center into the bowl of coating and turn it over with a dipping fork—here, a loop-tipped type. Lift the coated center out of the bowl, wipe the fork against the rim of the bowl to remove excess coating, and set the coated center on the prepared tray. Dip two more centers in the same way.

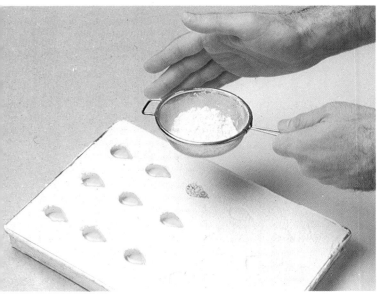

3 **Covering with cornstarch.** Remove the bowl of reserved cornstarch from the oven. Put a portion of the cornstarch into a fine-meshed sieve. Holding the sieve about 2 inches [5 cm.] above the molding bed, tap the sieve gently to sift cornstarch evenly over the whole pan to a depth of about ⅛ inch [3 mm.].

9 **Turning over the centers.** Leave the pan containing the molded centers in a draft-free place for at least 12 hours. To ensure that the shells forming around the centers thicken evenly, gently turn the centers with a spoon or fork after six hours.

2 **Decorating.** Immediately after dipping three centers, decorate them *(page 76).* Here, the dipping loop is pressed against each candy to create a ridge. Continue in this way until all the centers are coated. When the chocolates have set, serve them or store them in a cool place.

Molding a Hollow Easter Egg

Pouring a melted-and-tempered dipping chocolate or a melted chocolate-flavored coating around the inside of two halves of a mold to set will produce identical chocolate shapes. Because chocolate shrinks as it sets, the shapes can easily be lifted from the mold and joined together to form freestanding sculptures.

Molds, which are sold at candymaking-supply stores, are most commonly used to make Easter eggs *(right),* but they also come in other shapes—various animal forms, for instance. Most molds are available in both metal and plastic. The easiest to use are made of transparent plastic, which will enable you to see when the chocolate has shrunk away from the sides. Whatever material you do choose, thoroughly polish the mold's interior before you pour in the coating; the glossier the inside of the mold, the glossier the candy's surface is likely to be.

The amount of coating you need depends on the size of your mold—and not just because of surface area: The larger the confection, the thicker the shell will need to be to withstand unmolding and handling. But coating poured in a single thick layer will not set evenly. To make a strong shell, apply several thin layers of coating to the mold. The 8-inch [20-cm.] Easter egg shown here was made with ¾ pound [350 g.] of chocolate-flavored coating, applied in two layers. For a larger object, three layers might be needed.

After completing each layer, invert the mold onto a flat surface; some of the coating will drain downward to form a sturdy, flat rim. Let each layer of coating set before you add the next. When the chocolate halves are unmolded, the two rims can be joined. If you like, you can fill the molded shape with small candies before you bond the two halves together.

To decorate an Easter egg, fill a piping bag with melted coating, and pipe a design *(pages 16-17)* around the seam at which the two molded halves are joined. If you want to emphasize the decoration, you can use coating of a contrasting color. When stored in a cool place, chocolate shapes will keep indefinitely.

1 Polishing the mold. Hold each half of a metal or plastic mold by its outer edge and use a soft, dry cloth—here, a square of muslin—to polish the inner surface to a high gloss.

2 Spooning in coating. Line a tray with wax paper. Melt chocolate-flavored coating *(pages 74-75)*. Keep the melted chocolate over hot water as you work, stirring it from time to time with a wooden spoon. To coat each half of the mold, support it in your palm and ladle in several spoonfuls of coating.

6 Freeing the edges. When the coating has hardened—this usually takes at least two hours—it will shrink away from the mold halves. Use a plastic scraper to trim dry coating from the outer edge of each mold. Run your thumbnail around the rim between the coating and the mold to free any bits of coating stuck to the mold.

7 Unmolding the chocolate. To detach each half of the chocolate shell from its mold, press down at one side of the chocolate shell's rim until the shell moves slightly in the mold. Place the fingers of one hand inside the shell and, balancing it on your finger tips, lift it free of the mold. Place the shell, rounded side down, on the wax paper.

3 **Coating the mold.** Hold the outer edges of the mold half with both hands. Working quickly so that the coating does not set, tilt the mold and rotate it so that the melted coating runs around the inside, coating it completely.

4 **Tipping out the excess.** Tip the mold to pour any excess coating back into the bowl. When no more drips out, invert the mold on the tray; leave it until the coating is firm. The egg shown here set in 20 minutes, but the time taken will vary according to the thickness of the layer, the mold material, and the heat and humidity of the room.

5 **Spooning in a second layer.** Lift each mold from the wax paper and spoon in sufficient coating to form a second layer. Rotate each mold so that the coating runs around to coat the layer that has already set. Tip the excess coating back into the bowl. Invert the mold and place it on the tray.

8 **Assembling the Easter egg.** Cut out two rectangles of wax paper. Melt chocolate-flavored coating. Using the wax paper, pick up one of the chocolate shells. With a small spatula, spread melted coating around the shell's rim. Use the second piece of wax paper to pick up the other half of the egg and press the halves together to seal them.

9 **Finishing the egg.** Prepare a piping bag; fit it with a star nozzle *(inset)* and fill it with coating. Balance the egg on the finger tips of one hand or, if your hands are damp, support it with wax paper to avoid marking the surface. Pipe coating over the seam, then pipe a small circle on the egg's rounded end to form a base. Stand the egg on a sheet of wax paper *(above)*.

Fashioning Soft-centered Chocolate Cups

Using the basic technique of molding *(pages 84-85)*, you can fashion individual chocolate cups and fill them with a variety of centers. For such small shapes, rigid molds are not necessary; foil candy cups provide enough support. The molds are attractive enough to be left on the finished chocolates, or you can peel them off once the chocolate has set.

A chocolate cup may contain either a soft center, such as the fondant chosen for this demonstration *(pages 30-31)*, or a stiffer center, such as a nut or chocolate paste *(pages 56-59 and 64-67)*. For more flavor and texture, you can add chopped nuts or candied fruit peel, a whole nut or half of a small fruit; here, brandied raspberry halves are used *(recipe, page 159)*.

Fondant—and any other filling that has to be melted over heat—should be cooled before it is spooned into a cup; otherwise it may melt the chocolate. Firmer fillings can be spooned or piped into the cups; if they are piped, they will set with decorative tops. Alternatively, top the confection with a layer of chocolate.

1 **Lining cups.** Melt chocolate-flavored coating *(pages 74-75)*. Using a teaspoon, half-fill a foil cup with coating. Rotate the cup to coat the sides and bottom *(above)*; invert it over the chocolate to tip out excess. Place the cups on a tray and let the coating set for two to five minutes, until it is firm.

2 **Filling cups.** Melt fondant *(page 33)*. Drain and halve brandied raspberries. Spoon a little melted fondant into a chocolate cup and place a raspberry half on top of the fondant. Cover the raspberry with another layer of fondant.

3 **Sealing the cups.** When the surface of the fondant is firm, spoon a layer of coating over it *(inset)*. Tilt the cup so that the coating spreads evenly over the fondant. Serve the chocolates *(right)* as soon as they are hard or—to store them for a few days—pack them in a box between sheets of wax paper.

Anthology of Recipes

rawing upon the cooking literature of more than 25 countries, ｭe editors and consultants for this volume have selected 253 ｭblished recipes for the Anthology that follows. The selections ｭnge from the familiar to the exotic—from 19 variations of ｭlled candy to an Indian fudge decorated with edible silver ｭaf. Many of the recipes were written by world-renowned expoｭents of the culinary art, but the Anthology also includes selecｭons from rare and out-of-print books and from works that have ｭever been published in English. Whatever the sources, the ｭmphasis in these recipes is always on techniques that are pracｭcal for the home cook.

Since many early recipe writers did not specify amounts of ｭgredients, sizes of pans, or even cooking times and temperaｭres, the missing information has been judiciously added. In ｭme cases, clarifying introductory notes have also been supｭlied; they are printed in italics. Modern recipe terms have been ｭbstituted for archaic language; but to preserve the character ｭf the original recipes and to create a true anthology, the auｭhors' texts have been changed as little as possible.

In keeping with the organization of the first half of the book, ｭost of the recipes in the Anthology are categorized according to ｭhe technique and the ingredients. Recipes for standard prepｭrations—fondant and nut pastes among them—appear at the ｭnd of the Anthology. Unfamiliar cooking terms and uncommon ｭgredients are defined or explained in the combined General ｭndex and Glossary.

All ingredients are listed within each recipe in order of use, ｭith both the customary United States measurements and ｭhe metric measurements provided. All quantities reflect the ｭmerican practice of measuring such solid ingredients as sugar ｭr cocoa powder by volume rather than by weight, as is done in ｭurope. White granulated sugar is simply referred to as sugar ｭhroughout the Anthology, unless brown sugar or confectioners' ｭugar is called for in the same recipe. All measures given for ｭuts are for shelled nuts.

To make the quantities simpler to measure, many of the ｭigures have been rounded off to correspond to the gradations ｭn U.S. metric spoons and cups. (One cup, for example, equals ｭ37 milliliters; however, wherever practicable in these recipes, ｭhe metric equivalent of 1 cup appears as a more readily meaｭured 250 milliliters—¼ liter.) Similarly, the weight, ovenｭemperature and linear metric equivalents have been rounded ｭff slightly. Thus the American and metric figures do not exactｭy match, but using one set or the other will produce the same ｭood results. Candy-thermometer temperatures, however, have ｭot been rounded off, since precision is critical.

Simple Boiled-Sugar Candy

Clear Fruit Drops

To make ½ pound [¼ kg.]

1 cup	sugar	¼ liter
2 tsp.	liquid glucose or light corn syrup	10 ml.
⅓ cup	water	75 ml.
	food coloring and flavoring	

Over medium heat, dissolve the sugar and liquid glucose or corn syrup in the water. Bring this syrup to a boil, and boil it to a temperature of 296° to 298° F. [147° to 148° C.]. Add the food coloring and flavoring, and boil the syrup to 300° F. [149° C.] *(hard-crack stage, pages 8-11).*

Remove the pan from the heat at once. Pour the syrup immediately into an oiled jelly-roll pan, or drop it by spoonfuls onto an oiled marble slab. If the mixture is poured into a pan, score it at once to form squares, and break it into pieces when it is cold. The mixture sets very quickly.

D. F. HUTTON AND E. M. BODE
SIMPLE SWEETMAKING

Horehound Candy

Horehound is an herb that grows wild in Europe, Asia and America. The leaves, which have a distinctive bitter flavor, can be bought dried from food shops specializing in herbs.

To make 1¾ pounds [875 g.]

1¼ cups	water	300 ml.
2 cups	fresh horehound leaves or 1 cup [¼ liter] dried horehound	½ liter
4 cups	brown sugar	1 liter
¼ cup	light corn syrup	50 ml.

Put the water into a saucepan and bring it to a boil. Reduce the heat, add the horehound, cover the pan and simmer for 15 minutes. Remove the pan from the heat and let the mixture stand for one hour to infuse. Strain the liquid and discard the horehound. Add the sugar and the corn syrup to the liquid, and boil it to the hard-crack stage—300° F. [149° C.] on a candy thermometer *(pages 8-11).* Pour the syrup into a buttered pan measuring 8 by 12 inches [20 by 30 cm.]. When the candy begins to set, mark it into squares. Cut the candy into pieces when cold.

DOROTHY HALL
THE BOOK OF HERBS

Licorice Drops

To make about ½ pound [¼ kg.]

1 cup	granulated sugar	¼ liter
¼ cup	brown sugar	50 ml.
¼ cup	water	50 ml.
¼ cup	light corn syrup	50 ml.
1 tbsp.	black food coloring	15 ml.
¼ tsp.	anise extract or pulverized anise seeds	1 ml.

Put the sugars, water and corn syrup into a pot, set the pot over medium heat, and stir. When the batch has boiled for the first time, wash the sugar crystals down from the sides of the pot. Put the thermometer in the pot, and cook without further stirring to 290° F. [143° C.] *(soft-crack stage, pages 8-11).* Then take the pot from the heat, and add the food coloring and the anise flavoring, and stir them in gently.

With a teaspoon, drop round patties about the size of quarters onto a greased baking sheet. If the candy in the pot gets too firm for spooning, reheat it gently until it softens.

Cool the drops completely by placing the sheet near an open window or in a cool room, but not in the refrigerator, or the pieces will stick. Soon the drops will be firm and will come off the sheet easily.

Wrap the drops individually in wax paper or cellophane.

MARTIN K. HERRMANN
THE ART OF MAKING GOOD CANDIES AT HOME

Raspberry Candy

Bonbons Framboises

To make raspberry-vinegar syrup, crush 1 cup [¼ liter] of raspberries, put them in a jar, and cover them with 2 cups [½ liter] of distilled white vinegar or white wine vinegar. Let them rest for six days at room temperature, stirring each day. Then strain the mixture and mix it with 1 cup of sugar, stirring over low heat until the sugar dissolves. Boil for 10 minutes; skim off any scum. Cool the syrup, then refrigerate it.

To make about ¼ pound [125 g.]

½ cup	sugar	125 ml.
¼ cup	water	50 ml.
1 tbsp.	raspberry-vinegar syrup	15 ml.
1 tsp.	brandy	5 ml.

Dissolve the sugar in the water and bring to a boil over high heat. When the syrup is cooked to the point where it will crack between the teeth when cooled *(hard-crack stage, pages 8-11),* add the raspberry-vinegar syrup. Bring the mixture back to a boil and add the brandy. Pour the mixture onto an oiled marble slab. When it is cooled but not completely set, cut it into pieces with an oiled knife.

MME. JEANNE SAVARIN (EDITOR)
LA CUISINE DES FAMILLES

Red-Grape Candy

Conserva di Uva Rossa

To make about 2 pounds [1 kg.]

1½ lb.	red grapes, stems removed (about 5 cups [1¼ liters])	¾ kg.
1½ cups	water	375 ml.
2 cups	sugar	½ liter

Put the grapes in an enameled, tinned or stainless-steel saucepan with half of the water, and boil them until their juice begins to flow— about 15 minutes. Strain the grapes through a fine sieve lined with cheesecloth to remove the skins and seeds. Put the strained juice back in the pan. Boil for another 15 minutes, or until the mixture jells.

In a deep, heavy pan, heat the sugar and the remaining water until the sugar dissolves, then boil the syrup to the hard-crack stage *(pages 8-11)*. Immediately remove the pan from the heat, add the jelled grape juice, and stir well until the mixture foams up. Pour the mixture into a buttered pan 15 inches [38 cm.] square and score it into 1-inch [2½-cm.] squares. Separate the pieces when cold.

IPPOLITO CAVALCANTI
CUCINA TEORICO-PRATICA

———————◆———————

Rock Candy

To make about 1 pound [½ kg.]

1¾ cups	sugar	425 ml.
½ cup	water	125 ml.
½ cup	light corn syrup	125 ml.
	salt	
	food coloring (optional)	
¼ tsp.	flavoring	1 ml.
	confectioners' sugar	

In a small saucepan, combine the sugar, water, corn syrup and a dash of salt, and stir until the sugar dissolves. Cover

the pan and bring the mixture to a rolling boil. Remove the lid, place a thermometer in the pan, and cook the mixture to 250° F. [121° C.] *(hard-ball stage, pages 8-11)*. Add the food coloring, if using, and continue cooking until the mixture reaches 285° to 290° F. [140° to 143° C.]. Remove the pan from the heat and let the mixture cool a few minutes. Add the flavoring and cover for five minutes. Pour into a buttered pan measuring 7 by 10 inches [18 by 25 cm.]. Cut the candy into strips with oiled scissors as soon as it is cool enough to handle. Then cut it into squares or diamond shapes. When the candy is cold, dust it with confectioners' sugar to prevent sticking.

MILDRED BRAND
IDEALS CANDY COOKBOOK

———————◆———————

Wintergreen Candy

Wintergreen—or checkerberry—is an evergreen shrub that grows in woods ranging from Canada to Georgia. The leaves are available in health-food stores.

Wintergreen candy is a favorite with most youngsters, and an extract may be made from checkerberries or their leaves. Berries are gathered in the early fall, but if the dried leaves are preferred, they should be picked and dried in the spring while they are still tender and filled with oil.

Steep the checkerberries or their leaves in boiling water, or boil if necessary, until 3 tablespoons [45 ml.] of strong tea have been secured.

To make about ½ pound [¼ kg.]

2 cups	brown sugar	½ liter
3 tbsp.	strong checkerberry tea	45 ml.
1 tbsp.	vinegar	15 ml.

Add the sugar to the tea and stir until the sugar is dissolved. Boil the syrup until it tests for a hard ball *(pages 8-11)*. Add the vinegar to the syrup, boil for one minute more, and pour the syrup onto a well-buttered platter. When cold, break the candy into small pieces.

GRACE FIRTH
A NATURAL YEAR

Barley Sugar

The technique of making barley sugar is shown on pages 24-25. In this recipe, be especially careful to remove the pan from the heat to stop the cooking as soon as the syrup reaches the hard-crack stage—otherwise the syrup will caramelize. Since this mixture cools and hardens rapidly, it may be advisable to ask a friend to help you twist the barley sugar into strips, lest the last strips become too stiff to twist. If the mixture does harden too fast to make twisted strips, it can be broken into small pieces for eating.

	To make about 1 pound [½ kg.]	
2 cups	sugar	½ liter
⅔ cup	water	150 ml.
½	lemon, the peel thinly pared in one continuous strip, the juice strained to remove pulp	½
	cream of tartar	

In a heavy pan, heat the sugar and water until the sugar has completely dissolved. Add the lemon peel and a pinch of cream of tartar. Boil the syrup until it reaches the soft-ball stage *(pages 8-11)*. Add the lemon juice and boil the syrup to the hard-crack stage. Stop the cooking by dipping the base of the pan into ice water; remove the lemon peel.

Pour out the syrup in a thin layer onto a lightly oiled work surface. Let the mixture cool for a few minutes, then use a narrow-bladed spatula to fold the sides in toward the middle. Oil scissors and use them to cut the mixture into strips. Twist the strips rapidly while they are still warm.

GOOD HOUSEKEEPING INSTITUTE
GOOD HOUSEKEEPING'S BASIC COOKERY

Old-fashioned Barley Sugar

The quantity of barley water used in this recipe can be halved in order to reduce the cooking time of the syrup.

	To make about 2 pounds [1 kg.]	
½ cup	pearl barley	125 ml.
1	lemon, half the peel thinly pared, the juice squeezed and its pulp strained out	1
5 cups	cold water	1¼ liters
4 cups	sugar	1 liter

Into a saucepan, put the barley and the lemon peel. Pour in the cold water, bring the mixture to a boil and simmer it, covered, for two hours. Remove the pan from the heat, and let the barley water stand for about 30 minutes so that the solids settle to the bottom of the pan. Ladle off enough clear liquid from the top of the barley water to make 2½ cups [625 ml.] of liquid.

Pour the barley water into a saucepan and add the sugar. Set the pan over low heat and stir until the sugar has dis-

solved; then let the syrup boil without stirring. Add the lemon juice, and boil the syrup again until it begins to crack *(hard-crack stage, pages 8-11)*.

Pour the syrup onto a buttered platter or buttered marble slab. When the candy is cool enough to handle, cut it quickly into short strips with oiled scissors, then hold each strip by its ends and twist the ends in opposite directions.

MAY BYRON (EDITOR)
PUDDINGS, PASTRIES AND SWEET DISHES

Dotty Dimple's Vinegar Candy

Instructions for making pulled candy are on pages 26-29.

Rebecca Sophia Clarke (Sophie May) of Norridgewock, Maine, wrote more than 40 books for children, including the six-volume series, the *Dotty Dimple Stories*, published from 1867 to 1869. This candy became as popular with children as did the books.

	To make 1½ pounds [¾ kg.]	
3 cups	sugar	¾ liter
1½ cups	vinegar	375 ml.

Combine the sugar with the vinegar and cook over low heat, stirring constantly, until the sugar is dissolved. Continue cooking until the syrup reaches the soft-crack stage—270° to 290° F. [132° to 143° C.]—or until a few drops tested in cold water separate into threads that are hard but not brittle *(pages 8-11)*.

Pour the syrup onto a large buttered platter, and let the candy cool until it can be handled comfortably. Butter your hands, and pull the taffy until it is white and almost firm. Stretch it into a rope about 1 inch [2½ cm.] in diameter, and snip off pieces with oiled scissors.

THE EDITORS OF AMERICAN HERITAGE
THE AMERICAN HERITAGE COOKBOOK

Vinegar Candy

The technique of making pulled candy is demonstrated on pages 26-29.

	To make about 2½ pounds [1¼ kg.]	
1 cup	cider vinegar	¼ liter
4 quarts	molasses	1 liter

Stir the cider vinegar into the molasses. Boil the mixture until it reaches the point where a little dropped into cold water becomes very hard and brittle *(hard-crack stage, pages 8-11)*. Pour the mixture onto buttered platters and let it cool until it can be handled. Form the candy into a large roll; then pull it to any size and cut it into sticks.

HOW TO MAKE CANDY

Honey Taffy

For a change of taste, add 1 teaspoon [5 ml.] of instant-coffee crystals to the boiling syrup. Or melt 3 ounces [90 g.] of semi-sweet chocolate with 1 tablespoon [15 ml.] of butter and let cool; after cutting the taffy into pieces, dip one end of each piece into the cooled chocolate mixture, covering about half of the piece. Let the chocolate-coated taffy dry on sheets of wax paper before wrapping.

To make 2 pounds [1 kg.]

2 cups	sugar	½ liter
2 cups	honey	½ liter
1 cup	water	¼ liter
¼ tsp.	salt	1 ml.
2 tsp.	vanilla extract	10 ml.

Lightly oil the inside of a 3-quart [3-liter] saucepan. Combine the sugar, honey, water and salt in the pan. Cook the mixture over medium heat, stirring constantly until the sugar is completely dissolved and the syrup comes to a boil. Wipe down the sugar crystals above the liquid line, using a clean pastry brush dipped in cold water. Without stirring, continue boiling the syrup until a candy thermometer registers 280° F. [138° C.] *(soft-crack stage, pages 8-11)*. Stir in the vanilla extract. Pour the syrup into an oiled jelly-roll pan that has been set on a wire rack.

Let the taffy cool until it can be handled comfortably — about three minutes — then start working it. Shape the taffy into a ball, then start pulling. Form a long rope; double it. Redouble the rope; pull it out again. When the taffy feels light and pliable, shape it into a long rope about ½ inch [1 cm.] in diameter. Using well-oiled scissors, cut the rope into 1-inch [2½-cm.] pieces. Wrap each piece in cellophane or wax paper. Store the pieces of candy in an airtight container in a cool place.

MIRIAM LOWENBERG
CREATIVE CANDY MAKING

Edinburgh Rock

The original Edinburgh rock is a pulled taffy made by Ferguson's. Sold in boxes printed with the Ferguson or Royal Stewart tartan, it is shipped all over the world. The rock should be pastel-colored and lightly flavored. Traditionally, plain white rock is flavored with lemon, vanilla or peppermint; pink rock is flavored with raspberry extract or rose water; pale brown rock is flavored with ground ginger; and yellow rock is flavored with orange-flower water or orange extract.

To make 1½ pounds [¾ kg.]

3 cups	sugar	¾ liter
1 tbsp.	liquid glucose or light corn syrup	15 ml.
1¼ cups	water	300 ml.
¼ tsp.	cream of tartar	1 ml.
	food coloring and flavoring	

In a heavy saucepan, dissolve the sugar in the glucose or corn syrup and water over medium heat. Add the cream of tartar, and boil the syrup to 275° F. [135° C.] *(soft-crack stage, pages 8-11)*. Pour the syrup onto a buttered marble slab. Add the coloring and flavoring. Fold the edges of the mixture to the center as they cool.

As soon as the candy is cool enough, pull it for about 15 minutes. Then pull the rock into sticks, being careful not to twist it, and, when cold, break it into pieces. Leave it exposed to the air for at least 24 hours in a warm place, until the process of granulation is complete and the rock is powdery and soft. Store it in tins.

BEATRICE MANDERS AND E. M. MILLNER
THE ART OF SWEET-MAKING

French Taffy

Berlingots

This recipe produces a pale yellow, lemon-flavored taffy. For other colors and flavors, substitute the combinations suggested on pages 14-15 for the lemon juice and peel.

To make about 2 pounds [1 kg.]

4 cups	sugar	1 liter
2 cups	tepid water	½ liter
1½ tbsp.	fresh lemon juice, pulp strained out	22 ml.
1 tsp.	grated lemon peel	5 ml.

In a saucepan, combine the sugar, water and lemon juice. Stir over medium heat until the sugar dissolves, then increase the heat and cook this syrup to the soft-ball stage *(pages 8-11)*. Add the lemon peel. Cook the mixture to the hard-crack stage.

Pour the syrup onto an oiled work surface. Use a narrow-bladed spatula to fold the mixture quickly toward the center as it spreads out. As soon as the syrup is cool enough to handle, pull and knead it in your hands until it becomes opaque. Then roll it between your hands until it forms one long strip the thickness of a finger. With oiled scissors, cut the strip into small pieces the size of hazelnuts. Store the candy in a dry place.

MME. ROSALIE BLANQUET
LE PÂTISSIER DES MÉNAGES

Berlingots

The technique of making pulled candy is shown on pages 26-29. If preferred, you can cook the red and white portions of syrup to the same temperature. In that case, food coloring can be added to the second portion of syrup while it is in the pan.

To make 1 pound [½ kg.]

2 cups	sugar	½ liter
1 tbsp.	liquid glucose or light corn syrup	15 ml.
⅔ cup	water	150 ml.
	red food coloring	

Boil the sugar, glucose or corn syrup, and the water to 250° F. [121° C.] *(hard-ball stage, pages 8-11)*. Pour half of the syrup in a thin stream onto an oiled area of a marble slab. Add a few drops of red food coloring, and fold in the edges of the syrup as they spread.

Meanwhile, boil the remainder of the syrup to 300° F. [149° C.] *(hard-crack stage)* and pour it onto another oiled area of the slab. When this second portion of the syrup is cool enough, pull it until it is white.

Working rapidly, form the red portion into an egg shape and fold the white part around it, gradually working the ball into a two-colored cylinder ½ inch [1 cm.] thick. Use oiled scissors to cut the stick into pieces 1 inch [2½ cm.] long. Roll the pieces between your palms to make them spherical.

BEATRICE MANDERS AND E. M. MILLNER
THE ART OF SWEET-MAKING

Bull's-Eyes

The original version of this turn-of-the-century recipe used tartaric acid to make the finished candy creamier. Citric acid has replaced tartaric acid in modern candymaking and is readily available at pharmacies. The technique of making pulled candy is demonstrated on pages 26-29.

To make 2 pounds [1 kg.]

about 5 cups	dark brown sugar (about 2 lb. [1 kg.])	about 1¼ liters
1 cup	water	¼ liter
	cream of tartar	
½ tsp.	lemon extract	2 ml.
¼ tsp.	citric acid	1 ml.

Dissolve the brown sugar in the water over medium heat, add a pinch of cream of tartar, and boil the syrup to the soft-crack stage *(pages 8-11)*. Pour the syrup onto a buttered platter or marble slab. As the syrup cools and hardens, slice off one quarter to one half of the mixture, and pull it until it is white and opaque. Pull the white mixture into a thin rope, and cut it into short lengths.

To the remaining syrup, add the lemon extract and citric acid, and mix well. Lay the lengths of the white mixture on the brown unpulled mixture at about 1-inch [2½-cm.] intervals. Fold the brown mixture in half lengthwise. Pull the folded candy, and break or cut it into strips. Twist the strips, holding them by both ends and turning each end in the opposite direction. Then, using buttered scissors, cut the strips into small, equal pieces.

MAY BYRON (EDITOR)
PUDDINGS, PASTRIES AND SWEET DISHES

Bristol Mints

The technique of making pulled candy is shown on pages 26-29. The plain and the colored sugar syrups should be cooked simultaneously so that neither has a chance to harden before it can be pulled or shaped. It is advisable to ask a friend to help you so that the pulling can be done before the syrups become hard and brittle.

This candy is smartly striped in brown and white like a fine French ribbon.

To make 1 pound [½ kg.]

1 cup	granulated sugar	¼ liter
1 cup	water	¼ liter
	cream of tartar	
1 tsp.	peppermint extract	5 ml.
1⅓ cups	dark brown sugar	325 ml.
	brown food coloring	

Dissolve the granulated sugar in half of the water over medium heat. Add a pinch of cream of tartar and cook the syrup to 300° F. [149° C.] *(hard-crack stage, pages 8-11)*. Add half of the peppermint extract. Remove the pan from the heat and pour the syrup onto one area of a buttered marble slab or work surface. Let the syrup cool until it can be handled—two to three minutes—then pull and work it until it is white and opaque. With an oiled spatula, shape it into a square.

Meanwhile, add the brown sugar to the rest of the water, stirring constantly over medium heat until the sugar has dissolved. Boil the brown sugar syrup to 300° F., and add the rest of the peppermint extract and the brown food coloring. Pour the syrup onto the buttered marble slab, keeping it separate from the white syrup. With an oiled spatula, shape the cooled brown syrup into a square.

Cut the white and the brown squares in half, pile them on top of each other—brown, white, brown, white—and press them together. Then cut them into strips with a sharp, oiled knife. With oiled scissors, cut the strips into small squares. Let the mixture set.

NELL HEATON (EDITOR)
HOME-MADE SWEETS

Stick Candy

The technique of making pulled candy is demonstrated on pages 26-29.

	To make 1 pound [½ kg.]	
2 cups	sugar	½ liter
½ cup	light corn syrup	125 ml.
½ cup	water	125 ml.
1	lemon, the peel grated, the juice squeezed and its pulp strained out	1
1 tsp.	lemon extract, or 1 tsp. [5 ml.] peppermint extract and a few drops of red food coloring	5 ml.

In a saucepan, dissolve the sugar in the corn syrup and water over medium heat. Bring the mixture to a boil, and boil the syrup without stirring until a few drops become brittle in cold water *(hard-crack stage, pages 8-11)*. Stir in the lemon peel and juice. Remove the pan from the heat.

For lemon sticks, add the lemon extract and pour the candy onto a buttered platter. When the candy is cool enough to handle, after a few minutes, pull it until it is opaque, roll it into sticks, and cut the sticks into pieces with oiled scissors.

For peppermint sticks, add the peppermint extract and pour half of the syrup onto a buttered platter. Add the red coloring to the other half of the syrup and pour the red syrup onto another buttered platter. When the syrups are cool enough to handle, pull them separately, then twist one around the other. Form them into canes or sticks.

MRS. SIMON KANDER (EDITOR)
THE SETTLEMENT COOK BOOK

Striped Candies
Polkagrisar

To make about 1 pound [½ kg.]

2 cups	sugar	½ liter
1 tbsp.	liquid glucose or light corn syrup	15 ml.
1 cup	water	¼ liter
2 tsp.	malt vinegar	10 ml.
	peppermint extract	
	red food coloring	

In a saucepan, mix the sugar, glucose or corn syrup, water and vinegar. Dissolve the sugar over medium heat, stirring constantly; then bring to a boil, without stirring. Boil the syrup to a temperature of 275° F. [135° C.], or until the mixture becomes brittle when dropped into cold water *(soft-crack stage, pages 8-11)*. Remove the pan from the heat and let it cool for three to four minutes.

Pour three quarters of the syrup onto an oiled marble slab or baking sheet. Add a few drops of peppermint extract

and, with a spatula, turn the edges of the mixture constantly toward the center until the extract is well incorporated and the taffy is cool enough to handle.

Oil your hands, and stretch and pull the taffy, folding, stretching and folding until it is opaque and white. Then pull the taffy into one long strip and lay it on an oiled marble slab or baking sheet.

Color the reserved syrup in the pan with a few drops of the red coloring. Pour this syrup onto the slab or baking sheet in two strips, one on each side of the pulled taffy. Working quickly, twist the three strips together. Use oiled scissors to cut the twisted taffy immediately into sections.

SAM WIDENFELT (EDITOR)
FAVORITE SWEDISH RECIPES

Maple-flavored Fondant

For this recipe it is important to use pure maple syrup and not maple-flavored pancake syrup.

	To make about 1 ½ pounds [¾ kg.]	
2½ cups	sugar	625 ml.
1 cup	pure maple syrup	¼ liter
½ cup	water	125 ml.
⅛ tsp.	cream of tartar	½ ml.

In a saucepan, mix the ingredients, and dissolve the sugar over medium heat, stirring constantly. Boil the mixture, without stirring, to a temperature of approximately 230° F. [110° C.]; reduce the heat and cook the syrup until it reaches a temperature of 234° to 236° F. [112° to 113° C.] or forms a very soft ball with the water test *(pages 8-11)*. Wipe the crystals from the pouring side of the saucepan and pour the hot syrup into a shallow bowl. Let it cool undisturbed to a temperature of 110° F. [43° C.]; then stir it with a heavy spoon or spatula until the fondant is thoroughly creamed and the whole mass has a cheeselike consistency. Knead it until the fondant is soft and plastic. Store it in a covered container or shape it into pieces of candy.

WALTER W. CHENOWETH
HOW TO MAKE CANDY

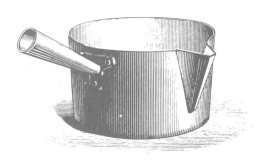

Pure Maple Fondant

It is important to use pure maple syrup, not maple-flavored pancake syrup, for this recipe.

To make about ½ pound [¼ kg.]		
2 cups	pure maple syrup	½ liter

In a saucepan, boil the maple syrup to a temperature of 234° F. [112° C.], or to a very soft ball by the water test *(pages 8-11)*. Wipe the crystals from the inside of the saucepan and pour the hot syrup into a shallow, heatproof bowl.

Let the syrup cool, undisturbed, to a temperature of 105° to 110° F. [40° to 43° C.]. Stir the mixture until it is thick and grainy, then knead it until it is soft and plastic. Store the fondant in a covered container.

WALTER W. CHENOWETH
HOW TO MAKE CANDY

Ginger Fondant

Gemberborstplaat

The original version of this recipe specified that the fondant be formed in ring-shaped candy molds.

To make about 1 pound [½ kg.]		
1 tsp.	ground ginger	5 ml.
2 cups	sugar	½ liter
½ cup	water	125 ml.
2 oz.	candied ginger in syrup, drained, finely shredded and the syrup reserved	60 g.

Combine the ground ginger and sugar in a saucepan, add the water, and set the pan over medium heat. Cook this mixture, stirring continuously, until the sugar has dissolved. Then boil the syrup without stirring for 10 minutes *(soft-ball stage, pages 8-11)*. Add the shredded ginger and its syrup, and let the mixture boil for one to two minutes more. Remove the pan from the heat and stir the mixture continuously until it thickens.

Shape the mixture into balls about 1 inch [2½ cm.] in diameter. Flatten the balls slightly and let the candy set. As soon as the top surfaces of the pieces are firm, turn the pieces over and let them firm on the opposite surfaces. Do not leave the pieces too long on one side, or the bottom surfaces of the fondant will stick to the paper.

C. J. WANNÉE (EDITOR)
KOOKBOEK VAN DE AMSTERDAMSE HUISHOUDSCHOOL

Anise-Honey Chews

Star anise is easily ground in a blender, both seeds and pods together. You can substitute any other flavoring, herb, or spice for the star anise.

To make about ½ pound [¼ kg.]		
1 cup	honey	¼ liter
1½ tsp.	star anise, finely ground	7 ml.

In a small saucepan, cook the honey and anise together over low heat until the mixture reaches the firm-ball stage *(pages 8-11)*. Pour the mixture into a very lightly greased soup bowl and allow it to cool somewhat in the bowl. When the honey mixture is cool enough to handle, tear off bits and shape them into balls between the palms of your hands, then place them on a dry plate to set. When the candy is well set, wrap each piece in wax paper.

STAN AND FLOSS DWORKIN
NATURAL SNACKS 'N' SWEETS

Enriched Boiled-Sugar Candy

Molasses Taffy

The technique of making pulled candy is demonstrated on pages 26-29.

To make about 1 pound [½ kg.]		
4 cups	molasses	1 liter
1 cup	brown sugar	¼ liter
½ cup	water	125 ml.
3 tbsp.	butter	45 ml.
½ tsp.	baking soda	2 ml.

Combine the molasses, sugar and water. Cook the mixture over low heat until it reaches the soft-crack stage—272° F. [133° C.] *(pages 8-11)*. Remove the pan from the heat; add the butter and baking soda. Pour the mixture into a buttered pan 8 inches [20 cm.] square and let the candy stand until it is cool enough to handle. Gather the candy into a ball and pull it until it is opaque. With oiled scissors, cut the taffy into 1-inch [2½-cm.] pieces.

MARY MARGARET MC BRIDE
HARVEST OF AMERICAN COOKING

Lellie Ishmael's Cream Candy

The technique of making pulled candy is demonstrated on pages 26-29.

After the candy has been standing three to four hours in a warm room, it becomes creamy, but at first it is chewy.

To make about 2 pounds [1 kg.]

4 cups	sugar	1 liter
1 cup	water	¼ liter
½ tsp.	salt	2 ml.
⅛ tsp.	baking soda	½ ml.
1 cup	light cream	¼ liter

In a heavy metal pan, combine the sugar, water, salt and baking soda. Do not stir these ingredients. Put the pan on high heat. When the mixture begins to form large, clear bubbles, and will spin a hair thread 3 to 6 inches [8 to 15 cm.] long *(soft-crack stage, pages 8-11)*, add the cream, drop by drop, as if you were making a mayonnaise. The syrup must never stop boiling, and this process of adding the cream cannot be rushed. After the last drop of cream has been added, reduce the heat, and simmer until the mixture turns pale brown and will once more spin a thread 3 to 6 inches long. The whole cooking process takes about 15 to 20 minutes.

In a warm place, such as near the open door of a heated oven or by a fire, pour the syrup in a thin, narrow stream about 6 to 8 inches [15 to 20 cm.] long onto a buttered marble slab or enameled tabletop. Leave a space and pour out another narrow stream of syrup next to it, and so on until the syrup is used up. Do not scrape the pan, because the scrapings will crystallize.

Begin to pull the candy immediately. Beginning with the first thin strip of syrup, start pulling, then add the next and incorporate that, and so on until all of the candy is used up. Continue to pull until the candy turns white, or the palest ivory color, and is too stiff to continue pulling. When pulling the candy, it will be found that two people can handle the stiff candy better than one.

When the candy becomes too stiff to pull any longer, twist it into a rope about 1½ inches [4 cm.] thick, and cut it with kitchen scissors into pieces 1 to 1½ inches [2½ to 4 cm.] wide; then spread it out on the buttered work surface. It is necessary to work quickly, as the candy gets hard very suddenly, and again, two pairs of hands are better than one. One person can cut from one end of the rope, another from the other end. Either let the candy soften to a creamy consistency on the work surface or pack it into tin boxes, putting a sheet of wax paper or foil between the layers.

MARION FLEXNER
OUT OF KENTUCKY KITCHENS

Welsh Toffee

Cyflaith

Noson Gyflaith (the Toffee Evening) was a traditional part of Christmas or New Year festivities in some areas of north Wales earlier this century. Families would invite friends to their homes for supper and the meal would be followed by merriment, playing games, making toffee, and storytelling. When the required ingredients for the toffee had boiled to a certain degree, the toffee was poured onto a well-greased slate or stone slab. The hearthstone itself was used for this purpose in some houses. Members of the happy gathering would then cover their hands with butter and attempt to pull the warm toffee until it became golden yellow in color.

To make about 3 pounds [1 ½ kg.]

8 cups	dark brown sugar	2 liters
⅔ cup	boiling water	150 ml.
3 tbsp.	fresh lemon juice, pulp strained out	45 ml.
16 tbsp.	salted butter (½ lb. [¼ kg.]), softened	240 ml.

Using an enameled or stainless-steel saucepan over low heat, gradually dissolve the sugar in the boiling water. Stir it continuously with a wooden spoon until the sugar is thoroughly dissolved. This usually takes from 20 to 30 minutes. Remove the saucepan from the heat, add the lemon juice and the softened butter, and stir them into the sugar. Boil this mixture fairly briskly, without stirring it, for 15 minutes.

Gently drop a teaspoonful of the mixture into a cupful of cold water; if it hardens at once, it has reached the required consistency *(soft-crack stage, pages 8-11)*. Pour the mixture slowly onto a buttered marble slab or large flat dish. Do not scrape the pan clean as the scrapings might turn the toffee back into sugar.

Use extra butter to butter your hands. Pull the taffy into long golden strands while it is still hot. Cut the taffy into smaller pieces.

S. MINWEL TIBBOTT
WELSH FARE

Golden Honeycomb Pulled Taffy

Yellow-Man (Traditional)

The golden syrup can be replaced by molasses to make a dark brown honeycomb taffy.

This is a universal favorite in Northern Ireland and to this day is found on stalls at country fairs. It is usually brought to the fairs in one large lump and broken as it is sold.

To make about 1 ¼ pound [600 g.]

2 tbsp.	butter	30 ml.
1 cup	Demerara or turbinado sugar	¼ liter
2 tbsp.	water	30 ml.
1 ⅓ cups	English golden syrup	325 ml.
1 tsp.	baking soda	5 ml.

Melt the butter in a pan and tip the pan to grease it evenly. Then add the Demerara or turbinado sugar, the water, and the golden syrup. Stir until the sugar has dissolved. Bring the syrup to a boil, and boil without stirring until the syrup is crisp and brittle when tested in cold water *(hard-crack stage, pages 8-11)*. Stir in the baking soda, and quickly pour the mixture onto a buttered or oiled marble slab or platter. Turn the edges of the mixture to the center, and pull the taffy as soon as it is cool enough—about three minutes. Pull the taffy until it is pale in color.

FLORENCE IRWIN
THE COOKIN' WOMAN

Candy Balls

Stroopballetjes

This candy will be soft and sticky. Enclose each one in plastic wrap before storing the candy.

To make about 1 pound [½ kg.]

2 cups	molasses	½ liter
9 tbsp.	sugar	135 ml.
2 tsp.	butter	10 ml.

In a heavy pan, warm the molasses over medium heat. Add the sugar and the butter, and stir until the sugar dissolves. Without stirring, boil the mixture until it has the consistency of a thick syrup *(soft-ball stage, pages 8-11)*. Pour the syrup onto an oiled marble slab or baking sheet. As soon as the syrup begins to set, form it into a ball and pull it into a thick strip. Cut the strip into small pieces and roll these into little balls.

C. J. WANNÉE (EDITOR)
KOOKBOEK VAN DE AMSTERDAMSE HUISHOUDSCHOOL

Salt-Water Taffy

The technique of making pulled candy is demonstrated on pages 26-29.

This famous candy is sold all along the boardwalk at Atlantic City and, it is claimed, is made with sea water.

To make about 10 ounces [300 g.]

1 cup	sugar	¼ liter
1 tbsp.	cornstarch	15 ml.
⅔ cup	light corn syrup	150 ml.
1 tbsp.	butter	15 ml.
½ cup	water	125 ml.
¼ tsp.	salt	1 ml.
	food coloring and flavoring	

Mix the sugar and cornstarch in a saucepan. Stir in the corn syrup, butter, water and salt. Cook the mixture over moderate heat until it reaches 254° F. [123° C.] or until a few drops tested in cold water form a hard ball that holds its shape *(pages 8-11)*. Remove the pan from the heat, add a few drops of food coloring and flavoring, and pour the taffy onto a buttered platter. Cool the taffy until it can be handled comfortably, about two to three minutes. Butter your hands, and pull the taffy until it is light in color and firm enough to hold a shape. Stretch it into a roll about 1 inch [2½ cm.] in diameter and snip off bits with oiled kitchen scissors. Wrap each piece in wax paper.

THE EDITORS OF AMERICAN HERITAGE
THE AMERICAN HERITAGE COOKBOOK

White House Molasses Candy

The technique of making pulled candy is shown on pages 26-29. Flavoring is discussed on pages 14-15. Either orange or peppermint flavoring would complement the strong taste of the molasses.

To make about 2 pounds [1 kg.]

1 cup	dark brown sugar	¼ liter
1 quart	molasses	1 liter
4 tbsp.	butter	60 ml.
½ tsp.	baking soda	2 ml.
	flavoring (optional)	

Put the sugar, molasses and butter into a large, heavy pan. Cook them over low heat, stirring frequently to dissolve the sugar and prevent burning. Boil until the mixture thickens. Test the mixture by taking some out and dropping a few drops in a cup of cold water. If the drops harden quickly and break short between the teeth *(soft-crack stage, pages 8-11),* the mixture is boiled enough. Remove the pan from the heat. Now put in the baking soda and stir the candy well.

Pour the candy onto a buttered jelly-roll pan or cookie sheet. After about two to three minutes, when the candy is cool enough to handle, put a couple of drops of flavoring—if using—on top of it. Butter your hands well. Pull the candy, fold it in half, then pull and double it again until the candy turns whitish yellow. The candy may then quickly be cut into strips and rolled or twisted.

FANNY LEMIRA GILLETTE AND HUGO ZIEMANN
THE WHITE HOUSE COOKBOOK

Taffy and Fanny

Taffi a Ffani

To make about ¾ pound [350 g.]

2⅔ cups	dark brown sugar (1 lb. [½ kg.])	650 ml.
1 cup	cold water	¼ liter
2 tsp.	vinegar	10 ml.
2 tbsp.	butter	30 ml.
	peppermint extract	

Put the sugar, water, vinegar and butter into a cast-iron saucepan and cook them over medium heat, stirring constantly until the sugar has dissolved. Bring the mixture to a boil, and boil it for 15 minutes. Test a teaspoonful of the boiling mixture in cold water; if it hardens at once *(soft-crack stage, pages 8-11)*, remove the mixture from the heat.

Pour the bulk of the mixture onto a buttered or oiled platter or marble slab, but retain a little in the saucepan, and keep the saucepan in a larger pan filled with warm water to prevent the taffy mixture from hardening.

Grease your hands with butter and, as quickly as possible, pull the poured taffy while it is hot, adding a few drops of peppermint extract while pulling. Continue pulling until the taffy turns a creamy color, then pull it into long, flat strips about 1 inch [2½ cm.] wide.

Butter or oil the slab or dish again. Lay the taffy strips on the slab or dish. Pour the reserved taffy mixture in a thin stream onto the taffy strips to form a thin brown line along the center of each one. Cut the taffy into small pieces before it hardens.

S. MINWEL TIBBOTT
WELSH FARE

Peanut Butter-filled Velvet Molasses Kisses

Sorghum is a dark syrup made from a grain called sorgo rather than from sugar cane.

To make about ¾ pound [350 g.]

1 cup	light molasses or sorghum	¼ liter
⅔ cup	sugar	150 ml.
½ cup	light corn syrup	125 ml.
½ cup	hot water	125 ml.
¼ tsp.	cream of tartar	1 ml.
2 tbsp.	butter, cut into small pieces	30 ml.
½ tsp.	salt	2 ml.
½ tsp.	vanilla extract	2 ml.
½ cup	peanut butter	125 ml.

In a 4-quart [4-liter] saucepan (do not use a smaller pan or the mixture will boil over), combine the molasses or sorghum, sugar, corn syrup, water and cream of tartar. Mix until thoroughly blended. Place the mixture over medium heat and stir until the sugar is dissolved. Wash down the sides of the pan whenever necessary with a brush dipped in hot water. Increase the heat only enough to prevent the mixture from boiling over, and cook it without stirring to 242° F. [117° C.]. Add the butter, a little at a time, and the salt. Continue to cook the mixture over medium heat to 254° F. [122° C.], the hard-ball stage *(pages 8-11)*, stirring often to prevent scorching.

When the syrup reaches 254° F., remove the pan from the stove and let it stand until the boiling ceases; then pour the candy onto a lightly oiled marble slab. While it cools, gently turn the edges of the syrup toward the center several times with a candy scraper. This is to prevent the edges from becoming too cool and to keep the batch even in consistency and temperature. Let the candy cool for about 30 minutes undisturbed. When very cool, add and fold in the vanilla.

Cut the candy into several pieces. On an ungreased part of a cool marble slab, roll the candy with a rolling pin; roll each piece (or stretch with fingers) into strips that measure about 3½ inches [9 cm.] wide and about ⅛ inch [3 mm.] in thickness. With a piping bag and a plain tip, pipe a thick roll of peanut butter in the center of each strip. Enclose the peanut butter by overlapping the candy; then gently form the candy into a long, uniform roll about 1 inch [2½ cm.] wide. With oiled scissors or a sharp knife, cut the candy into individual pieces, and wrap in wax paper.

ANTOINETTE AND FRANÇOIS POPE
ANTOINETTE POPE SCHOOL NEW CANDY COOKBOOK

Maple Cream Candy

This candy is short-lived when cut into pieces and exposed to the air, but if left in the pan with a wax-paper cover, it may be kept for a few weeks in good condition.

To make about 1 1/2 pounds [3/4 kg.]

2 cups	sugar	1/2 liter
1 cup	pure maple syrup	1/4 liter
1/2 cup	light cream	125 ml.
1/2 cup	water	125 ml.
2 tbsp.	butter	30 ml.
1 oz.	nuts, finely chopped (about 1/4 cup [50 ml.]) (optional)	30 g.

In a saucepan, mix the sugar, maple syrup, cream and water. Stir over medium heat until the sugar dissolves, and then boil without stirring to approximately 230° F. [110° C.].

Add the butter and reduce the heat; boil the mixture to 236° F. [113° C.], or to a soft ball by the water test *(pages 8-11)*. With a damp cloth, wipe away the crystals from the inside of the pan, and pour the hot syrup into a shallow bowl. Let it cool, undisturbed, to a temperature of 110° to 115° F. [43° to 46° C.].

Stir the cooled syrup with a heavy spoon or spatula until it is well creamed; add the nuts, if using. Continue to stir until the mixture has a soft, doughlike consistency. Knead it in your hands or on a board until it is soft and plastic.

Place the mixture in a pan 8 inches [20 cm.] square that has been lightly buttered or lined with wax paper. Press the mixture down to form a sheet of uniform thickness, and smooth off the top by gently patting it with your fingers. Cover it with wax paper. After it stands a few minutes, the candy may be removed from the pan and cut into pieces suitable for serving.

WALTER W. CHENOWETH
HOW TO MAKE CANDY

Preserved Ginger Fondant

Ingwer-Fondant

To make about 1 1/2 pounds [3/4 kg.]

3 cups	light brown sugar	3/4 liter
1 cup	milk	1/4 liter
2 tbsp.	butter	30 ml.
2 tbsp.	finely chopped preserved ginger	30 ml.

In a large pan, bring the sugar and milk to a boil, stirring constantly. Stir until the syrup reaches a temperature of 234° F. [112° C.] *(soft-ball stage, pages 8-11)*. Remove the pan

from the heat, stir in the butter, and let the fondant mixture cool until lukewarm. Then beat the fondant until it is creamy. Finally, stir in the chopped ginger.

Butter a baking sheet. Spread the fondant on the sheet to a thickness of 3/4 inch [2 cm.]. Let the fondant cool completely. When it is cold, cut the fondant into cubes with a knife dipped into hot water after each cut.

MARGRET UHLE AND ANNE BRAKEMEIER
KONFEKT ZUM SELBERMACHEN

Sour-Cream Fondant

The handling of dipping chocolate and chocolate-flavored coating is demonstrated on pages 74-75.

To make about 1 1/2 pounds [3/4 kg.]

3 cups	light brown sugar	3/4 liter
1 cup	sour cream	1/4 liter
8 tbsp.	butter	120 ml.
1 tsp.	vanilla extract	5 ml.
	chopped pecans (optional)	
	dipping chocolate or chocolate-flavored coating	

Cook the brown sugar and sour cream to 240° F. [116° C.] *(soft-ball stage, pages 8-11)*. When this temperature is reached, remove the mixture from the heat; add the butter and vanilla without stirring. Let the mixture stand until the butter has melted, then pour the mixture out onto a cold marble slab. The butter will separate from the syrup. Cool the mixture until lukewarm, then work it with a spatula or paddle. When it is creamy and holds its shape, work in the nuts, if desired, and form the mixture into a mound on the slab. Let the mixture set until it is firm enough to shape into 3/4-inch [2-cm.] balls, or pat it into a buttered pan 8 inches [20 cm.] square. Dip the balls into melted and tempered dipping chocolate or melted chocolate-flavored coating. Or, if the candy has been put in a pan, cut it into squares.

MILDRED BRAND
IDEALS CANDY COOKBOOK

Italian Cream

To make about 1 pound [½ kg.]

⅓ cup	light brown sugar	75 ml.
1 cup	superfine sugar	¼ liter
2 tbsp.	warm water	30 ml.
¾ cup	liquid glucose or light corn syrup	175 ml.
⅔ cup	heavy cream	150 ml.
	vanilla extract	
⅓ cup	fondant *(recipe, page 166)*, cut into small pieces	75 ml.
3 oz.	walnuts, chopped (about ¾ cup [175 ml.])	90 g.

Put the sugars, water, glucose or corn syrup, and cream into a saucepan. Dissolve the sugars carefully over low heat, stirring all the time. Boil the mixture to 236° F. [113° C.] *(softball stage, pages 8-11)*.

Remove the pan from the heat and let the mixture cool for two to three minutes. Add the vanilla extract, fondant and walnuts. Stir the mixture with a wooden spoon or spatula until it begins to look grainy. Do not overstir, or the candy will become grainy and its smooth texture will be spoiled.

Pour the candy into a pan 7 to 8 inches [18 to 20 cm.] square that has been lined with wax paper. When the candy has set, cut it into squares. It should cut smoothly, like cheese. Wrap the candy in wax paper and aluminum foil. It keeps well for months.

D. F. HUTTON AND E. M. BODE
SIMPLE SWEETMAKING

Almond Pralines

Amandes Pralinées

These sugared almonds may turn pale brown during cooking, but this will not impair their flavor.

Peanuts may be made into delightful candy by following the same procedures outlined here.

To make about 2 pounds [1 kg.]

1 lb.	almonds, blanched and peeled (about 3 cups [¾ liter])	½ kg.
2 cups	superfine sugar	½ liter
	red food coloring (optional)	

Put the almonds into a skillet with the sugar, and add a dash of red food coloring if you wish to tinge them to a beautiful rose. But they are very beautiful when a snowy white. Place the skillet over very low heat, stirring all the time until the almonds make a loud crackling sound. Then take the skillet off the heat and stir until the sugar becomes sandy and detached from the almonds. Put the almonds in a colander with large holes and shake off the loose sugar. Reserve the sugar.

Return the almonds to the heat, stirring them lightly with a spoon as they again pick up the sugar. Pay strict attention to the heat, that it be not too high. When the almonds have taken up this part of the sugar, put in the reserved sugar and continue to cook the almonds, stirring lightly until they have taken up all of the sugar. Then take a piece of paper and put it in the colander and throw the almonds upon it; shake the nuts around so as to separate those that still cling together. Each almond must be separate and encrusted with sugar.

THE PICAYUNE'S CREOLE COOK BOOK

Burnt Almonds

Gebrannte Mandeln

To make about 2 pounds [1 kg.]

2 cups	sugar	½ liter
2 to 3 tbsp.	water	30 to 45 ml.
1 lb.	almonds (about 3 cups [¾ liter])	½ kg.
1 tsp.	ground cinnamon (optional)	5 ml.

In a saucepan set over medium heat, dissolve the sugar in the water and boil the syrup to the thread stage *(pages 8-11)*. Tip in the almonds, and use a wooden spatula to stir them constantly until they have absorbed the syrup. Remove the pan from the heat and stir the almonds continuously until they are dry; return the pan to the heat, and stir until the almonds are glazed and their sugar coating has browned lightly. Remove the pan from the heat. Stir in the cinnamon, if using. Tip the glazed almonds onto a buttered platter and separate the almonds.

HENRIETTE DAVIDIS
PRAKTISCHES KOCHBUCH

Candied Almonds

Amandes à la Siamoise

This recipe for candied almonds is adapted from a book written in 1698 by the chef to King Louis XIV of France. It is not clear why the almonds are referred to as Siamese style.

To make about 2½ pounds [1¼ kg.]

2 cups	sugar	½ liter
½ cup	water	125 ml.
1 lb.	almonds, blanched, peeled, halved and lightly toasted (about 4 cups [1 liter])	½ kg.
about 1 cup	coarse white or colored sugar	about ¼ liter

Dissolve the sugar in the water over medium heat and cook the syrup to the hard-ball stage *(pages 8-11)*. Remove the pan from the heat and add the toasted almonds.

You may pour the mixture onto a sheet of buttered or oiled parchment paper that has been spread out on a rack, and then let the candy harden before breaking it into pieces. Or you may remove the almonds one by one from the syrup with a spoon and roll them in the coarse sugar before letting them dry on parchment paper.

NOUVELLE INSTRUCTION POUR LES CONFITURES,
LES LIQUEURS ET LES FRUITS

Poor Man's Almond Roca

To make about ¾ pound [350 g.]

3 oz.	almonds or walnuts, coarsely chopped (about ¾ cup [175 ml.])	90 g.
8 tbsp.	butter	120 ml.
¾ cup	brown sugar	175 ml.
6 oz.	semisweet chocolate, coarsely chopped	175 g.

Sprinkle the chopped nuts over the bottom of a well-greased 9-inch [23-cm.] piepan. In a 2-quart [2-liter] saucepan, melt the butter. Add the brown sugar, and then stir constantly for seven minutes. Pour the mixture over the nuts in the pan, and immediately top with the chopped chocolate. Let the chocolate melt, and then spread it over the sugar-butter mixture with the flat side of a table knife. Place the pan in the freezer for about 20 minutes so it will set. Then cut the candy into squares. Store the candy in the refrigerator.

RONA COHEN (EDITOR)
RECIPES TO RONA

Chocolate Almond Brittle

To make about 1½ pounds [¾ kg.]

2 cups	sugar	½ liter
⅓ cup	light corn syrup	75 ml.
⅔ cup	water	150 ml.
4 tbsp.	butter	60 ml.
2 oz.	semisweet chocolate, grated	60 g.
1 tsp.	vanilla extract	5 ml.
½ tsp.	baking soda	2 ml.
6 oz.	almonds, blanched, peeled, toasted and coarsely chopped (about 1½ cups [375 ml.])	175 g.

In a saucepan, combine the sugar with the corn syrup, water and butter. Cook over medium heat, stirring until the sugar has dissolved. Without stirring, continue cooking until a temperature of 300° F. [149° C.] is reached—the hard-crack stage *(pages 8-11)*. Remove the pan from the heat. Stirring the mixture rapidly, add the grated chocolate, vanilla extract, baking soda and toasted almonds. Pour the mixture in a thin layer onto a greased baking sheet. When it is cool enough to handle, pull the candy outward at two opposite edges to make the layer thin; rest the extra width on a second greased baking sheet. Let the brittle cool. When it is cold, break it into pieces with a hammer.

JULIETTE ELKON
THE CHOCOLATE COOKBOOK

Sugared Almonds

The author recommends cooking the sugar-coating mixture in a copper bowl, but an untinned copper saucepan or other heavy pan can be substituted.

To make 3 pounds [1½ kg.]

4 cups	sugar	1 liter
1 cup	water	¼ liter
1 lb.	almonds (about 3 cups [¾ liter])	½ kg.

In a copper bowl, dissolve 3 cups [¾ liter] of the sugar in about ⅔ cup [150 ml.] of the water over medium heat. Bring the syrup to a boil; boil to the soft-ball stage, 240° F. [116° C.] *(pages 8-11)*.

Off the heat, add the almonds and, with a wooden spoon, stir until the syrup sets. Continue stirring until the sugar grains and looks like powder. Turn the mixture out onto a marble slab and pick out all of the almonds, or put the mixture into a coarse sieve so that the sugar passes through the sieve and the almonds remain.

Return this almond sugar to the copper bowl, add half of the remaining water, and wash down the sides of the bowl with a wet pastry brush while boiling the syrup until it reaches the soft-ball stage. Add the almonds, stir the mixture until the sugar separates and crystallizes again, and remove the almonds from the sugar as before.

Put the reserved cup [¼ liter] of sugar into the pan, add the strained cooked sugar and the remaining water, wash down the sides of the pan as before while cooking, and cook the syrup to the soft-ball stage. Add the almonds. Stir as before, and continue stirring until the syrup sets and looks a little powdery, as before. Continue stirring over the heat until you notice that the crystallized sugar on the sides of the pan is starting to melt and that the almonds look shiny.

Now, without delay, turn all of the contents of the pan onto a marble slab and separate the almonds to prevent them from sticking to one another. Within a few minutes, the almonds will be ready to serve.

E. J. KOLLIST
FRENCH PASTRY, CONFECTIONERY AND SWEETS

Honey-Almond Candy

Sohan Asali

The quantity of saffron specified in this recipe will color the candy bright orange yellow. If a paler color is desired, use only 1 teaspoon [5 ml.] of saffron.

To make about 1 pound [½ kg.]

1 cup	sugar	¼ liter
2 tbsp.	honey	30 ml.
3 tbsp.	butter	45 ml.
6 oz.	almonds, blanched, peeled and slivered (about 1½ cups [375 ml.])	175 g.
1 tbsp.	ground saffron, dissolved in 2 tbsp. [30 ml.] hot water	15 ml.
about ¼ cup	chopped pistachios, or 2 tbsp. [30 ml.] almonds, blanched, peeled and slivered	about 50 ml.

Place the sugar, honey and butter in a saucepan over medium heat, stirring occasionally until the sugar dissolves, about 10 minutes. Add the 1½ cups [375 ml.] of almonds, and stir occasionally until the almonds turn golden brown, about 10 minutes. Do not stir too much, or the butter may separate. Add the saffron and remove the pan from the heat. Let the mixture cool until lukewarm, then drop it by teaspoonfuls onto a buttered baking sheet. Sprinkle each piece of candy with a few chopped pistachios or slivered almonds. When the pieces are completely cool and firm, use a narrow-bladed spatula to lift them off the baking sheet. Store the candy in an airtight container.

NESTA RAMAZANI
PERSIAN COOKING

Christmas Almond Brittle

Makagigi

The technique of cooking sugar to a caramel without water is demonstrated on page 9.

To make 1½ pounds [¾ kg.]

¼ cup	sugar	50 ml.
½ cup	honey	125 ml.
10 tbsp.	butter	150 ml.
1 lb.	walnuts or almonds, chopped (about 4 cups [1 liter])	½ kg.

Put the sugar into a heavy frying pan. Heat the sugar over low heat until it has melted and is delicately browned *(caramel stage, pages 8-11)*. Add the honey and butter, and simmer for 20 minutes. Stir in the nuts and cook for 10 minutes. Line a platter or pan with wax paper and drop tablespoons of the brittle onto the paper. Let the brittle harden.

SAVELLA STECHISHIN
TRADITIONAL UKRAINIAN COOKERY

Cracknel

Croquante

This candy, similar to nougat, is made in Provence at Christmas time. Originally it was made only with almonds and honey—sugar was not introduced into Europe until the time of the Crusades.

To make about 14 ounces [400 g.]

¾ cup	superfine sugar	175 ml.
5 oz.	almonds, chopped (about 1¼ cups [300 ml.])	150 g.
about 5 tbsp.	honey	about 75 ml.

Put the sugar, almonds and 5 tablespoons [75 ml.] of the honey into a saucepan, and cook over high heat, stirring constantly, until the mixture reaches the hard-crack stage *(pages 8-11)*. If the mixture becomes too thick to stir, add another tablespoon [15 ml.] of honey during the cooking.

Pour the mixture out onto an oiled marble slab, and spread it out with an oiled rolling pin or a large, smooth potato until it forms an even layer about ¼ inch [6 mm.] thick. With a sharp, oiled knife, cut the mixture into 2-inch [5-cm.] squares before it has completely cooled.

LOUIS GINIÉS
CUISINE PROVENÇALE

Italian Cracknel

Croccante

The technique of caramelizing sugar without water is demonstrated on page 9.

To make about ½ pound [¼ kg.]		
¼ lb.	almonds, blanched, peeled and slivered (about 1 cup [¼ liter])	125 g.
½ cup	superfine sugar	125 ml.
2 tbsp.	butter (optional)	30 ml.
½	lemon	½

Toast the slivered almonds in a heavy pan over very low heat, turning them frequently until they are yellowish in color but not browned.

Put the sugar into a heavy saucepan and melt it over very low heat, rotating the pan as the sugar melts. When the sugar is bubbly, stir in the hot almonds. Add the butter if you want a richer candy. Continue cooking the mixture until it turns a cinnamon color. Immediately dip the bottom of the pan in cold water to stop the cooking. Then slowly pour the mixture into a buttered or oiled pan measuring 8 by 12 inches [20 by 30 cm.]. Use the cut side of the lemon to spread the mixture evenly and push it into the corners of the pan.

Let the cracknel cool completely. To unmold it, loosen the edges with a sharp knife, then invert the pan. If unmolding is difficult, briefly dip the base of the pan into boiling water. Break the unmolded cracknel into pieces.

PELLEGRINO ARTUSI
LA SCIENZA IN CUCINA E L'ARTE DI MANGIAR BENE

Cashew Brittle

Raw cashews are sold in health-food stores.

To make about 1 pound [½ kg.]		
¾ cup	honey	175 ml.
¼ cup	water	50 ml.
1 cup	raw cashews	¼ liter
1 tbsp.	butter	15 ml.
½ tsp.	vanilla extract	2 ml.
1 tsp.	baking soda	5 ml.

Boil the honey and the water until the syrup forms a soft ball when dropped into cold water or reaches 234° F. [112° C.] on a candy thermometer *(pages 8-11)*. Add the nuts and, stirring constantly, boil the mixture until it turns golden brown—10 to 12 minutes. Remove the pan from the heat, and add the butter, vanilla and baking soda. Mix well, then pour the brittle onto a buttered baking sheet. When it cools, break the brittle into pieces.

FAYE MARTIN
RODALE'S NATURALLY DELICIOUS DESSERTS AND SNACKS

Coconut Brittle

To make about 1 ½ pounds [¾ kg.]		
2 cups	sugar	½ liter
½ cup	light corn syrup	125 ml.
½ cup	water	125 ml.
2 tbsp.	butter	30 ml.
¼ tsp.	salt	1 ml.
⅛ tsp.	baking soda	½ ml.
1 ½ cups	freshly grated coconut	375 ml.

Combine the sugar, corn syrup and water, and bring to a boil, stirring constantly. Stop stirring, and boil the syrup until a soft ball is formed when the syrup is tried in water *(pages 8-11)*—the temperature of the syrup will be 234° to 240° F. [112° to 116° C.]. Add the butter and salt. Continue boiling until a hard ball is formed—250° to 264° F. [121° to 130° C.]. Add the baking soda and coconut. Pour the brittle mixture into a buttered pan 8 inches [20 cm.] square and let it cool.

ALLEN PRESCOTT
THE WIFESAVER'S CANDY RECIPES

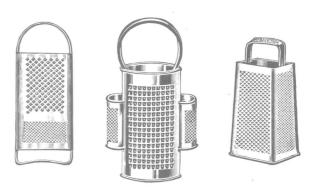

Peanut-Molasses Brittle

To make about 1 ¾ pounds [875 g.]		
2 cups	sugar	½ liter
½ cup	molasses	125 ml.
½ cup	water	125 ml.
5 tbsp.	butter	75 ml.
1 tsp.	baking soda	5 ml.
10 oz.	unsalted peanuts (about 2 cups [½ liter]), blanched, peeled and roasted	300 g.

Put the sugar, molasses and water into a saucepan and cook them, stirring until the sugar is dissolved. Continue cooking very slowly until the temperature of 300° F. [149° C.] is reached (*hard-crack stage, pages 8-11*).

Remove the pan from the heat, stir in the butter, and then beat in the baking soda. Add the peanuts and mix them in well. Pour the mixture in a thin layer onto a well-greased cold work surface or baking sheet. Smooth the candy out with a metal spatula. If you like, pull it into a thin sheet that will be easy to break into pieces. Or leave it unpulled and score it into 1-inch [2½-cm.] squares. In either case, loosen the brittle from the work surface or baking sheet with the spatula while the candy is still warm. When cold, break the brittle into squares or pieces.

MAY B. VAN ARSDALE AND RUTH PARRISH CASA EMELLOS
CANDY RECIPES & OTHER CONFECTIONS

Maine Peanut Brittle

The technique of cooking sugar to a caramel without water is demonstrated on page 9.

	To make about 1 pound [½ kg.]	
5 oz.	peanuts, toasted, peeled and chopped (about 1 cup [¼ liter])	150 g.
2 cups	sugar	½ liter

Spread the peanuts in a buttered pan 9 inches [23 cm.] square. Put the sugar in a heavy saucepan and cook it over low heat, stirring constantly, until it melts into a thin syrup, about 10 minutes. Pour the syrup over the nuts. When the brittle is nearly cold, mark it into squares.

WILMA LORD PERKINS (EDITOR)
THE FANNIE FARMER COOKBOOK

Old-fashioned Molasses Candy

	To make about 1 pound [½ kg.]	
½ cup	dark brown sugar	125 ml.
1½ cups	molasses	375 ml.
1 tbsp.	butter	15 ml.
1 tbsp.	vinegar	15 ml.
1 tsp.	baking soda	5 ml.
3 oz.	peanuts, coarsely chopped (about ½ cup [125 ml.]) (optional)	90 g.

Stir the brown sugar, molasses, butter and vinegar together. Boil them to a temperature of 260° F. [127° C.], or until a drop will form a hard ball in cold water (*pages 8-11*). Add the baking soda and stir rapidly. Turn the mixture at once into a buttered shallow pan 8 inches [20 cm.] square. If desired, spread chopped peanuts over the top. Cool the candy and break it into pieces for serving.

MILDRED GROSBERG BELLIN
THE JEWISH COOK BOOK

Pecan Pralines, New Orleans-Style

	To make about 2 pounds [1 kg.]	
2 cups	sugar	½ liter
¾ cup	water	175 ml.
½ tbsp.	vinegar	7 ml.
1 lb.	pecans, halved (about 4 cups [1 liter])	½ kg.

Boil the sugar, water and vinegar together until this syrup makes a soft ball when a drop is tested in a cup of cold water (*pages 8-11*). Put in the pecans and cook until the candy forms a hard ball when tested in a cup of cold water.

Have ready large buttered platters or cookie sheets; drop onto them tablespoonfuls of the candy, spaced about 6 inches [15 cm.] apart. Let the pralines cool. When they are cold and hard, run a knife under the pralines and put them on a plate.

A BOOK OF FAMOUS OLD NEW ORLEANS RECIPES

Pecan Pralines

Pralines aux Pacanes

	To make 1½ pounds [¾ kg.]	
½ lb.	pecans (about 2 cups [½ liter])	¼ kg.
2⅔ cups	dark brown sugar (1 lb. [½ kg.])	650 ml.
¼ cup	water	50 ml.

Cut some of the pecans into fine pieces, others into halves and others again into demihalves. Thoroughly dissolve the sugar in the water, then bring the syrup to a boil. Add the pecans. Let all boil, stirring constantly, until the mixture begins to thicken, and then take it off the stove.

Drop the mixture on a buttered marble slab or platter by spoonfuls, spreading them out with a fork until each forms a neat, round cake about ½ inch [1 cm.] thick and 4 to 5 inches [10 to 12½ cm.] in diameter. Let the pralines dry, then lift them off the slab or platter with a narrow-bladed spatula.

THE PICAYUNE'S CREOLE COOK BOOK

Peanut Candy

The technique of caramelizing sugar without water is demonstrated on page 9. For this recipe you will need a baking pan 8 inches [20 cm.] square, well buttered and warmed in a 200° F. [100° C.] oven.

To make about 1 ¼ pounds [600 g.]

3½ oz.	peanuts, chopped (about ¾ cup [175 ml.])	105 g.
¼ tsp.	salt	1 ml.
2 cups	sugar	½ liter

Heat the peanuts and the salt together. Put the sugar in a heavy pan, place it over low heat, and stir it constantly until the sugar changes to a light brown syrup. Add the chopped peanuts and the salt, stirring them in as quickly as possible. Pour the mixture immediately into a hot buttered pan and, with a buttered knife, divide it into squares.

A BOOK OF FAMOUS OLD NEW ORLEANS RECIPES

Molasses Toffee

La Colle

It is most important to dissolve the sugar thoroughly. The finished toffee should have the thick, smooth consistency implicit in the French name for this confection: La colle means "glue." It was a Creole specialty of New Orleans.

To make about 2 pounds [1 kg.]

5 cups	dark brown sugar or 2 cups [½ liter] dark molasses	1 ¼ liters
½ lb.	pecans or peanuts, coarsely chopped (about 2 cups [½ liter])	¼ kg.

Dissolve the sugar in ¼ cup [50 ml.] of water and bring the mixture—or the molasses alone—to a boil. Stir in the chopped nuts and cook the syrup until it reaches the soft-crack stage *(pages 8-11)*. Pour the mixture into paper cups or molds measuring 2 by 4 inches [5 by 10 cm.], making each piece of candy about ¼ to ½ inch [6 mm. to 1 cm.] thick. Let them cool.

THE PICAYUNE'S CREOLE COOK BOOK

Pine-Nut Candy

Pinocchiate

Pinocchiate is candy from the Umbria region of Italy and is made for Christmas in Assisi, Gubbio and Perugia. The method of preparation, shape and ingredients vary, but the candy usually is diamond-shaped and wrapped in pairs, one plain and one chocolate-flavored. To flavor *pinocchiate*, add ⅔ cup [150 ml.] of cocoa powder to the basic mixture.

To make about 4 pounds [2 kg.]

4 cups	sugar	1 liter
1 ¼ cups	water	300 ml.
	cream of tartar	
1 ¾ lb.	pine nuts	875 g.
1 tbsp.	flour	15 ml.

In a large pan, dissolve the sugar in the water, then add a pinch of cream of tartar. Boil the syrup to the soft-crack stage *(pages 8-11)*. Remove the pan from the heat, and add the pine nuts and flour. Mix well with a wooden spoon. When the ingredients are thoroughly blended, turn the mixture out onto a buttered or oiled marble slab. Use a spatula to flatten the candy until it is about ½ inch [1 cm.] thick. Immediately cut the candy into 1½-inch [4-cm.] diamonds.

PIERO LUIGI MENICHETTI AND LUCIANA MENICHETTI PANFILI
VECCHIA CUCINA EUGUBINA

Spiced English Walnuts

To make about 1 ¼ pounds [600 g.]

1 cup	sugar	¼ liter
¼ tsp.	salt	1 ml.
1 tsp.	ground cinnamon	5 ml.
½ cup	milk	125 ml.
¾ lb.	walnuts (about 3 cups [¾ liter])	350 g.
1 tsp.	vanilla extract	5 ml.

In a heavy saucepan, combine the sugar, salt, cinnamon and milk. Stirring constantly, cook over medium heat until the sugar dissolves, then boil without stirring until the syrup forms a soft ball in cold water *(pages 8-11)*. Remove the pan from the heat, and add the nuts and vanilla extract. Spread the candy out on wax paper and let it cool before cutting it into squares.

LOUIS SZATHMÁRY (EDITOR)
FIFTY YEARS OF PRAIRIE COOKING

Nut Candy

Nuent

To make about 2 ½ pounds [1 ¼ kg.]

½ cup	sugar	125 ml.
2 cups	honey	½ liter
1 ½ lb.	walnuts or pecans, finely chopped (about 6 cups [1 ½ liters])	¾ kg.

Bring the sugar and honey to a boil; boil them for 10 minutes. Slowly add the nuts. Cook the mixture until it is thick, or until a candy thermometer registers the soft-crack stage *(pages 8-11)*. Spoon the mixture out onto a wet marble slab or wooden board. Dip your hands in ice water, and pat the mixture into a square about 1 inch [2½ cm.] thick. Let the square cool slightly. Using a sharp, wet knife, cut it into squares or diamonds.

SARA KASDAN
LOVE AND KNISHES

Sesame Crunch

Gajjak

Raw sesame seeds are sold at health-food stores.

To make about ½ pound [¼ kg.]

1 cup	raw sesame seeds	¼ liter
1 tbsp.	water	15 ml.
1 tbsp.	butter	15 ml.
½ cup	sugar	125 ml.
½ tsp.	fresh lemon juice, pulp strained out	2 ml.

Grind the sesame seeds to a fine powder using a coffee grinder or an electric blender.

Heat the water and butter in an enameled pan over medium-low heat. When the butter melts, add the sugar. Stirring constantly to prevent burning, cook the mixture until it turns a butterscotch color—10 to 15 minutes.

Add the lemon juice and stir rapidly for five seconds; the candy will sizzle. Add the sesame powder. Mix vigorously for 15 seconds, then immediately pour the mixture onto a greased marble slab or wooden board in a square about 9 inches [23 cm.]. Place a 9-inch-square piece of greased wax paper (greased side down) over the sesame mixture. Using a rolling pin, roll the mixture into a sheet ⅛ inch [3 mm.] thick. Working quickly while the mixture is still warm, peel off the wax paper, and use a sharp knife to cut the candy into 2-inch [2½-cm.] squares or diamond-shaped pieces. The en-

tire process—from pouring the sesame mixture through cutting the shapes—must be done very quickly, without interruption; otherwise the mixture will cool and become brittle and impossible to handle.

When the candy has cooled, separate the pieces. Wrap each one in decorative silver paper or in foil. Store the pieces in an airtight container. *Gajjak* keeps indefinitely.

JULIE SAHNI
CLASSIC INDIAN COOKING

Sesame Candy

Semesmyah

To make about 9 ounces [275 g.]

6 oz.	sesame seeds (about 1 cup [¼ liter])	175 g.
3 tbsp.	brown sugar	45 ml.
3 tbsp.	honey	45 ml.

To toast the sesame seeds, spread them evenly in a 10-inch [25-cm.] frying pan. Stirring constantly, cook the seeds over fairly low heat for about five minutes. Remove the pan from the heat and let it stand.

In a small pan, combine the sugar and the honey. Stirring constantly, cook them over low heat until thick, about five minutes. Add the sesame seeds and mix thoroughly.

Put a piece of wax paper on a board or kitchen table and empty the sesame-seed mixture into the center. Cover it with another piece of wax paper and, with a rolling pin, roll out the mixture to a thickness of about ¼ inch [6 mm.]. Remove the paper. Cut the candy into square or diamond shapes. Let the candy cool, then separate the pieces and store them in a tightly covered box or jar.

DAISY INY
THE BEST OF BAGHDAD COOKING

Sesame Snaps

Halawet Sumsum

To make about 2 pounds [1 kg.]

2 cups	sugar	½ liter
1 lb.	sesame seeds (about 3 cups [¾ liter])	½ kg.

Place the sugar and sesame seeds in a saucepan. Let them simmer over very low heat, stirring gently all the time, until the sugar is melted and the whole turns slightly brown, about 10 minutes. Pour the mixture onto a buttered baking sheet or metal tray. Spread it out in a layer about ¼ inch [6 mm.] thick. While it is still warm and before it becomes brittle, slice the mixture with a sharp knife. Wrap the pieces separately in parchment or wax paper. This candy will keep indefinitely.

MARGARET JOY PHILIPPOU
101 ARABIAN DELIGHTS

Sesame Squares

To toast sesame seeds, pour them into a dry skillet and, stirring constantly, cook them over medium heat for about 10 minutes until they begin to release their aroma.

This candy is chewy, but becomes brittle if the syrup is cooked to 300° F. [149° C.]. Remember, moisture is the enemy of brittles, so store the candy in an airtight container!

To make about 1 ¼ pounds [600 g.]

¾ lb.	toasted sesame seeds (about 2 cups [½ liter])	350 g.
1 ½ cups	honey	375 ml.
1 tbsp.	fresh lemon juice, pulp strained out	15 ml.

Lightly oil the inside of a 3-quart [3-liter] saucepan. Combine the sesame seeds, honey and lemon juice in the saucepan. Over medium heat, cook the mixture to the boiling point. Then, stirring constantly, boil it to 280° F. [138° C.], the soft-crack stage *(pages 8-11)*. Pour the mixture immediately into an oiled jelly-roll pan. As the mixture cools, flatten the edges. When the candy has cooled completely, cut it into 2-inch [5-cm.] squares or 2-by-4-inch [5-by-10-cm.] bars. Wrap each piece in wax paper or plastic wrap. Store the pieces in an airtight container.

MIRIAM LOWENBERG
CREATIVE CANDY MAKING

Poppy-Seed Candy

Mohnelech

To make about 3 pounds [1 ½ kg.]

4 cups	poppy seeds, covered with boiling water, soaked overnight and drained	1 liter
½ cup	sugar	125 ml.
2 cups	honey	½ liter
½ lb.	pecans or walnuts, chopped (about 2 cups [½ liter])	¼ kg.

Pound the poppy seeds with a pestle or other heavy instrument for at least 10 minutes. (Pounding cracks the seeds and releases the flavor.) Large poppy seeds can be run through a food grinder.

Cook the sugar and honey over low heat until the sugar dissolves. Add the poppy seeds and, stirring frequently, cook the mixture until it is thick. This may take 30 to 40 minutes. Test the mixture by dropping a spoonful onto a wet work surface; if it holds its shape, it is ready for the next step. Stir in the nuts. Cook for one minute longer.

Turn the mixture out onto a wet work surface. Dip your hands in ice water, and pat the mixture to a thickness of ½ inch [1 cm.]. Let it cool for five to 10 minutes. With a sharp knife dipped in hot water, cut the candy into about 50 pieces.

SARA KASDAN
LOVE AND KNISHES

Polish Poppy-Seed Candy

Makagigi

To make about 1 pound [½ kg.]

½ cup	sugar	125 ml.
¾ cup	honey	175 ml.
5 oz.	poppy seeds, ground (about 1 cup [¼ liter])	150 g.

Stirring continuously, cook the ingredients over low heat. When the mixture is lightly browned, after about 15 minutes, pour it onto an oiled marble slab or platter. Use an oiled, narrow-bladed spatula to spread the mixture into a thin layer. Let the candy set and, when it is firm but not cold, cut it into 1-inch [2½-cm.] squares.

JAN CZERNIKOWSKI
CIASTA, CIASTKA, CIASTECZKA

Corn Balls

To make about 2 pounds [1 kg.]

2 cups	sugar	½ liter
1 ½ cups	water	375 ml.
½ cup	light corn syrup	125 ml.
⅓ tsp.	salt	1 ½ ml.
⅓ tsp.	vinegar	1 ½ ml.
1 tbsp.	vanilla extract	15 ml.
5 quarts	freshly popped popcorn, made from ½ cup [125 ml.] dried popcorn	5 liters

Bring the sugar, water and corn syrup to a boil and, without stirring, boil the mixture for 10 minutes. Add the salt, vinegar and vanilla, and boil for another 10 minutes. The mixture should be brittle when tested in cold water *(hard-crack stage, pages 8-11)*.

Have the corn in a large pan; gradually pour the syrup, using a spoon all of the time to turn the popcorn so that it may be evenly coated. Shape the mixture into balls and let them stand in a cold place until brittle. Wrap the balls in wax paper and tie them at the throat with colored thread.

AMY B. W. MILLER AND PERSIS W. FULLER (EDITORS)
THE BEST OF SHAKER COOKING

Cracker Jacks

To make about 1 pound [½ kg.]

2 quarts	freshly popped popcorn, made from ¼ cup [50 ml.] dried popcorn	2 liters
¼ tsp.	salt	1 ml.
½ lb.	shelled peanuts (about 2 cups [½ liter])	¼ kg.
1 cup	molasses	¼ liter
½ cup	brown sugar	125 ml.
½ tsp.	vinegar	2 ml.

Salt the popcorn, and mix it with the toasted peanuts in a roasting pan.

Combine the molasses, sugar and vinegar in a heavy saucepan, and cook the mixture over low heat, stirring constantly to prevent burning. When the mixture spins a thread or reaches 250° F. [121° C.] on a candy thermometer *(pages 8-11)*, remove it from the stove and pour it over the popcorn-peanut mixture. Stir the ingredients well, then let them harden and cool completely. Break the mass of candy into small chunks.

LYDIA SAIGER
THE JUNK FOOD COOKBOOK

Butterscotch

To make about 1 pound [½ kg.]

⅔ cup	water	150 ml.
1 lb.	Demerara or turbinado sugar	½ kg.
4 tbsp.	butter	60 ml.

Pour the water into a saucepan and bring it to a boil. Add the sugar and the butter, reduce the heat, and cook the mixture slowly, stirring constantly until the sugar dissolves and the butter melts. Bring the mixture to a boil, cover the pan, and simmer for two minutes. Uncover the pan, and continue to boil without stirring for about 12 minutes, or until a little of the mixture dropped into a cup of cold water separates into hard, brittle threads *(hard-crack stage, pages 8-11)*. The temperature on the candy thermometer should register 300° F. [149° C.].

Pour the mixture into a buttered pan 6 inches [15 cm.] square and let it rest at room temperature until it is almost set. Butter a knife and use it to mark the butterscotch into squares or bars. When the butterscotch has hardened, break it along the marked lines and wrap each piece in wax paper.

SONIA ALLISON
THE DAIRY BOOK OF HOME COOKERY

Old-fashioned Butterscotch

To make about 1 pound [½ kg.]

2 cups	sugar	½ liter
⅔ cup	heavy cream	150 ml.
⅔ cup	water	150 ml.
	cream of tartar	
6 tbsp.	butter, cut into small pieces	90 ml.
½ tsp.	vanilla extract	2 ml.

Place the sugar in a saucepan, add the cream and the water, and stir until the sugar dissolves. Add a pinch of cream of tartar, place over medium heat, and boil the mixture very slowly until its temperature measures 240° F. [116° C.] on a candy thermometer *(soft-ball stage, pages 8-11)*. Add the butter and boil the mixture until it reaches 280° F. [138° C.]—the soft-crack stage. Remove the pan from the heat and add the vanilla extract.

Pour the mixture into a deep, buttered pan 7 inches [18 cm.] square. When the butterscotch is nearly cold, use the point of a buttered or oiled knife to mark it into bars or squares. When the butterscotch is quite cold and set, break it up, wrap each piece in wax paper, and keep the candy in an airtight container.

SONIA AGNEW
SWEET-MAKING FOR EVERYWOMAN

Swedish Cream Toffee
Knäck

To make about 1¾ pounds [875 g.]

1¾ cups	sugar	425 ml.
1¼ cups	heavy cream	300 ml.
1¼ cups	English golden syrup	300 ml.
¼ cup	dry bread crumbs, sifted	50 ml.
5 oz.	almonds, blanched, peeled and finely chopped (about 1½ cups [375 ml.])	150 g.

Stir the sugar, cream and golden syrup together in a saucepan. Place the pan over medium heat and cook until the mixture reaches the hard-ball stage *(pages 8-11)*. This may take about 15 to 20 minutes. Add the bread crumbs and boil the mixture for another five minutes *(soft-crack stage)*. Stir in the almonds and let the mixture come to a boil again quickly. Pour it into little fluted paper cups.

INGA NORBERG (EDITOR)
GOOD FOOD FROM SWEDEN

Dark Everton Toffee

To make about 1 pound [½ kg.]

1¼ cups	Demerara or turbinado sugar	300 ml.
¼ cup	water	50 ml.
2 tbsp.	English golden syrup	30 ml.
1 tbsp.	molasses	15 ml.
7 tbsp.	butter	105 ml.

Put all of the ingredients into a saucepan. Heat the mixture slowly, stirring, until the butter melts and the sugar dissolves. Bring the mixture to a boil. Cover the pan. Boil gently for about two minutes. Uncover the pan and continue to boil the mixture, stirring it occasionally, for 10 to 15 minutes until a little of the mixture dropped into a cup of cold water separates into hard and brittle threads *(hard-crack stage, pages 8-11)*. The temperature on a candy thermometer should read 300° F. [149° C.]. Pour the mixture into a buttered pan 6 inches [15 cm.] square. Let the toffee harden, then turn it out onto a board and break it into pieces with a small hammer.

SONIA ALLISON
THE DAIRY BOOK OF HOME COOKERY

Everton Toffee

The technique of making toffee is shown on pages 34-35. The lemon juice may be added at the end of cooking to minimize loss of flavor by evaporation.

To make about 1¼ pounds [600 g.]

2 cups	sugar	½ liter
8 tbsp.	butter	120 ml.
1 tsp.	fresh lemon juice, pulp strained out	5 ml.
1¼ cups	water	300 ml.

Put all of the ingredients into a heavy pan. Stir them over medium heat until the sugar has dissolved, about 10 to 15 minutes. Then, without stirring, boil until the mixture reaches a temperature of 290° F. [143° C.] *(soft-crack stage, pages 8-11)*. Pour the mixture into a buttered or oiled pan measuring 8 by 12 by 1¼ inches [20 by 30 by 3 cm.], and let the toffee cool until it is almost firm to the touch. Then mark it into 1-inch [2½-cm.] squares with a very sharp knife. When it is completely cold, break the toffee into pieces and wrap them in wax paper.

WINIFRED GRAHAM
CHOCOLATES AND CANDIES FOR PLEASURE AND PROFIT

Passover Ginger Candy

Passover Ingberlech

Matzo meal —ground matzos —is obtainable wherever Jewish foods are sold.

To make about 1½ pounds [¾ kg.]

1 cup	sugar	¼ liter
⅔ cup	honey	150 ml.
2 oz.	almonds, blanched, peeled and chopped (about ½ cup [125 ml.])	60 g.
1½ tbsp.	ground ginger	22 ml.
1 cup	matzo meal	¼ liter
2	eggs, beaten	2
¼ cup	sugar, mixed with 1 tsp. [5 ml.] ground ginger	50 ml.

In a deep saucepan, combine the cup [¼ liter] of sugar and the honey, stir over low heat, and bring the mixture to a boil. Reduce the heat and simmer for 10 minutes. Remove the pan from the heat. Mix the almonds, ground ginger and the matzo meal with the eggs; mix well, using a fork. Add the mixture to the syrup. Stirring constantly, cook over low heat until a candy thermometer registers the soft-crack stage *(pages 8-11)*.

Turn the mixture out onto a wet marble slab or board. Dip your hands in ice water; use the palms of your hands to flatten the mixture to a thickness of ½ inch [1 cm.]. Sprinkle the mixture with the ginger-flavored sugar and let it cool slightly. With a sharp, wet knife, cut the candy into about 25 squares or diamonds.

SARA KASDAN
LOVE AND KNISHES

Golden Honeycomb Taffy

Yellow-Man (Modern)

To make about 1¾ pounds [875 g.]

8 tbsp.	butter	120 ml.
2 tbsp.	vinegar	30 ml.
⅔ cup	molasses	150 ml.
⅔ cup	English golden syrup	150 ml.
2 cups	Demerara or turbinado sugar (1 lb. [½ kg.])	½ liter
½ tsp.	baking soda	2 ml.

In a saucepan over medium heat, melt the butter. Add the vinegar, molasses, golden syrup, and Demerara or turbinado sugar. Stir the mixture until the sugar has dissolved. Without stirring, boil the mixture until it is crisp when tested in cold water *(hard-crack stage, pages 8-11)*. Remove the pan from the heat and stir in the baking soda. When the mixture foams up, stir it again. Pour the mixture quickly into a buttered pan 8 inches [20 cm.] square. Let the taffy cool. When it is cool, mark the surface of the taffy into 1-inch [2½-cm.] squares. Leave it until cold, cut it into squares, and store the taffy in a tightly closed tin.

FLORENCE IRWIN
THE COOKIN' WOMAN

Dutch Coffee Candy

Haags Hopje

The use of confectioners' bars is demonstrated on page 19.

To make about 10 ounces [300 g.]

⅞ cup	sugar	200 ml.
5 tbsp.	English golden syrup	75 ml.
⅓ cup	strong black coffee	75 ml.
4 tbsp.	butter	60 ml.
4 tbsp.	heavy cream	60 ml.

In a large saucepan, stir the sugar together with the golden syrup and coffee until the sugar dissolves. Bring the mixture to a boil. Add the butter and cream, taking care not to let the mixture boil over, as it will bubble up quickly to the top of the pan. Cook, stirring constantly, until the temperature of the mixture reaches 278° F. [137° C.]—the soft-crack stage *(pages 8-11)*.

Pour the mixture onto a buttered marble slab between confectioners' bars arranged in a 6-inch [15-cm.] square. As soon as the mixture begins to harden, in 15 to 20 minutes, mark it into ¾-inch [2-cm.] squares. When the mixture has cooled completely, break it into the little squares.

C. A. H. HAITSMA MULIER-VAN BEUSEKOM (EDITOR)
CULINAIRE ENCYCLOPÉDIE

Macadamia Toffee

To make about ¾ pound [350 g.]

1 cup	butter	¼ liter
1 ¼ cups	sugar	300 ml.
½ lb.	macadamia nuts (about 1 ½ cups [375 ml.]), half finely chopped	¼ kg.
1 oz.	semisweet chocolate, melted	30 g.

In a heavy skillet, melt the butter. Add the sugar. Stir the mixture over high heat until it foams vigorously; then stir over low heat for five minutes. Add the whole nuts; stir over high heat until the mixture begins to smoke. Reduce the heat to low; stir for seven minutes. If the mixture darkens too quickly, remove it from the heat, but still stir it for a full seven minutes.

Quickly pour the mixture into a pan measuring 9 by 13 inches [23 by 32 cm.]. Let it cool. Spread half of the chocolate over the candy, then sprinkle with half of the chopped nuts, and cool. Flip the sheet of candy out of the pan. Spread the second side with the remaining chocolate, and sprinkle with the remaining nuts. Let it cool, and then break the candy into pieces. Store the candy in a covered metal container lined with wax paper.

DOROTHY C. FRANK
COOKING WITH NUTS

Swedish Toffee

Knäck

To make about ¾ pound [350 g.]

½ cup	sugar	125 ml.
⅓ cup	heavy cream	75 ml.
⅓ cup	dark molasses	75 ml.
2 tbsp.	butter	30 ml.
1 oz.	almonds, blanched, peeled and chopped (about ¼ cup [50 ml.])	30 g.

In a heavy saucepan, heat the sugar, cream and molasses slowly, stirring until the sugar has dissolved. Without stirring, cook the mixture over medium heat until it reaches a temperature of 248° F. [120° C.]—the firm-ball stage *(pages 8-11)*. Remove the pan from the heat and then stir in the butter and almonds.

Quickly pour the mixture into a buttered, shallow baking pan 4 by 8 inches [10 by 20 cm.]. When the toffee is lukewarm, use a greased knife to mark it into 1-inch [2½-cm.] squares. Remove the toffee from the pan when it is completely cold, and cut or break it into squares. Wrap each square of toffee in wax paper.

GUNNEVI BONEKAMP
SCANDINAVIAN COOKING

Farfel Candy

Matzo farfel are made by mixing water and matzo meal into a paste, shaping the paste into small pieces and baking or frying them. They are obtainable ready-made where Jewish foods are sold.

To make about 2 pounds [1 kg.]

1⅓ cups	honey	325 ml.
½ cup	sugar	125 ml.
¾ cup	matzo farfel	175 ml.
¾ lb.	chopped nuts (about 3 cups [¾ liter])	350 g.

Dissolve the honey and the sugar over low heat. Bring them to a boil, and boil until they are light brown or until a candy thermometer registers the soft-crack stage *(pages 8-11)*. Stir in the farfel and the nuts. Pour the mixture out onto a wet marble slab or board. Wet your hands with ice water, and pat the candy into a square about ¾ inch [2 cm.] thick. Let it cool slightly. Then cut it with a sharp, wet knife into about 50 squares or diamonds.

SARA KASDAN
LOVE AND KNISHES

Toffee

To make about ¾ pound [350 g.]

1¼ cups	superfine sugar	300 ml.
1¼ cups	heavy cream	300 ml.
2 tsp.	vanilla extract	10 ml.
2 tsp.	Scotch whisky	10 ml.

In a clean, unlined copper saucepan, dissolve the sugar in the cream over medium heat and bring the mixture to a boil, stirring occasionally. Reduce the heat and simmer, without stirring: The mixture will first become quite liquid, and afterward it will gradually thicken. When it has thickened—after 15 to 20 minutes—add the vanilla extract and the whisky. About five minutes later, when the mixture becomes very frothy and draws away from the edges of the pan, pour it quickly onto a flat buttered dish—the toffee should set at once. Cut it into 1-inch [2½-cm.] squares. The toffee should be quite smooth and of a creamy white; it should be rich without being at all crisp or crumbly.

THE KING'S COLLEGE HOSPITAL BOOK OF COOKING RECIPES

Toffee-Butter Crunch

To make about 2½ pounds [1¼ kg.]

½ lb.	almonds, blanched and peeled (about 1½ cups [375 ml.])	¼ kg.
16 tbsp.	butter (½ lb. [¼ kg.])	240 ml.
1½ cups	sugar	375 ml.
3 tbsp.	water	45 ml.
1 tbsp.	light corn syrup	15 ml.
1 lb.	milk chocolate, broken into pieces	½ kg.

Chop half of the almonds coarse, the other half fine, and spread them on a baking sheet. Toast the nuts in a preheated 350° F. [180° C.] oven for five minutes, or until they are lightly browned.

In a large saucepan, melt the butter. Add the sugar, water and corn syrup. Stirring occasionally, cook the mixture over medium heat until it reaches the hard-crack stage—300° F. [149° C.] *(pages 8-11)*. Quickly stir in the coarsely chopped almonds. While it is still hot, spread the mixture onto a well-greased baking sheet measuring 9 by 13 inches [23 by 32 cm.]. Cool this candy thoroughly. Then turn it out onto wax paper.

In a bowl set in a saucepan of hot water, melt the chocolate. Spread half of the melted chocolate over the candy and sprinkle it with half of the finely chopped almonds. Cover the top with wax paper, and turn the candy over. Spread the other side with the remaining chocolate and sprinkle it with the remaining almonds. Chill the toffee to firm it, then break it into about 24 pieces.

JUNIOR LEAGUE OF JACKSON, MISSISSIPPI
SOUTHERN SIDEBOARDS

Black Nougat with Pine Honey

Le Nougat Noir au Miel de Pin

Nougat noir is a French name for dark nut toffee.

Pine honey, which is a specialty of the Chartreuse Valley, may be replaced by any good flower honey. This candy will have a different flavor for each kind of honey used.

To make about 1½ pounds [¾ kg.]

1 lb.	whole almonds	½ kg.
2 cups	honey	½ liter
1	small handful fresh thyme	1

Make sure the almonds are perfectly dry before using. Into a 1½-quart [1½-liter] heavy iron saucepan, put the honey and heat it slowly. As the temperature of the honey begins to rise, drop in the thyme and the almonds with their skins on. Continue cooking the mixture slowly, increasing the temperature and stirring the contents almost continuously until the honey begins to turn dark brown and the almonds begin to crackle. This will usually take about 30 minutes.

Line a shallow pan 9 inches [23 cm.] square with well-buttered aluminum foil or wax paper. Pour the almonds and honey into the pan. Press another piece of buttered paper or foil on top of the mixture. On top of that, place a light wooden board of a size just to fit inside the pan, and put a 2-pound [1-kg.] weight or can on top of the board so that the mixture will be pressed down and solidified. Let the candy cool gradually to room temperature. Do not refrigerate it. The cooling will take at least four hours.

When the nougat is cold, take it out of the pan and peel off the coverings. Lay the nougat on a wooden board and, with a heavy, sharp knife, cut it up into bite-sized squares. Store these in a tightly lidded jar. At room temperature they will be chewy. From the refrigerator they will be crackly.

ROY ANDRIES DE GROOT
THE AUBERGE OF THE FLOWERING HEARTH

Chocolate Nougat

Although this candy is called a nougat, it more closely resembles a caramel or toffee. The authors suggest that the nougat can also be dipped in chocolate; this technique is demonstrated on pages 74-75.

To make about ¾ pound [350 g.]

1 oz.	unsweetened or semisweet chocolate	30 g.
1 cup	superfine sugar	¼ liter
1 tsp.	liquid glucose or light corn syrup	5 ml.
5 tbsp.	water	75 ml.
2 tbsp.	butter	30 ml.
½ tsp.	vanilla extract	2 ml.
½ cup	hazelnuts, toasted, peeled and chopped, or almonds, blanched, peeled, toasted and chopped, or walnuts, chopped, or a mixture of the three	125 ml.
	edible rice paper	

Melt the chocolate over a pan of hot water and keep it warm.

Combine the sugar, glucose or corn syrup, water and butter in a saucepan, and dissolve them carefully. Put a candy thermometer into the saucepan and boil the mixture until it reaches 236° to 238° F. [113° to 114° C.] *(soft-ball stage, pages 8-11)*. Remove the pan from the heat and let the mixture cool for 15 to 20 minutes. When the candy is just warm to the touch, add the vanilla and the melted chocolate. Stir until the mixture forms a thick paste. Let the mixture stand for 30 minutes, covered with wax paper and a thick cloth so that it cools very slowly.

Pour the mixture out onto a board, and knead it until it is soft and smooth. (If it is not thick enough to knead, stir it well with a wooden spoon or spatula.) Return the mixture to a clean saucepan and melt it over boiling water, stirring

constantly, until it is soft enough to pour. Remove the pan from the heat and add the nuts.

Pour the nougat into a pan measuring 4 by 6 inches [10 by 15 cm.] and lined with edible rice paper. Brush another piece of rice paper with cold water and place it on top of the nougat. When the nougat is cold and set, cut it into 1-inch [2½-cm.] squares or 1-by-2-inch [2½-by-5-cm.] rectangles. Wrap the pieces in wax paper.

D. F. HUTTON AND E. M. BODE
SIMPLE SWEETMAKING

Dark Nougat
Nougat Noir

Although this candy is called a nougat, it more closely resembles a caramel or toffee. This nougat is one of the 13 traditional Provençal Christmas desserts.

To make about 4 pounds [2 kg.]

2 cups	superfine sugar	½ liter
1⅓ cups	honey (1 lb. [½ kg.])	325 ml.
2 lb.	almonds, blanched and lightly toasted (about 6 cups [1½ liters])	1 kg.
1 tbsp.	orange-flower water	15 ml.

In a saucepan, combine the sugar, honey, almonds, and orange-flower water. Stirring frequently, bring the mixture to a boil over low heat, and cook until the almonds crackle under a spatula and the honey turns pale golden brown.

Pour the nougat into two oiled pans 8 inches [20 cm.] square and allow it to cool. Then unmold the nougat and break it into pieces.

CÉLINE VENCE
ENCYCLOPÉDIE HACHETTE DE LA CUISINE RÉGIONALE

Cream Bonbons
Nidelzeltli

To make about 2 pounds [1 kg.]

2¼ cups	sugar	550 ml.
2 cups	milk, combined with 2 cups cream, or 4 cups [1 liter] milk and 2 tsp. [10 ml.] butter	½ liter

In a 4-quart [4-liter] saucepan, bring the sugar and the combination of milk and cream, or milk and butter, to a boil. Stir constantly until the mixture is reduced to a thick, yellowish brown paste that comes away easily from the bottom of the saucepan. Pour the paste into a buttered jelly-roll pan measuring 8 by 12 inches [20 by 30 cm.]. Spread out the paste to a thickness of about ½ inch [1 cm.] and let it cool for 10 minutes. Dip the tip of a knife in oil and cut the paste into 1-inch [2½-cm.] squares. Let the candy cool before breaking it into pieces and serving it.

EVA MARIA BORER
TANTE HEIDI'S SWISS KITCHEN

111

American Caramels

This recipe is from a book written for professional candy-makers—and produces a commercial-sized batch of caramels. The quantities can safely be halved or quartered, keeping them in the proportions listed, to yield a smaller batch. The author suggests that the vanilla extract can be replaced with strawberry or raspberry flavoring.

To make 12 pounds [5 kg.]

12 cups	sugar	3 liters
4 cups	liquid glucose or light corn syrup	1 liter
2 quarts	heavy cream	2 liters
1½ lb.	butter	¾ kg.
¼ cup	vanilla extract	50 ml.

Put the sugar, the glucose or corn syrup, and the cream into a pan; put the pan on low heat and stir constantly until the sugar has dissolved. Without stirring, boil the syrup to the firm-ball stage *(pages 8-11)*. Add the butter, stir until it is well mixed into the syrup, then remove the pan from the heat. Flavor the caramel mixture with the vanilla extract. Pour the caramel onto an oiled marble slab or into six oiled pans, each measuring 8 inches [20 cm.] square.

Let the caramel set before marking it into 1-inch [2½-cm.] squares. When the caramel is cold, cut it into squares with a sharp knife and wrap each square in wax paper.

SKUSE'S COMPLETE CONFECTIONER

Vanilla Cream Caramels

Caramels are soft candies for which sugar syrup is cooked to either the firm-ball or hard-ball stage; these caramels are not to be confused with the liquid brown caramel—sugar cooked to a much higher temperature—that is used for dipping or coating. The technique of making caramels is demonstrated on pages 36-37.

To make about ½ pound [¼ kg.]

1 cup	sugar	¼ liter
1 cup	heavy cream	¼ liter
2 tbsp.	butter	30 ml.
3 tbsp.	honey	45 ml.
½	vanilla bean, slit lengthwise	½

Mix the sugar, cream, butter, honey and the vanilla bean in a medium-sized copper pan. Place the pan over medium heat, and stir until the sugar has dissolved, occasionally brushing down the sides of the pan with a wet pastry brush to remove any crystals that form. When the sugar has completely dissolved, place a candy thermometer in the pan and bring the mixture to a boil. Boil the mixture steadily, stirring occasionally, until the candy thermometer registers 250° F. [121° C.] *(hard-ball stage, pages 8-11)*. Quickly test the consistency of the mixture by dropping a teaspoonful of it into a bowl of ice water. Remove the test sample from the bowl with your fingers—it should be cold and firm enough to shape into a ball. The syrup will now have the consistency of the finished candy. If the syrup is too soft, cook it a little longer. If it is just right, quickly remove the pan from the heat and dip the base in a bowl of ice water to stop further cooking. Use a fork to remove the vanilla bean and quickly pour the syrup into a buttered pan 8 inches [20 cm.] square or onto buttered wax paper, containing the candy with confectioners' bars.

Let the caramel cool. It should take about two hours at room temperature. When it has cooled and set, unmold the caramel and cut it into 1-inch [2½-cm.] strips, using an oiled or buttered knife. Chop the strips into 3-inch [8-cm.] nuggets. Caramels become sticky if left in contact with the air, so wrap them in pieces of cellophane.

PETITS PROPOS CULINAIRES VI

Milk Peppermint Lozenges

To make 1 pound [½ kg.]

2 cups	superfine sugar	½ liter
⅔ cup	milk or light cream	150 ml.
about 1 tsp.	peppermint extract or crème de menthe	about 5 ml.

Dissolve the sugar in the milk or light cream over medium heat, and boil the syrup for about 10 minutes *(firm-ball stage, pages 8-11)*. Take the pan off the heat and stir in the peppermint extract or liqueur. Beat the mixture until it is cool and firm enough to be dropped by the teaspoonful onto wax paper without running. Do this, as quickly as possible, as soon as the mixture begins to set in the pan. If it sets too firmly to drop, warm the mixture again for a moment.

MRS. M. E. RATTRAY
SWEETMEAT-MAKING AT HOME

Chocolate Caramels

To make 2½ pounds [1¼ kg.]

3 cups	light brown sugar	¾ liter
1½ cups	molasses	375 ml.
12 tbsp.	butter	180 ml.
3 tbsp.	flour	45 ml.
6 oz.	unsweetened chocolate	175 g.
1½ cups	milk	375 ml.
1½ tsp.	vanilla extract	7 ml.
about 30	almonds (optional)	about 30

In a saucepan, combine the sugar, molasses, butter and flour. Dissolve the sugar, stirring over medium heat, and bring the mixture to a boil. Boil it for five minutes, without stirring, then add the chocolate and milk. Cook, stirring frequently, until a small amount of the mixture forms a firm ball when dropped into very cold water—248° F. [120° C.] on a candy thermometer *(pages 8-11)*. Add the vanilla extract and pour the mixture into a buttered pan 9 inches [23 cm.] square. Let the caramel cool before cutting it into squares. Put the squares into individual paper cups and top each with an almond. Or wrap the caramels in a long strip of plastic wrap, twisting the wrap between the caramels and tying the twisted sections with ribbon to separate the squares.

WOMAN'S DAY COLLECTOR'S COOK BOOK

Ohio Chocolate Caramels

To make about 1 pound [½ kg.]

½ cup	milk	125 ml.
1 cup	sugar	¼ liter
3½ oz.	unsweetened chocolate, grated (about 1 cup [¼ liter])	100 g.
1 cup	molasses	¼ liter
2 tbsp.	butter	30 ml.

In a saucepan, heat the milk and add the sugar, chocolate and molasses; stir the mixture over medium heat until the sugar has dissolved and the chocolate has melted. Add the butter. Do not stir the mixture after it begins to boil, for that will make it grain. The mixture is done when it hardens and becomes brittle when dropped in cold water *(hard-ball stage, pages 8-11)*.

Pour the mixture onto buttered plates, making a layer about ½ inch [1 cm.] thick. When the caramel is nearly cold, cut it with a buttered knife into 1-inch [2½-cm.] squares.

THE BUCKEYE COOK BOOK

Bordeaux Chocolate Squares

Niniches Bordelaises

To make about ¾ pound [350 g.]

3 oz.	semisweet chocolate, grated	90 g.
½ cup	superfine sugar	125 ml.
3 tbsp.	butter	45 ml.
⅓ cup	honey	75 ml.
¾ cup	milk	175 ml.

In a saucepan, combine the grated chocolate and all of the other ingredients. Set the pan over medium heat and stir the mixture constantly. When the mixture begins to thicken, let a drop fall from a spoon into a bowl of ice water. If the drop dissolves in the water, continue to cook the mixture, still stirring it constantly. Repeat the process until the drop of mixture falls to the bottom of the bowl like a little pearl— the temperature will be 217° to 221° F. [103° to 105° C.] *(pages 8-11)*. Remove the pan from the heat.

Pour the mixture onto an oiled marble slab or platter, and spread it out with a narrow-bladed spatula. Score the candy into ¾-inch [2-cm.] squares with an oiled knife. Let the candy cool. When cold, cut it out along the scored lines.

CÉLINE VENCE
ENCYCLOPÉDIE HACHETTE DE LA CUISINE RÉGIONALE

Kinuski Caramels

Kinuskikola

To make about ¾ pound [350 g.]

¾ cup	sugar	175 ml.
3 tbsp.	cocoa powder	45 ml.
3 tbsp.	molasses	45 ml.
¾ cup	milk	175 ml.
2 tbsp.	butter	30 ml.
	vanilla extract	

In a heavy saucepan, mix the sugar and cocoa. Add the molasses, milk and butter, and heat the mixture slowly, stirring until the sugar has dissolved. Without stirring, simmer the mixture over medium heat until it reaches a temperature of 248° F. [120° C.]—the firm-ball stage *(pages 8-11)*. Remove the pan from the heat and stir in a few drops of vanilla extract. Quickly pour the mixture into a shallow, buttered baking pan 4 by 8 inches [10 by 20 cm.].

When the candy has cooled until lukewarm, cut it into 1-inch [2½-cm.] squares. Wrap each of these in wax paper.

GUNNEVI BONEKAMP
SCANDINAVIAN COOKING

Chocolate Fudge

The technique of making fudge is shown on pages 38-39.

To make about 1½ pounds [¾ kg.]

2 cups	sugar	½ liter
½ cup	milk	125 ml.
2 tbsp.	butter	30 ml.
6 oz.	semisweet chocolate, grated or chopped	175 g.

Put the sugar into a saucepan, and mix it with the milk to form a thick paste. Add the butter, and stir in the grated or chopped chocolate. Put the pan over low heat and cook, stirring constantly. Do not let the contents of the saucepan come to a boil until the sugar has dissolved and the chocolate has melted. Then increase the heat slightly and let the mixture boil for about five minutes, or until it reaches the soft-ball stage *(pages 8-11)*. Take the fudge off the heat, beat it until it is thick, and pour it into a buttered pan 8 inches [20 cm.] square. Cut the fudge into 1-inch [2½-cm.] squares before it has time to get cold.

MRS. C. F. LEYEL AND MISS OLGA HARTLEY
THE GENTLE ART OF COOKERY

Banana-Chocolate Fudge

To make about 1½ pounds [¾ kg.]

1	medium-ripe banana, mashed	1
2 oz.	unsweetened chocolate, broken into pieces	60 g.
½ cup	brown sugar	125 ml.
1½ cups	granulated sugar	375 ml.
¾ cup	milk	175 ml.
⅛ tsp.	salt	½ ml.
2 tbsp.	light corn syrup	30 ml.
3 tbsp.	butter	45 ml.
½ tsp.	vanilla extract	2 ml.
½ cup	chopped walnuts (optional)	125 ml.

In a saucepan, combine the banana, chocolate, brown and granulated sugars, milk, salt and corn syrup. Stirring con-

stantly, cook the mixture over medium heat until the sugars dissolve. If sugar crystals form on the sides of the pan, wipe them off with a pastry brush dipped in water. Cook over medium heat, stirring the mixture occasionally to prevent sticking, until it reaches the soft-ball stage—236° F. [113° C.] *(pages 8-11)*. Remove the pan from the heat. Add the butter without stirring; cool the mixture until lukewarm—110° F. [43° C.].

Add the vanilla extract; beat the fudge until it loses its gloss and starts to thicken. Pour it into a buttered loaf pan measuring 4½ by 8½ inches [11 by 21 cm.]. Sprinkle the fudge with the chopped walnuts, if using, gently pressing them into the fudge with a spoon. When it is cool and firm, cut the fudge into 32 pieces.

NELL B. NICHOLS (EDITOR)
HOMEMADE CANDY

Chocolate Log Cabin Rolls

To make about 1½ pounds [¾ kg.]

1 cup	light brown sugar	¼ liter
¾ cup	granulated sugar	175 ml.
½ cup	maple syrup	125 ml.
1 cup	light cream	¼ liter
2 tbsp.	butter	30 ml.
	salt	
1½ oz.	unsweetened chocolate, broken into small pieces	45 g.
1	egg white, lightly beaten	1
4 oz.	pecans, broken into pieces (about 1 cup [¼ liter])	125 g.

In a heavy 3-quart [3-liter] saucepan, combine the sugars, maple syrup, cream, butter, a pinch of salt and the chocolate. Stirring constantly, bring the mixture to the boiling point over low heat. Cover the pan and cook the mixture for five minutes. Remove the lid and continue to cook the mixture, stirring occasionally, until it forms a soft ball in cold water—a temperature of 236° F. [113° C.] on a candy thermometer *(pages 8-11)*.

Remove the pan from the heat and allow the contents to cool to about 110° F. [43° C.], or until the bottom of the pan feels lukewarm. Beat the fudge vigorously until it begins to lose its gloss and will hold its shape. Turn it out onto a buttered work surface.

Keeping your hands well buttered, knead the fudge until it can be shaped into two 9-inch [23-cm.] rolls. Brush the rolls with the beaten egg white and roll them in the broken nuts, pressing the nuts into the roll to make them adhere.

Enclose the rolls in plastic wrap or wax paper, and chill them. To serve, cut each roll of fudge into about 18 slices.

JOSH GASPERO (EDITOR)
HERSHEY'S 1934 COOKBOOK

Mexican Penuche

Dark brown sugar takes a long time to dissolve; make sure it has completely dissolved before letting the mixture boil.

To make about 1 ½ pounds [¾ kg.]

3 cups	dark brown sugar	¾ liter
1 cup	milk	¼ liter
½ oz.	unsweetened chocolate, melted	15 g.
1 tbsp.	butter	15 ml.
1-inch	piece vanilla bean, split lengthwise	2½-cm.
6 oz.	nuts, coarsely chopped (about 1½ cups [375 ml.])	175 g.

In a saucepan over medium heat, dissolve the sugar in the milk, and add the chocolate, stirring constantly. Reduce the heat and add the butter and vanilla bean. Bring the mixture slowly to a boil. Stir until the mixture reaches the soft-ball stage *(pages 8-11)* and remove the pan from the heat.

Discard the vanilla bean. Add the nuts, mixing them in thoroughly and beating until the candy begins to harden. Turn the candy out into a buttered pan 8 inches [20 cm.] square. When it is completely cold, cut the candy into 1-inch [2½-cm.] squares.

CORA, ROSE AND BOB BROWN
THE SOUTH AMERICAN COOK BOOK

Alice's Pecan Patés

To make about 1 ½ pounds [¾ kg.]

1 cup	granulated sugar	¼ liter
2 cups	dark brown sugar	½ liter
1 tbsp.	butter	15 ml.
⅛ tsp.	salt	½ ml.
1 cup	light cream	¼ liter
2 tsp.	vanilla extract	10 ml.
¼ lb.	pecans, coarsely chopped (about 1 cup [¼ liter])	125 g.
¼ tsp.	cream of tartar	1 ml.

In a saucepan, combine the granulated and brown sugars with the butter, salt and cream. Stir to dissolve the sugars. Set over medium heat and boil, stirring occasionally, until a little of the mixture dropped into ice water makes a firm ball *(pages 8-11)*.

Remove the pan from the heat. Add the vanilla, pecans and cream of tartar to the mixture, and beat it hard until it becomes stiff and creamy. Drop tablespoons of the mixture

onto a buttered platter or marble slab. (If the mixture hardens too quickly, pour it onto the platter or slab, and cut it into 1-inch [2½-cm.] squares when it is cold.) Wrap each piece separately in wax paper. The candy will keep for a long time in a tin box if the box is tightly closed.

MARION FLEXNER
OUT OF KENTUCKY KITCHENS

Smith College Fudge

Fudge was popular in the late 19th Century in American women's colleges. Sometimes cooked over the gaslight which hung from the center of the ceiling, it was used as the excuse for parties after lights-out. This fudge recipe was given by Maria Parloa; it appeared in a booklet distributed in 1905 by a chocolate manufacturer.

To make about 1 ¼ pounds [600 g.]

1 cup	granulated sugar	¼ liter
1 cup	brown sugar	¼ liter
¼ cup	molasses	50 ml.
½ cup	light cream	125 ml.
2 oz.	unsweetened chocolate, coarsely chopped	60 g.
4 tbsp.	butter	60 ml.
1½ tsp.	vanilla extract	7 ml.

In a saucepan, combine the two sugars, the molasses, cream and chocolate. Cook them over medium heat, stirring until the sugar and the chocolate have melted. Continue cooking, without stirring, until the mixture reaches 238° F. [115° C.] or until a few drops tested in cold water form a soft ball *(pages 8-11)*. Remove the pan from the heat, stir in the butter and vanilla, and cool slightly, until the mixture is tepid. Then beat it until the fudge begins to harden. Pour it out onto a buttered dish, and cut it into squares before the fudge is completely hard.

THE EDITORS OF AMERICAN HERITAGE
THE AMERICAN HERITAGE COOKBOOK

Chocolate Pecan Pralines

To make about 1 ½ pounds [¾ kg.]

1 cup	granulated sugar	¼ liter
1 cup	light brown or maple sugar	¼ liter
½ cup	light cream	125 ml.
¼ tsp.	salt	1 ml.
2 oz.	unsweetened chocolate, broken into small pieces	60 g.
1 tbsp.	butter	15 ml.
¼ lb.	pecans, broken into small pieces (about 1 cup [¼ liter])	125 g.
1 tsp.	vanilla extract	5 ml.

In a heavy saucepan, combine the sugars, the cream and the salt. Stirring constantly, cook the mixture over medium heat until it reaches a temperature of 228° F. [109° C.] on a candy thermometer. Add the chocolate, butter and pecans, and—stirring constantly—cook the mixture to the soft-ball stage—234° F. [112° C.] *(pages 8-11).*

Remove the pan from the heat and add the vanilla extract; let the candy cool for five minutes. Beat the candy for 10 to 15 seconds, or until it thickens slightly. Immediately— using a large spoon—drop the mixture in mounds onto buttered plates or wax paper. If the mixture becomes too thick to drop, stir in a tablespoonful of hot water to thin it.

JOSH GASPERO (EDITOR)
HERSHEY'S 1934 COOKBOOK

Milk Fudge

The technique of making fudge is shown on pages 38-39. This recipe can be varied by adding ½ cup [125 ml.] of chopped dried fruit, chopped nuts, a mixture of fruit and nuts, 3 table-spoons [45 ml.] of grated fresh coconut, or 4 ounces [125 g.] of grated chocolate to the mixture just before it is poured out to cool. Vanilla sugar (page 15) can be used instead of the plain granulated sugar and the vanilla extract.

To make 2 pounds [1 kg.]

1 ¼ cups	milk	300 ml.
3 ½ cups	sugar	875 ml.
8 tbsp.	butter	120 ml.
2 tsp.	vanilla extract	10 ml.

Put the milk in a heavy saucepan. Stirring all the time, add the sugar and the butter, and heat the mixture slowly until the sugar dissolves and the butter melts. Bring the mixture to a boil and cover the pan with a lid. Boil it for two minutes and then uncover it. Without stirring, boil the mix-

ture steadily for 10 to 15 minutes, or until it reaches the soft-ball stage *(pages 8-11).*

Remove the mixture from the heat, dip the base of the pan briefly in cold water, stir in the vanilla extract and let the fudge cool until it is lukewarm. Beat the fudge until it loses its glossy appearance and is thick and creamy. Pour it into a greased pan 8 inches [20 cm.] square. Let the fudge cool completely before marking it into 1-inch [2½-cm.] squares with a sharp knife.

MARY NORWAK
TOFFEES, FUDGES, CHOCOLATES AND SWEETS

Maple Fudge

This fudge is particularly good when made with walnuts. Add 1 cup [¼ liter] of broken walnuts to the fudge just before spreading it out to cool.

To make 1 pound [½ kg.]

2 cups	sugar	½ liter
½ cup	pure maple syrup	125 ml.
1 cup	milk	¼ liter
2 tbsp.	light corn syrup	30 ml.
	salt	
2 tbsp.	butter	30 ml.
1 tsp.	vanilla extract	5 ml.

Lightly oil the inside of a 1½- to 2-quart [1½- to 2-liter] saucepan. Combine the sugar, maple syrup, milk, corn syrup and a pinch of salt in the pan. Cook the mixture over low heat until the sugar dissolves completely and the mixture boils. Wipe down the sugar crystals above the liquid line with a clean pastry brush that has been dipped in cold water.

Cook the mixture, without stirring, until the soft-ball stage is reached—238° F. [114° C.] *(pages 8-11).* Remove the pan from the heat immediately. Add the butter, but do not stir. Cool the fudge to 110° F. [43° C.] or until the bottom of the pan feels barely warm to the touch. Add the vanilla extract. Beat the fudge vigorously until it is thick and has lost its glossy look. Immediately spoon the fudge into an oiled pan 8 inches [20 cm.] square and spread it evenly to cool. When the fudge is cold, cut it into squares.

MIRIAM LOWENBERG
CREATIVE CANDY MAKING

Grand Operas

If you wish to coat the candy with chocolate, use 8 ounces [¼ kg.] of dipping chocolate or chocolate-flavored coating, and follow the technique shown on pages 74-75.

To make 1 ½ pounds [¾ kg.]

2 cups	sugar	½ liter
3 tbsp.	light corn syrup	45 ml.
½ cup	heavy cream	125 ml.
1½ cups	milk	375 ml.
¼ tsp.	salt	1 ml.
1 tsp.	vanilla extract	5 ml.

Put all of the ingredients except the vanilla into a saucepan, and cook them over low heat, stirring constantly, until the temperature of 238° F. [115° C.] is reached *(soft-ball stage, pages 8-11)*. It is better to cook the mixture rather slowly so that some of the sugar in the milk will caramelize.

Pour the mixture into a bowl. Cool the mixture until it is lukewarm—about 110° F. [43° C.]. Beat it with a wooden spatula until it becomes thick and creamy and has lost its shiny appearance—about three to four minutes.

Press the candy into a lightly oiled pan 8 inches [20 cm.] square. When the candy is completely cold, cut it into 1-inch [2½-cm.] squares.

MAY B. VAN ARSDALE AND RUTH PARRISH CASA EMELLOS
CANDY RECIPES & OTHER CONFECTIONS

Buttermilk Candy

This candy can be made by substituting plain yogurt for the buttermilk.

To make about 1 ½ pounds [¾ kg.]

1 cup	buttermilk	¼ liter
1 tsp.	baking soda	5 ml.
2 cups	sugar	½ liter
2 tbsp.	light corn syrup	30 ml.
4 tbsp.	butter	60 ml.
¼ lb.	pecans, chopped (about 1 cup [¼ liter])	125 g.

In a heavy 3-quart [3-liter] saucepan, combine the buttermilk and the baking soda. Let the mixture stand for 20 minutes. Add the sugar and the corn syrup to the buttermilk. Bring the mixture to a boil over medium heat, stirring until the sugar has dissolved. When the mixture boils, add the butter and cook, stirring from time to time, to the soft-ball stage—236° to 238° F. [113° to 114° C.] *(pages 8-11)*. The mixture will become medium brown in color.

Remove the pan from the heat and cool the candy to lukewarm—110° F. [43° C.]. Beat the candy until it loses its gloss and starts to thicken. Stir in the pecans. Pour the candy into a buttered pan 8 inches [20 cm.] square. Cool the candy until it is firm; then cut it into 36 pieces.

NELL B. NICHOLS (EDITOR)
HOMEMADE CANDY

Almond Cream Fudge

Badaam Barfi

To make about 1 ¾ pounds [875 g.]

1 lb.	almonds, blanched and peeled (about 3 cups [¾ liter])	½ kg.
2 cups	half-and-half cream	½ liter
¾ cup	sugar	175 ml.
2 tbsp.	*ghee*	30 ml.
2	sheets of edible silver leaf, or *vark* (optional)	2

Put the almonds in the container of an electric blender or food processor, and grind them to a fine powder. Set the ground almonds aside until needed.

Bring the cream to a boil in a heavy saucepan. Cook over high heat, uncovered, for 10 minutes, or until it has thickened to the consistency of a cream soup, stirring constantly to prevent burning. Reduce the heat to medium, add the sugar, and cook for an additional two minutes, or until all of the sugar has dissolved. Add the ground almonds and the *ghee*. Stir vigorously and constantly as the mixture begins to lump up and stick to the spoon. Release the fudge from the spoon by scraping it off with a knife or a teaspoon. Continue cooking the mixture for three minutes.

Pour the fudge onto the center of a greased square of wax paper or a pan 8 inches [20 cm.] square. Working deftly and quickly, flatten and spread it to an even thickness within the square. If you are using edible silver leaf, place it over the fudge, and gently press it to make it adhere. While the fudge is still warm, cut it into neat diamond-shaped pieces measuring 1 by 2 inches [2½ by 5 cm.], using a sharp knife dipped in cold water.

This fudge keeps for three weeks if it is stored in a tightly sealed container at room temperature and for several months in the refrigerator.

JULIE SAHNI
CLASSIC INDIAN COOKING

Toasted Almond Bark

The technique of toasting nuts is shown on page 13.

To make about 1 1/2 pounds [3/4 kg.]

2 cups	sugar	1/2 liter
2/3 cup	milk	150 ml.
1 tbsp.	light corn syrup	15 ml.
1/4 tsp.	salt	1 ml.
2 tbsp.	butter	30 ml.
1 tsp.	vanilla extract	5 ml.
5 oz.	almonds, toasted (about 1 cup [1/4 liter])	150 g.

In a heavy saucepan, combine the sugar, milk, corn syrup and salt. Stirring constantly, cook the mixture until the sugar dissolves and the syrup comes to a boil. Then cook without stirring to the soft-ball stage—234° F. [112° C.] *(pages 8-11).*

Remove the pan from the heat; add the butter, but do not stir. Let the mixture cool until lukewarm—110° F. [43° C.]. Then add the vanilla. Beat until the mixture thickens and is creamy. Add the toasted almonds. Then spread out the mixture on a baking sheet lined with wax paper, forming a layer of candy about 1/2 inch [1 cm.] thick. Let the candy cool, then break it into pieces.

NELL B. NICHOLS (EDITOR)
HOMEMADE CANDY

Coconut Sanduskys

The techniques of grating fresh coconut and preparing coconut milk are demonstrated on page 13.

This is a rather soft candy. If you wish to have a firmer candy cook the mixture to about 238° F. [115° C.].

To make about 3/4 pound [350 g.]

1 cup	granulated sugar	1/4 liter
1 cup	brown sugar	1/4 liter
1 cup	freshly grated coconut	1/4 liter
1/2 cup	coconut milk	125 ml.
1/4 cup	water	50 ml.
1 tsp.	vanilla extract	5 ml.

Cook the sugars, grated coconut, coconut milk, water and vanilla extract together over medium heat, stirring occasionally to prevent burning. Cook the mixture to a temperature of 236° F. [113° C.] *(soft-ball stage, pages 8-11).*

Remove the pan from the heat, and let the mixture cool to 120° F. [49° C.]. Beat the mixture until it is thick and creamy, about five to 10 minutes. Pour the mixture into a greased pan 8 inches [20 cm.] square. When the candy has set, cut it into about 12 squares.

MAY B. VAN ARSDALE AND RUTH PARRISH CASA EMELLOS
CANDY RECIPES & OTHER CONFECTIONS

Coconut Penuche Patties

Originally from Mexico, penuche is a type of fudge. The technique of opening a coconut and grating the flesh is demonstrated on page 13.

To make about 1 1/2 pounds [3/4 kg.]

1 1/2 cups	granulated sugar	375 ml.
1 cup	light brown sugar	1/4 liter
3 tbsp.	light corn syrup	45 ml.
1 cup	light cream	1/4 liter
1 cup	finely grated coconut	1/4 liter
1 tsp.	vanilla extract	5 ml.
4 tbsp.	butter	60 ml.
about 18	pecans, halved	about 18

In a heavy saucepan, combine the sugars, the corn syrup and the cream. Bring the mixture to a boil over low heat, stirring constantly. Continue to boil gently, without stirring, until a small amount of the mixture forms a soft ball in cold water—or to a temperature of 234° F. [112° C.] *(pages 8-11).* Remove the pan from the heat.

Add the coconut, the vanilla extract and the butter. Do not stir. Cool the mixture until lukewarm—120° F. [49° C.]—without stirring. Then stir to blend the ingredients. Quickly drop the mixture by heaping teaspoonfuls onto wax paper. Press a pecan half onto each patty, and let the patties stand until they are firm, about three hours. Wrap the patties in wax paper to store them.

JASPER GUY WOODROOF
COCONUTS: PRODUCTION PROCESSING PRODUCTS

Foamy Coconut Fudge

Narial Barfi

The technique of grating coconut is demonstrated on page 13. Raw cashews are sold at health-food stores.

Use only freshly grated coconut. The dry flaked coconut available in supermarkets simply does not taste as good. For a combination flavor, add 2 tablespoons [30 ml.] of roasted unsalted chopped cashew nuts with the coconut.

To make about 1 1/2 pounds [3/4 kg.]

3 cups	freshly grated coconut (flesh of 1 medium coconut)	3/4 liter
2 cups	sugar	1/2 liter
	cream of tartar (optional)	
1 cup	cold water	1/4 liter
1/4 tsp.	ground cardamom	1 ml.
2 tbsp.	*ghee* or light vegetable oil	30 ml.

Heat a large, heavy saucepan over medium heat for one minute. Add the grated coconut, and fry it, stirring constantly, until it looks dry and flaky but is still snow-white—five to seven minutes. Transfer the coconut to a bowl.

Combine the sugar, cream of tartar if you are using it, and cold water in the pan, and bring the mixture to a boil, stirring. Let the syrup continue to boil over medium heat, uncovered, for seven to 10 minutes, or until the syrup is thickened and looks frothy and full of bubbles. Add the coconut and ground cardamom, and cook for two to five minutes, stirring rapidly and vigorously. Stir in the *ghee* or vegetable oil, and continue cooking until the mixture begins to foam and stick to the bottom of the pan—about one minute. Do not stop stirring the fudge during this last critical minute for any reason whatsoever, or you may end up with crystals of candy instead of flaky-textured fudge.

Immediately pour the mixture into a greased pan 9 inches [23 cm.] square or onto a square of greased paper, and working deftly and quickly, spread the fudge to form an even layer, patting it gently with a flat spatula. Do not pack too much or the fudge will become dense. The fudge should be light and foamy, filled with air pockets. Let it cool for five minutes. Then cut it into neat 1½-inch [4-cm.] square pieces.

This fudge keeps well for several months if stored in tightly sealed containers.

JULIE SAHNI
CLASSIC INDIAN COOKING

Yogurt Toffee

To make about 1½ pounds [¾ kg.]

1 lb.	plain yogurt	½ kg.
2 cups	sugar	½ liter
2 tbsp.	slivered almonds	30 ml.
2 tbsp.	slivered cashews	30 ml.
¼ tsp.	ground saffron, dissolved in 2 teaspoons [10 ml.] hot milk	1 ml.
1 tbsp.	pistachios	15 ml.
10	whole cardamoms, seeds removed and separated	10

Hang the yogurt in a cheesecloth bag suspended over a bowl, refrigerate and let the yogurt drip overnight.

The next day, gently heat the thickened yogurt in a pan with the sugar, almonds and cashews. Stir continuously until the mixture thickens and comes away from the sides of the pan, about 15 minutes. Stir in the saffron and mix well. Spoon the candy into a buttered dish or pan 8 inches [20 cm.] square, and flatten its surface.

Grind the pistachios and the cardamom seeds together in a mortar or food processor, then sprinkle the mixture over the surface of the candy. Let the candy cool. Store it in an airtight container.

JACK SANTA MARIA
INDIAN SWEET COOKERY

Maylie's Restaurant New Orleans Pralines

To make about 2½ pounds [1 kg.]

2 cups	brown sugar	½ liter
1 cup	light molasses	¼ liter
2 cups	heavy cream	½ liter
4 tbsp.	butter	60 ml.
1 tsp.	vanilla extract	5 ml.
1 lb.	pecans, halved (about 4 cups [1 liter])	½ kg.

Boil the brown sugar, molasses, cream and butter together, stirring all the time, until the sugar dissolves. Continue boiling without stirring until a soft ball is formed when a drop is placed in cold water *(pages 8-11)*. Remove from the heat, add the vanilla and the nuts, and stir the mixture until it begins to crystallize. Drop spoonfuls of the mixture in small heaps on buttered baking sheets, leaving enough room between the pralines for them to spread slightly.

MARY LAND
NEW ORLEANS CUISINE

White or Pink Pralines

Pralines Blanches ou Roses de Coco

These dainty white or pink pralines are peculiar to Creole confections and are much sought after by strangers visiting New Orleans.

To make about 1½ pounds [¾ kg.]

2 cups	sugar	½ liter
¼ cup	water	50 ml.
4 cups	freshly grated coconut	1 liter
½ tsp.	red food coloring (optional)	2 ml.

Use a copper or other heavy saucepan. Put the sugar into the saucepan with the water and let it boil well. When it begins to form a syrup, take it from the heat and stir in the grated coconut. Mix thoroughly and return the pan to the heat. Be careful to stir the mixture constantly from the time you add the coconut. Cook it for two to three minutes; it will begin to bubble and should have reached the thread stage *(pages 8-11)*. This will be sufficient cooking if you wish the pralines to be light and flaky. Add the coloring, if using, just before taking the mixture from the heat.

Have ready a wet marble slab or buttered platter. Take a kitchen spoon and use it to drop spoonfuls of the mixture onto the slab or platter, spreading them out with a fork until they form neat round cakes about ¼ inch [6 mm.] thick and 4 or 5 inches [10 or 13 cm.] in diameter. Let them dry, then take a knife and gently raise them from the slab or dish.

THE PICAYUNE'S CREOLE COOK BOOK

Pralines

The technique of cooking sugar to a caramel without water is shown on page 9.

To make about 2 pounds [1 kg.]

2½ cups	sugar	625 ml.
1 cup	light cream	¼ liter
1 tbsp.	butter	15 ml.
½ lb.	pecans, halved (2 cups [½ liter])	¼ kg.

In a heavy iron pan, combine 2 cups [½ liter] of the sugar with the cream and butter, and bring to a boil over medium heat. In a separate heavy pan, melt the rest of the sugar and cook it until it is caramel-colored. Add the cream, butter and sugar syrup to the caramel mixture. Add the pecan halves, and cook the mixture to the soft-ball stage, 235° F. [113° C.] on a candy thermometer *(pages 8-11)*. Remove the pan from the heat and beat the mixture until it thickens. Drop spoonfuls of the mixture onto wax paper to form pralines about 2 to 3 inches [5 to 8 cm.] in diameter. Let the pralines harden.

THE JUNIOR LEAGUE OF NEW ORLEANS
THE PLANTATION COOKBOOK

Orange Pralines

To make about 1½ pounds [¾ kg.]

2 cups	sugar	½ liter
¾ cup	half-and-half cream	175 ml.
¼ tsp.	salt	1 ml.
2½ tbsp.	light corn syrup	37 ml.
½ cup	fresh orange juice, pulp strained out	125 ml.
2 tbsp.	grated orange peel	30 ml.
4 tbsp.	butter	60 ml.
1 tsp.	vanilla extract	5 ml.
	orange food coloring (optional)	
½ lb.	pecans, chopped (about 2 cups [½ liter])	¼ kg.

Place the sugar, cream, salt and corn syrup in a saucepan and stir constantly until the mixture boils. Add the orange juice slowly and continue cooking until the mixture reaches the soft-ball stage—240° F. [116° C.] on a candy thermometer *(pages 8-11)*. Add the grated orange peel and cook until the thermometer again shows 240° F.

Remove the pan from the heat and stir in the butter, vanilla extract, and food coloring, if desired. Cool the mixture, then beat it until it holds its shape. Add the pecans. Drop bite-sized pieces of the mixture onto wax paper to dry. Store the pralines in a tin or plastic container.

THE JUNIOR LEAGUE OF JACKSON, MISSISSIPPI
SOUTHERN SIDEBOARDS

Candied Orange Pecans

To make 2 pounds [1 kg.]

3 cups	sugar	¾ liter
1 cup	fresh orange juice, pulp strained out	¼ liter
1½ tbsp.	butter	22 ml.
1 tsp.	grated orange peel	5 ml.
¾ lb.	pecans (about 3 cups [¾ liter])	350 g.

In a saucepan, combine the sugar and the orange juice. Using a candy thermometer, cook the mixture to the soft-ball stage, 236° F. [113° C.] *(pages 8-11)*.

Remove the saucepan from the heat, and immediately add the butter and orange peel. Beat with a wooden spoon until the mixture is thick and almost set. Quickly add the pecans and continue to beat the mixture until it becomes grainy. Quickly turn the mixture out onto a buttered or oiled baking sheet, and use the spoon to distribute the nuts evenly before the candy cools.

JEAN HEWITT
THE NEW YORK TIMES SOUTHERN HERITAGE COOKBOOK

Wagner's Pralines

To make about 2 pounds [1 kg.]

2 cups	sugar	½ liter
¾ tsp.	baking soda	4 ml.
1 cup	light cream	¼ liter
1½ tsp.	butter	7 ml.
½ lb.	pecans, halved (about 2 cups [½ liter])	¼ kg.

Combine the sugar and baking soda in a deep 3-quart [3-liter] saucepan. Mix well. Add the cream and stir well. Bring the mixture to a boil over medium heat, stirring to prevent scorching. Cook the mixture until it forms a soft ball when tested in water *(pages 8-11)*. Remove the pan from the heat and add the butter. Add the pecan halves, and beat the mixture until it is thick enough to drop from a spoon. Drop spoonfuls of the mixture onto wax paper.

MARY LAND
NEW ORLEANS CUISINE

Peanut Confection

Erdnusskonfekt

Ground walnuts or grated coconut can be substituted for the peanuts, in which case the salt should be omitted. If using coconut, add ½ teaspoon [2 ml.] of vanilla extract.

To make about 1 pound [½ kg.]

1 tbsp.	butter	15 ml.
2 cups	brown sugar	½ liter
½ cup	milk or light cream	125 ml.
6 oz.	peanuts, toasted, peeled and chopped (about ⅔ cup [150 ml.])	175 g.
¼ tsp.	salt	1 ml.

Melt the butter in a saucepan. Add the sugar and milk or cream. Bring the mixture to a boil, and simmer until it forms a soft ball when dropped into cold water *(pages 8-11)*. Remove the pan from the heat, and beat the mixture until it is thick and creamy. Sprinkle the nuts with the salt, and stir them into the mixture. Turn the mixture out onto a buttered baking sheet. Let it cool until it is just warm to the touch before cutting it into 1-inch [2½-cm.] squares.

ELIZABETH SCHULER
MEIN KOCHBUCH

Cashew Nut Fudge

Kajoo Barfi

Raw cashews are sold at health-food stores.

This technique, popular with Maharashtrians in southwestern India, produces a soft, chewy fudge with a grainy texture. Almonds, pistachios or walnuts may be substituted for the cashews.

To make about ¾ pound [350 g.]

½ lb.	raw cashews (about 2 cups [½ liter])	¼ kg.
¾ cup	sugar	175 ml.
1 tbsp.	butter	15 ml.
2 tsp.	rose water	10 ml.
3	sheets of edible silver leaf, or *vark* (optional)	3

Place the cashews in a bowl, cover them with boiling water, and soak them for one hour. Drain the nuts, put them in an electric blender or food processor, and reduce them to a fine paste (adding some milk or water if the paste begins to clog).

Heat a well-seasoned frying pan (at least 9 inches [23 cm.] in diameter) over medium heat for two minutes. Add the nut paste and sugar. Reduce the heat to medium low, and cook the mixture for about 20 minutes, stirring and scraping

the sides and bottom of the pan frequently. When the fudge is thick and sticky, stir in the butter.

Pour the fudge into a buttered pan 9 inches square. Spread the fudge evenly by patting it gently with a spatula.

When cool, brush the top of the fudge with the rose water and let it dry briefly. Press the edible silver leaf over the fudge, if using, and cut 1½-inch [4-cm.] square or diamond-shaped pieces using a knife dipped in cold water. This fudge keeps for three weeks if stored in a tightly sealed container at room temperature and will keep for several months if the container is stored in the refrigerator.

JULIE SAHNI
CLASSIC INDIAN COOKING

Walnut Roll

To make about 2 pounds [1 kg.]

2 cups	granulated sugar	½ liter
1 cup	brown sugar	¼ liter
½ cup	light corn syrup	125 ml.
1 cup	light cream	¼ liter
1 tsp.	vanilla extract	5 ml.
5 oz.	walnuts, chopped (about 1¼ cups [300 ml.])	150 g.

Combine the sugars, corn syrup and cream in a heavy saucepan. Cook the mixture over low heat, stirring constantly until the sugars dissolve. Bring the mixture to a boil and continue cooking it over low heat, without stirring, to the soft-ball stage—236° F. [113° C.] *(pages 8-11)*. Remove the pan from the heat and let the mixture cool to 110° F. [43° C.]. Add the vanilla extract. Beat the mixture until it stiffens and a spoon leaves a trail in it. Then cool the candy and knead it until it is firm. Shape the candy into rolls 1½ inches [3 cm.] in diameter. Coat the rolls in the chopped walnuts. Wrap the rolls in wax paper and chill them until they are firm. Slice the rolls into pieces ½ inch [1 cm.] thick.

MARY MARGARET MC BRIDE
HARVEST OF AMERICAN COOKING

Penuche

If desired, ½ cup [125 ml.] of chopped candied cherries may be substituted for ½ cup of the nuts and the mixture dropped by teaspoonfuls onto wax paper.

To make about 1 ½ pounds [¾ kg.]

3 cups	light brown sugar	¾ liter
1 cup	light cream	¼ liter
1 ½ tbsp.	butter	22 ml.
1 ½ tsp.	vanilla extract	7 ml.
4 oz.	walnuts, broken into pieces (about 1 cup [¼ liter])	125 g.

Cook and stir the light brown sugar and the cream together until the mixture boils. Cook without stirring until the soft-ball stage is reached—236° F. [113° C.] *(pages 8-11)*. Remove the pan from the heat and stir in the butter. Cool the mixture until it is lukewarm, and add the vanilla extract. Beat the mixture until it is creamy and thick; then add the walnuts. Pour the mixture into a buttered pan 8 inches [20 cm.] square, and let the candy cool until it is firm. Cut it into 1-inch [2½-cm.] squares.

MILDRED GROSBERG BELLIN
THE JEWISH COOK BOOK

Orange Caramel Fudge

To make about 1 pound [½ kg.]

2 cups	dark brown sugar	½ liter
½ cup	heavy cream	125 ml.
½ tsp.	baking soda	2 ml.
1 tsp.	butter	5 ml.
2 tbsp.	grated orange peel	30 ml.
¼ lb.	mixed nuts, coarsely chopped (about 1 cup [¼ liter])	125 g.
	salt	

In a saucepan, dissolve the sugar with the cream and baking soda over medium heat, stirring constantly. Bring the mixture to a boil and stop stirring. Continue to boil the mixture until it makes a thick syrup that forms a ball when dropped into cold water *(firm-ball stage, pages 8-11)*. Remove the pan from the heat, and add the butter, orange peel, nuts and a pinch of salt. Beat the mixture well until it becomes quite thick. Pour the fudge onto a buttered plate and, when cold, cut it into 1-inch [2½-cm.] squares; or drop teaspoons of the fudge onto a large buttered platter.

MARION FLEXNER
OUT OF KENTUCKY KITCHENS

Mexican Orange Candy

To give this caramel a more pronounced orange flavor, increase the quantity of grated orange peel to ¼ cup [50 ml.]. The technique of caramelizing sugar without water is demonstrated on page 9.

To make 2 pounds [1 kg.]

3 cups	sugar	¾ liter
1 ½ cups	milk, scalded	375 ml.
2 tbsp.	grated orange peel	30 ml.
⅛ tsp.	salt	½ ml.
8 tbsp.	butter	120 ml.
¼ lb.	nuts, chopped (about 1 cup [¼ liter])	125 g.

In a deep, heavy 4-quart [4-liter] saucepan, melt 1 cup [¼ liter] of the sugar, stirring constantly. When the sugar has melted to a light golden brown, take it off the heat and pour the milk into it all at one time. Stir the mixture quickly; it will foam up.

Return the saucepan to the heat, add the rest of the sugar and cook, stirring constantly, until the sugar dissolves. Continue cooking, without stirring, to the soft-ball stage—238° F. [114° C.] *(pages 8-11)*. Remove the pan from the heat; add the orange peel, salt and butter, but do not stir. Let the mixture stand until it is lukewarm—110° F. [43° C.]. Beat the mixture until it loses its gloss and starts to thicken. Add the nuts; stir to mix, then pour the mixture into a buttered pan 9 inches [23 cm.] square. Mark the candy into 49 pieces while it is still warm; cut it when it is cool and firm.

NELL B. NICHOLS (EDITOR)
HOMEMADE CANDY

Gold Nuggets

To make about 1 ¼ pounds [600 g.]

1 ½ cups	sugar	375 ml.
3 tbsp.	fresh orange juice, pulp strained out	45 ml.
¼ cup	warm water	50 ml.
¼ tsp.	ground cinnamon	1 ml.
¼ cup	grated orange peel	50 ml.
10 oz.	walnuts or other nuts (about 2½ cups [625 ml.])	300 g.

In a saucepan, mix the sugar and orange juice with the water. Over medium heat, dissolve the sugar, stirring constantly. Bring to a boil, cover the pan, and let the syrup boil for one minute to steam down sugar crystals from the sides of the pan. Remove the lid, and cook the mixture without stirring until a small amount forms a soft ball when dropped into very cold water—or until the mixture reaches 240° F. [116° C.] on a candy thermometer *(pages 8-11)*.

Remove the pan from the heat. Add the remaining ingredients. Stir with a fork until the mixture becomes creamy.

Turn it out onto a sheet of wax paper or a lightly buttered baking sheet. Separate the nuts with a fork. Cool the nuggets and store them in an airtight container.

WOMAN'S DAY COLLECTOR'S COOK BOOK

Pineapple Penuche

The technique of making candied pineapple is demonstrated on pages 50-51. The lemon extract can be replaced with 1 teaspoon [5 ml.] of finely grated lemon peel.

To make about 2 pounds [1 kg.]

3 cups	sugar	¾ liter
1 cup	milk	¼ liter
2 tbsp.	butter, softened and cut into small pieces	30 ml.
	lemon extract	
1½ cups	chopped candied pineapple	375 ml.

Melt the sugar in the milk over low heat, stirring until the sugar dissolves. Add the butter gradually, and stir constantly until the mixture begins to boil. Reduce the heat, cover the mixture and let it simmer for three minutes. Remove the lid, and boil the mixture rapidly until it reaches 238° F. [114° C.]—the soft-ball stage *(pages 8-11)*.

Lift the saucepan from the heat. Add a few drops of lemon extract and the candied pineapple. Beat the mixture until it is thick and creamy. Butter a baking pan measuring 8 by 12 by 1¼ inches [20 by 30 by 3 cm.] and pour the mixture into it. Let the mixture set, then cut it into ½-inch [1-cm.] squares.

ESMÉ GRAY BOOKER
SWEETS THAT HAVE TEMPTED ME

Ginger Cream Candy

To make about 1½ pounds [¾ kg.]

2 cups	granulated sugar	½ liter
1 cup	light brown sugar	¼ liter
¾ cup	milk	175 ml.
2 tbsp.	light corn syrup	30 ml.
2 tbsp.	butter	30 ml.
2 tbsp.	candied ginger, finely chopped	30 ml.
1 tsp.	vanilla extract	5 ml.

Combine in a saucepan the sugars, milk and corn syrup. Boil the mixture to the soft-ball stage, 238° F. [114° C.] on a candy thermometer *(pages 8-11)*. Remove from the heat. Add the butter and ginger. Do not stir. When the mixture has cooled to lukewarm, add the vanilla. Beat until creamy. Pour the mixture into two buttered pans 8 inches [20 cm.] square. When the candy is cool, cut it into squares.

RUTH GRAVES WAKEFIELD
TOLL HOUSE TRIED AND TRUE RECIPES

Sesame Pralines

To make about 1½ pounds [¾ kg.]

1½ oz.	sesame seeds (about ¼ cup [50 ml.])	40 g.
1 cup	granulated sugar	¼ liter
1 cup	dark brown sugar	¼ liter
1 cup	heavy cream	¼ liter
2 tbsp.	butter	30 ml.
½ lb.	pecans, halved (about 2 cups [½ liter])	¼ kg.

Toast the sesame seeds in a preheated 350° F. [180° C.] oven, stirring occasionally, for 10 to 15 minutes, or until they are golden brown. In a 3-quart [3-liter] saucepan, combine the sugars and the cream. Cook the mixture over medium heat, stirring until the sugar dissolves. Wash the crystals from the sides of the pan with a damp pastry brush until the syrup boils. Cook the mixture to 230° F. [110° C.], then add the butter, pecans and sesame seeds; stirring occasionally, continue cooking until the mixture reaches 234° F. [112° C.], the soft-ball stage *(pages 8-11)*. Remove the pan from the heat. Cool the mixture for two to three minutes, then stir it for two minutes, or until it thickens slightly. Working fast, drop the mixture from a spoon onto buttered wax paper, aluminum foil or a marble slab, spacing each praline slightly apart.

MC CORMICK'S SPICES OF THE WORLD COOKBOOK

Benne Candy

Sesame seeds were brought to Charleston, South Carolina, by African slaves around 1600, and their word for sesame—"benne"—still is used in the South. To toast sesame seeds, spread them evenly in a dry frying pan, and cook them over medium heat, stirring frequently, until they darken and give off a nutlike aroma.

To make about 1¾ pounds [875 g.]

2⅔ cups	brown sugar (1 lb. [½ kg.])	650 ml.
1 tbsp.	butter	15 ml.
½ cup	milk	125 ml.
1 tbsp.	vinegar	15 ml.
1½ cups	sesame seeds, toasted	375 ml.
1 tsp.	vanilla extract	5 ml.

In a saucepan, mix the brown sugar, butter, milk and vinegar together. Cook over medium heat, stirring, until the sugar has dissolved. Boil the mixture until it begins to thread *(firm-ball stage, pages 8-11)*. Remove from the heat and beat in the sesame seeds. Add the vanilla and beat the mixture until it is creamy. Drop a teaspoonful at a time onto a buttered dish or wax paper, and let the candy cool.

HARRIET ROSS COLQUITT (EDITOR)
THE SAVANNAH COOK BOOK

Foamy Candy

Marshmallows

The technique of making marshmallows is shown on pages 40-41. Food coloring and flavoring are explained on pages 14-15. Marshmallows can be dusted with a mixture of equal quantities of confectioners' sugar and cornstarch to give them a smooth, firm crust. A few chopped nuts or dried fruits or some dried, flaked coconut may be added while the mixture is still stiff but not set.

To make about 1¼ pounds [600 g.]

2 cups	granulated sugar	½ liter
1 tbsp.	liquid glucose or light corn syrup	15 ml.
1½ cups	water	375 ml.
4 tbsp.	unflavored powdered gelatin	60 ml.
2 tbsp.	orange-flower water	30 ml.
	food coloring and flavoring (optional)	
2	egg whites, stiffly beaten	2
	confectioners' sugar, sifted	
	cornstarch	

Over medium heat, combine the granulated sugar and the glucose or corn syrup with about ¾ cup [175 ml.] of the water. Stir constantly until the sugar is completely dissolved. Bring the syrup to a boil without stirring. Increase the heat and boil until the syrup reaches a temperature of 260° F. [127° C.]—the hard-ball stage *(pages 8-11)*.

In another pan, soften the gelatin in the remaining ¾ cup of water and the orange-flower water for five to 10 minutes. Set the pan over simmering water and, whisking constantly, dissolve the gelatin. Add coloring and flavoring, if using.

Whisk the dissolved gelatin mixture into the syrup. Whisking continuously, gradually pour this mixture onto the stiffly beaten egg whites. Continue whisking until the marshmallow mixture is a white opaque mass that is thick enough to hold its shape.

Lightly oil a pan that is 12 by 8 by 1¼ inches [30 by 20 by 3 cm.] and dust the pan with a combination of equal quantities of confectioners' sugar and cornstarch. Pour the marshmallow mixture into the pan, smooth it flat with a narrow-bladed spatula, and let it set for several hours. With a knife, loosen the marshmallow from the edges of the pan. Dust a work surface with confectioners' sugar and turn the marshmallow onto it. Dust the marshmallow thickly with confectioners' sugar, and leave the marshmallow for one hour to let it dry and to allow the confectioners' sugar to form a crust.

Then cut the marshmallow into squares or rounds. Alternatively, the marshmallow can be cut into shapes without being dusted with confectioners' sugar, then left to dry for about one hour.

HELEN JEROME
SWEET-MAKING FOR ALL

Divinity That Never Fails

Suitable flavoring is discussed on pages 14-15.

To make about 1¼ pounds [600 g.]

2½ cups	sugar	625 ml.
¾ cup	light corn syrup	175 ml.
¼ cup	water	50 ml.
2	egg whites, stiffly beaten	2
	flavoring	

Dissolve the sugar in the corn syrup and water over medium heat, stirring constantly. Bring the syrup to a boil, and boil it to the thread stage *(pages 8-11)*. Pour two thirds of the syrup in a thin stream over the beaten egg whites, whisking all the time. Put the rest of the syrup back on the heat and cook it to the soft-ball stage. Pour the syrup into the egg-white mixture, whisking constantly. Add the flavoring, and continue whisking until the mixture forms stiff peaks. Pour the mixture into a buttered pan 8 inches [20 cm.] square. Let the divinity cool and set, then cut it into squares.

LOUIS SZATHMÁRY (EDITOR)
FIFTY YEARS OF PRAIRIE COOKING

Yellow Divinity

To make about 1½ pounds [¾ kg.]

2 cups	sugar	½ liter
½ cup	light corn syrup	125 ml.
½ cup	milk	125 ml.
2	egg yolks	2
¼ lb.	nuts, coarsely chopped (about 1 cup [¼ liter])	125 g.
1 tsp.	vanilla extract	5 ml.

Combine the sugar, corn syrup and milk, and cook them until the mixture reaches 248° F. [120° C.] on a candy thermometer *(firm-ball stage, pages 8-11)*. While the syrup is cooking, whisk the egg yolks until they are thick and creamy. Slowly add the hot syrup to the egg yolks, whisking the mixture until it cools slightly. Add the chopped nuts and the vanilla extract. Drop the divinity in tablespoonfuls onto wax paper.

JUNIOR LEAGUE OF JACKSON, MISSISSIPPI
SOUTHERN SIDEBOARDS

Divinity

To make Sea Foam, a variation of this recipe, substitute light brown sugar for the granulated sugar and use only 1 table-spoon [15 ml.] of corn syrup.

To make about 13 ounces [375 g.]

1⅓ cups	sugar	325 ml.
¼ cup	light corn syrup	50 ml.
¼ cup	water	50 ml.
1	egg white	1
1 tsp.	vanilla extract	5 ml.
½ cup	chopped nuts	125 ml.

Put the sugar, corn syrup and water in a saucepan. Heat them, stirring, until the sugar has completely dissolved and the mixture starts to boil. Without stirring, cook the syrup to 256° F. [124° C.] *(hard-ball stage, pages 8-11).*

While the syrup is boiling, beat the egg white in a large bowl until it is very stiff. Slowly pour the hot syrup into the egg white in a thin stream, beating all the time you are pouring. Keep beating until the mixture is no longer shiny, about 10 minutes; by then the candy will be very stiff. Mix in the vanilla and chopped nuts, and drop the divinity by spoon-fuls onto wax paper.

CAROLYN MEYER
LOTS AND LOTS OF CANDY

Honey Almond Divinity

The technique of blanching almonds is shown on page 12.

To make about 1½ pounds [¾ kg.]

5 oz.	almonds, blanched, peeled and cut into coarse shreds (about 1¼ cups [300 ml.])	150 g.
2½ cups	sugar	625 ml.
1 cup	water	¼ liter
¼ cup	light corn syrup	50 ml.
¼ cup	honey	50 ml.
2	egg whites, stiffly beaten	2
½ tsp.	vanilla extract	2 ml.

Roast the shredded almonds in a preheated 250° F. [130° C.] oven for about 20 minutes, or until they are light brown.

In a saucepan, combine 1½ cups [375 ml.] of the sugar, ½ cup [125 ml.] of the water, the corn syrup and the honey. Stirring, cook over medium heat until the sugar is dissolved; then cook this syrup without stirring until a temperature of 246° F. [119° C.] is reached *(firm-ball stage, pages 8-11).*

While the syrup is cooking, combine the rest of the sugar and the water in another saucepan, and stir over medium heat until the sugar dissolves. While this mixture boils, pour the sugar-and-honey syrup slowly over the beaten egg whites, beating constantly during the addition.

Continue beating until the sugar-and-water syrup in the second saucepan reaches a temperature of 255° F. [124° C.] *(hard-ball stage).* Pour this hot syrup into the mixture of sugar, honey and egg, and beat until the candy does not stick to your finger when you gently touch the surface.

Stir in the vanilla and almonds, and pour the candy into a lightly buttered pan 8 by 12 by 1¼ inches [20 by 30 by 3 cm.]. When it is cold, cut the candy into 1-inch [2½-cm.] squares.

MAY B. VAN ARSDALE AND RUTH PARRISH CASA EMELLOS
CANDY RECIPES & OTHER CONFECTIONS

Divinity Drops

About ½ cup [125 ml.] of chopped candied fruit can be added along with the chopped nuts. To make chocolate-flavored drops, include 6 ounces [175 g.] of semisweet chocolate, broken into small pieces, when adding the nuts. To make ginger divinity drops, replace the vanilla extract with 1 tea-spoon [5 ml.] of ground ginger, and add ½ cup [125 ml.] of very finely chopped candied ginger when adding the nuts.

To make about 1½ pounds [¾ kg.]

2½ cups	sugar	625 ml.
½ cup	light corn syrup	125 ml.
¼ tsp.	salt	1 ml.
½ cup	water	125 ml.
2	egg whites, beaten until stiff but not dry	2
1 tsp.	vanilla extract	5 ml.
¼ lb.	nuts, coarsely chopped (about 1 cup [¼ liter])	125 g.
about 18	red candied cherries, halved	about 18
about 18	green candied cherries or pieces of angelica, chopped	about 18

In a saucepan, mix the sugar, corn syrup, salt and water. Cook, stirring, until the sugar dissolves. Continue cooking, without stirring, until a small amount of the mixture forms a firm ball when dropped in cold water—248° F. [120° C.] on a candy thermometer *(pages 8-11).*

Beating constantly, pour about half of the syrup over the egg whites. Cook the remainder of the syrup until a small amount forms hard threads in cold water—272° F. [133° C.] *(soft-crack stage).* Add the cooked syrup to the egg-white syrup, beating until the mixture holds its shape. Add the vanilla extract and the nuts. Drop tablespoonfuls of the mix-ture onto sheets of wax paper. Decorate the divinity with the red cherry halves and the chopped green cherries or angel-ica. Let the divinity stand until it is firm.

WOMAN'S DAY COLLECTOR'S COOK BOOK

Oklahoma Cherry Divinity

To make about 1¼ pounds [600 g.]

2 cups	sugar	½ liter
½ cup	light corn syrup	125 ml.
¼ tsp.	salt	1 ml.
½ cup	water	125 ml.
2	egg whites, stiffly beaten	2
1 tsp.	vanilla extract	5 ml.
¼ lb.	candied cherries, chopped (about 1 cup [¼ liter])	125 g.

Mix the sugar, syrup, salt and water in a saucepan and place it over low heat; stir until the sugar has dissolved. Wipe sugar crystals from the sides of the pan with a damp cloth. Without stirring, cook to the firm-ball stage, 248° F. [120° C.] on a candy thermometer *(pages 8-11)*.

Remove the pan from the heat and, beating constantly, gradually pour the syrup into the egg whites. Add the vanilla and beat until the mixture will hold its shape when dropped from a spoon. Add the cherries, mix well, and drop the mixture in spoonfuls onto wax paper.

THE EDITORS OF SOUTHERN LIVING
THE COOKIES AND CANDY COOKBOOK

Almond Nougat

To make about 1½ pounds [¾ kg.]

2 cups	sugar	½ liter
1½ cups	light corn syrup	375 ml.
¼ tsp.	salt	1 ml.
¼ cup	water	50 ml.
2	egg whites, stiffly beaten	2
½ tsp.	almond extract	2 ml.
	green food coloring	
4 tbsp.	butter, softened	60 ml.
¼ lb.	almonds, toasted (about 1 cup [¼ liter])	125 g.

In a heavy saucepan, mix the sugar, corn syrup and salt with the water. Cook, stirring, until the sugar dissolves. Continue to cook, without stirring, until a small amount of the mixture forms a hard ball when dropped in very cold water—250° F. [121° C.] on a candy thermometer *(pages 8-11)*.

Gradually beat about one quarter—not more—of the syrup into the beaten egg whites and continue beating until the mixture holds its shape. Cook the remaining syrup until a small amount separates into hard, brittle threads when dropped in very cold water—300° F. [149° C.]. Gradually beat this syrup into the egg-white mixture and continue beating until the mixture is thick and stiff. Add the almond flavoring and a few drops of coloring to tint the mixture to a delicate green. Beat in the butter and continue beating until the candy is very thick and satiny. Stir in the nuts and press the candy into a buttered pan 8 inches [20 cm.] square, smoothing the surface.

Let the candy stand until it is firm, then turn it out of the pan and cut it into 1-inch [2½-cm.] squares. Enclose each piece in wax paper or plastic wrap. For the best flavor, refrigerate the candy in an airtight container for several days.

WOMAN'S DAY COLLECTOR'S COOK BOOK

Nougat

Hylam

To make about 1 pound [½ kg.]

¼ lb.	walnuts, coarsely chopped (about 1 cup [¼ liter])	125 g.
1 cup	sugar	¼ liter
½ cup	honey	125 ml.
2 tbsp.	water	30 ml.
2	egg whites, stiffly beaten	2
1 tsp.	vanilla extract	5 ml.
	edible rice paper	

Bake the nuts in a preheated 250° F. [120° C.] oven for 15 to 20 minutes until they are dried out but not toasted. Mix the sugar, honey and water in a saucepan and, stirring constantly, cook over low heat until the sugar has dissolved. Then cook until a firm ball is formed when a little of the syrup is dropped into cold water *(pages 8-11)*.

Beating constantly, pour half of the syrup in a slow stream over the beaten egg whites. Return the remaining syrup to the heat and cook it to a temperature of 290° F. [143° C.] or until a cracking sound is heard when a little of it is dropped into cold water and knocked against the side of a cup *(soft-crack stage)*. Pour the syrup gradually over the egg-white mixture, beating constantly. Place the bowl with this nougat mixture in it over hot water and beat the mixture until it begins to harden. Beat in the nuts and the vanilla.

Line a pan 8 inches [20 cm.] square with edible rice paper and spread it with the mixture. Cover the nougat with rice paper and press down. When the mixture is cold, invert the pan to unmold the candy. Cut the nougat into bars. Wrap the bars in wax paper and store them in an airtight container.

SAVELLA STECHISHIN
TRADITIONAL UKRAINIAN COOKERY

Cremona Nougat

Torrone di Cremona

To make about 1¾ pounds [875 g.]

1 lb.	almonds, blanched, peeled, toasted and chopped (about 4 cups [1 liter])	½ kg.
1 cup	sugar	¼ liter
1 tsp.	finely chopped candied orange peel	5 ml.
½ tsp.	ground cinnamon	2 ml.
½ cup	honey	125 ml.
2	egg whites, stiffly beaten	2
	edible rice paper	

Pound the almonds in a mortar with the sugar, then stir in the candied peel and cinnamon. Put the honey in a heavy pan, add the almond mixture, and stir and cook until the mixture begins to brown *(soft-crack stage, pages 8-11)*. Remove the pan from the heat; quickly fold in the egg whites.

Pour the mixture into a shallow pan measuring 8 by 10 inches [20 by 25 cm.] and lined with edible rice paper. Let the candy cool, then cut it into small, rectangular pieces.

BERYL GOULD-MARKS
THE HOME BOOK OF ITALIAN COOKERY

Catalan Nougat

Turrón de Agramunt

When making nougat, the nuts should be warm. Cover freshly peeled nuts with foil to retain the warmth they gained in blanching or roasting; wrap previously peeled nuts in foil and warm them in a 200° F. [100° C.] oven for 15 minutes.

To make about 1 pound [½ kg.]

1⅓ cups	honey	325 ml.
2	egg whites, stiffly beaten	2
½ lb.	almonds, blanched, peeled and kept warm (about 1½ cups [375 ml.])	¼ kg.
3½ oz.	hazelnuts, roasted, peeled and kept warm (about ¾ cup [175 ml.])	100 g.
	edible rice paper	

Put the honey in a heavy saucepan and place over medium heat. Stir it with a wooden spoon and, when the honey begins to boil, remove the pan from the heat. Continue stirring until the honey thins to the consistency of pancake syrup. Stir in the egg whites and return the mixture to the heat;

continue cooking until it reaches a toffee-like consistency *(hard-ball stage, pages 8-11)*. Stir in the nuts and mix well.

Spread the mixture in a jelly-roll pan lined with edible rice paper. Cover with a second sheet of rice paper, and weight the top. Let it cool, then cut the nougat into 1-inch [2½-cm.] squares.

ANA MARIA CALERA
COCINA CATALANA

Macedonian Halvah

Mazedonische Halva

The technique of making nut brittle is demonstrated on page 35. Instead of crushing the brittle in a mortar, you can crush it in a plastic bag as for praline powder (page 78). In the Balkans, special rice-paper wafers are sold for making halvah, but you may substitute ordinary edible rice paper.

To make about 2 pounds [1 kg.]

2 cups	sugar	½ liter
6	egg yolks	6
5 oz.	hazelnuts, toasted, skinned and ground (about 2 cups [½ liter])	150 g.
3½ oz.	almonds, blanched, peeled and ground (about 1½ cups [375 ml.])	100 g.
16 tbsp.	butter (½ lb. [¼ kg.]), cut into small pieces	240 ml.
1 tsp.	vanilla extract	5 ml.
¼ cup	cocoa powder	50 ml.
	edible rice paper	

Cook half of the sugar without water to the caramel stage *(page 9)*, let it cool on a marble slab or platter sprinkled with water, and then pound it to a powder in a mortar.

Whisk the rest of the sugar with the egg yolks until the mixture is frothy. Add the ground nuts and the butter. Put the mixture into a bowl set over a saucepan of hot water, and beat it until it forms a thick paste. Add the vanilla extract and cocoa powder. Remove the bowl from the hot water, stir until the mixture cools, and then mix it thoroughly with the pounded caramelized sugar.

Spread the mixture over a piece of edible rice paper, place another piece of rice paper on top, and press the mixture down evenly with a heavy weight. Leave it in a cool place for a few hours. Remove the weight and cut the halvah into bars.

MARIA HORVÁTH
BALKAN-KÜCHE

Turkish Halvah

Türkische Halva

To make about 1 ¼ pounds [600 g.]

1 ¼ cups	sugar	300 ml.
5	egg whites, stiffly beaten	5
⅓ cup	honey, warmed	75 ml.
1 cup	almonds, blanched, peeled and coarsely chopped	¼ liter
3 ½ oz.	mixed candied fruit, finely chopped (about ¾ cup [175 ml.])	100 g.
	edible rice paper	

Beat the sugar into the egg whites, and continue to beat until the sugar has dissolved. Add the honey and put the mixture over a saucepan of hot water. Cook for 25 minutes, stirring constantly. When the mixture thickens to a paste, stir in the almonds and candied fruit.

Use a wet knife to spread the mixture on rice paper. Cover the mixture with another piece of rice paper and press it down evenly with a heavy weight. Let it sit in a cool place for a day. Remove the weight and cut the halvah into bars.

MARIA HORVÁTH
BALKAN-KÜCHE

Honey Nougat

To dry the almonds, spread them out on a baking sheet and bake them in a preheated 250° F. [120° C.] oven for about 20 minutes. Because this nougat is very sticky, you may want to replace the parchment paper with edible rice paper that does not have to be removed before eating the nougat. The rice paper, of course, should not be oiled.

To make about 4 pounds [2 kg.]

3 cups	sugar	¾ liter
2 cups	honey	½ liter
3	egg whites, stiffly beaten	3
	orange flavoring	
1 ½ lb.	almonds, blanched, peeled and dried (about 4 ½ cups [1 ⅛ liters])	¾ kg.

Put the sugar and honey in a saucepan over very low heat, and stir until the sugar dissolves. Cook the syrup until it becomes quite brittle (*soft-crack stage, pages 8-11*). Stirring all the while, gradually add the beaten egg whites. Stir in the orange flavoring and the almonds, and remove the pan from the heat.

Spread the nougat mixture in a jelly-roll pan or on two large pieces of oiled parchment paper contained by confec-

tioners' bars, forming layers about 2 inches [5 cm.] thick. Lay two more sheets of oiled parchment paper on top of the nougat. Lay two boards on top of the nougat, and set heavy weights on top of the boards. Let the nougat cool completely; then cut it into strips.

OSCAR TSCHIRKY
"OSCAR" OF THE WALDORF'S COOK BOOK

Chocolate Honey Nougat

Schokoladen-Nougat

The syrup for this nougat is cooked to a stage between the hard-ball and the soft-crack stages (pages 8-11). Most nougats are cooked to the hard-ball stage, but those containing a large proportion of honey must be cooked to a slightly higher temperature.

To make about 1 ¼ pounds [600 g.]

¾ cup	honey	175 ml.
1 cup	superfine sugar	¼ liter
2 ½ tbsp.	liquid glucose or light corn syrup	37 ml.
2 tbsp.	water	30 ml.
1	egg white, stiffly beaten	1
3 ½ oz.	semisweet chocolate, melted	100 g.
2 ½ oz.	hazelnuts, roasted, peeled and chopped (about ¾ cup [175 ml.])	75 g.
3 ½ oz.	almonds, blanched, peeled and chopped (about 1 cup [¼ liter])	100 g.

In a pan, melt the honey over low heat, stirring constantly. Put the pan in a bowl of hot water to keep the honey warm.

In a second pan over low heat, dissolve the sugar and the glucose or corn syrup in the water, stirring constantly. Boil the syrup without stirring until it registers 268° F. [131° C.] on a candy thermometer. Off the heat, gradually add the beaten egg white, then add the warm honey. Stirring constantly, cook the nougat mixture over low heat until it forms a stiff paste.

Remove the pan from the heat, and stir in the melted chocolate, the hazelnuts and almonds. Turn the hot nougat mixture onto a baking sheet lined with buttered aluminum foil. Using a knife dipped in boiling water, spread the mixture evenly. Let the nougat cool and harden before cutting it into squares, diamonds or bars.

MARGRET UHLE AND ANNE BRAKEMEIER
KONFEKT ZUM SELBERMACHEN

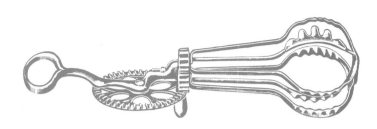

Italian Chocolate Nougat

Torrone di Cioccolato

This is a very hard, brittle nougat, cooked to the caramel stage (pages 8-11). Most nougats are cooked to the hard-ball stage.

To make 2 ½ pounds [1 ¼ kg.]

1 ½ cups	cocoa powder	375 ml.
2 tbsp.	water	30 ml.
1 cup	sugar	¼ liter
½ cup	honey	125 ml.
2	egg whites, stiffly beaten	2
1 lb.	hazelnuts, toasted, peeled and finely chopped (about 4 cups [1 liter])	½ kg.
	edible rice paper	

Mix the cocoa powder and water; cook them together, stirring constantly, until they form a smooth cream. Set it aside.

In a heavy saucepan, heat the sugar and honey together until they begin to brown. Gradually add the beaten egg whites; mix them in well. Remove the pan from the heat. Add the cocoa cream and the hazelnuts to the honey mixture. Pour the nougat into a pan measuring 8 by 10 inches [20 by 25 cm.] that has been lined with edible rice paper; the nougat will be about 2 inches [5 cm.] deep. Let it cool, then cut the nougat into small rectangles.

BERYL GOULD-MARKS
THE HOME BOOK OF ITALIAN COOKERY

Pistachio Nougat

The flavor of honey may be impaired by lengthy boiling; to preserve its flavor, the honey can be warmed separately and added when the sugar syrup reaches a temperature of 280° F. [138° C.]. To prevent the nougat mixture from cooling and setting prematurely, warm the chopped nuts in a 350° F. [180° C.] oven for five minutes before adding them.

To make about 1 ¾ pounds [875 g.]

1 cup	sugar	¼ liter
½ cup	honey	125 ml.
3 tbsp.	corn syrup	45 ml.
½ cup	water	125 ml.
2	egg whites, stiffly beaten	2
1 tsp.	vanilla extract	5 ml.
10 oz.	almonds, blanched, peeled, toasted and chopped (about 2 cups [½ liter])	300 g.
¼ lb.	pistachios, blanched, peeled and chopped (about 1 cup [¼ liter])	125 g.
	edible rice paper	

Put the sugar, honey, corn syrup and water into a saucepan, and stir them over medium heat until the sugar has dissolved. Without stirring, cook the syrup to a temperature of 290° F. [143° C.] *(soft-crack stage, pages 8-11).*

Remove the pan from the heat and, beating constantly, gradually pour the hot syrup onto the beaten egg whites. Beat the mixture thoroughly. Stir in the vanilla extract and the nuts. The mixture should be stiff. If it remains soft, put it in the top of a double boiler or in a pan over hot water, and beat it constantly until it dries out a little and becomes firm.

Pour the mixture into a pan 8 inches [20 cm.] square that has been lined with edible rice paper, and cover the surface with a layer of edible rice paper. Place a board on top of the nougat and place a heavy weight on the board. Let the nougat set for 15 hours. Remove the weight and cut the nougat into rectangular pieces.

MARY B. BOOKMEYER
CANDY AND CANDY-MAKING

Candy Jellies

Fresh-Fruit Candy Jellies

The technique of making fruit candy jellies is shown on pages 48-49. You may set batches of differently flavored candy jellies one on top of the other to make striped candy.

To make about 1 pound [½ kg.]

6 tbsp.	sugar	90 ml.
⅔ cup	fruit juice (lemon, orange or raspberry)	150 ml.
3 to 6 tbsp.	liquid glucose or light corn syrup	45 to 90 ml.
4 tbsp.	unflavored powdered gelatin, softened in ¼ cup [50 ml.] water	60 ml.
	food coloring (optional)	
	confectioners' sugar	

Put the sugar, fruit juice, and glucose or corn syrup in a pan and heat them slowly, stirring until the sugar dissolves. Add the gelatin and continue stirring the mixture until the gelatin dissolves. Food coloring can be added at this point. Pour the mixture into a dampened pan 6 inches [15 cm.] square and ¼ inch [6 mm.] deep, or into tiny dampened molds. Let the jelly set in a cool place for at least six hours.

When firm, cut the candy jelly into squares, or turn it out onto a work surface sprinkled with confectioners' sugar and use a cookie cutter to stamp out more elaborate shapes.

WINIFRED GRAHAM
CHOCOLATES AND CANDIES FOR PLEASURE AND PROFIT

Turkish Delight

To make about 1 pound [½ kg.]

2 cups	granulated sugar	½ liter
1¼ cups	water	300 ml.
1	lemon, the peel cut into strips, the juice squeezed and its pulp strained out	1
1	orange, the peel cut into strips, the juice squeezed and its pulp strained out	1
4 tbsp.	unflavored powdered gelatin	60 ml.
2 tbsp.	confectioners' sugar	30 ml.
1 tbsp.	cornstarch	15 ml.

Dissolve the granulated sugar in half of the water over medium heat. Add the strips of lemon and orange peel and the

juices. Bring the mixture to a boil and simmer for 15 minutes. Soften the gelatin by soaking it for five to 10 minutes in the rest of the water. Add the gelatin to the sugar syrup, stirring well, and boil for 20 minutes, until the syrup reaches the thread stage *(pages 8-11)*.

Strain the mixture into shallow dampened pans or onto platters, and let it set for 24 hours. Cut the candy into 1-inch [2½-cm.] squares. Sift the confectioners' sugar and cornstarch together into a shallow dish. Roll the pieces of candy in the mixture. Store the squares in boxes with more confectioners' sugar and cornstarch between each layer.

THE KING'S COLLEGE HOSPITAL BOOK OF COOKING RECIPES

Gumdrops

The author suggests that you choose cherry, peppermint, spearmint, orange or lemon extract as a flavoring, using it in the following amounts: 1 teaspoon [5 ml.] of cherry, peppermint or spearmint extract, and 2 teaspoons [10 ml.] of orange or lemon extract. In addition, the author suggests coloring the candy with the following amounts of food coloring: 7 drops of red for cherry; 7 drops of green for peppermint or spearmint; 7 drops of yellow and 1 drop of red for orange; and 10 drops of yellow for lemon.

To make about 1 pound [½ kg.]

1 cup	sugar	¼ liter
1 cup	light corn syrup	¼ liter
1¾ oz.	powdered fruit pectin (1 box)	52 g.
½ tsp.	baking soda	2 ml.
¾ cup	water	175 ml.
	sugar for coating	
	food coloring and flavoring	

Stir the sugar and syrup together in a 2-quart [2-liter] saucepan. In another 2-quart saucepan, mix together the pectin, baking soda and water; the mixture will foam. Place both of the pans over high heat. Cook both mixtures, stirring them simultaneously, until the foam thins in the pectin mixture and the sugar mixture comes to a rapid boil; this should take three to five minutes. Pour the pectin mixture in a slow, thin stream into the boiling sugar mixture; stir continuously as you pour, and take one full minute to make the transfer. Cook and stir the mixture for one more minute. Then remove it from the heat, and stir in flavoring and coloring.

Pour the mixture into a buttered loaf pan measuring 5 by 9 inches [13 by 23 cm.]. Let the candy stand at room temperature until cool and firm, about four hours. Cut the candy into squares, and roll them in sugar. Store the candy at room temperature in a loosely covered container.

DAPHNE METAXAS HARTWIG
MAKE YOUR OWN GROCERIES

Apple Candy

To make about 3 pounds [1½ kg.]

8	medium-sized apples, peeled, cored and cut into small pieces	8
½ cup	water	125 ml.
2 cups	light brown sugar	½ liter
2 tbsp.	unflavored powdered gelatin	30 ml.
¼ lb.	walnuts, chopped (about 1 cup [¼ liter])	125 g.
1 tbsp.	fresh lemon juice, pulp strained out	15 ml.
½ cup	confectioners' sugar	125 ml.
1 tbsp.	cornstarch	15 ml.

In a pan, combine the apples with half of the water, and cook the fruit until it is tender, about 20 to 25 minutes. Press the cooked apples through a sieve and add the brown sugar. Stirring often, cook the mixture over low heat until it is thick, about 30 minutes. Soften the gelatin in the rest of the water. Add the softened gelatin to the hot apple mixture and stir until the gelatin dissolves. Chill the mixture until it thickens slightly. Stir in the walnuts and the lemon juice.

Pour the candy into a dampened pan measuring 8 by 12 by 1¼ inches [20 by 30 by 3 cm.]. The candy layer should be about ½ inch [1 cm.] deep. Chill the candy thoroughly, then cut it into 1-inch [2½-cm.] squares. Combine the confectioners' sugar and the cornstarch, and roll the squares in this mixture.

DEMETRIA TAYLOR
APPLE KITCHEN COOK BOOK

Apple Candy Squares

To make about 2 pounds [1 kg.]

7	medium-sized tart apples, quartered, cored and cut into chunks (about 1¼ lb. [600 g.])	7
¼ cup	water	50 ml.
about 2 cups	granulated sugar	about ½ liter
⅛ tsp.	salt	½ ml.
3 tbsp.	unflavored powdered gelatin, softened in 6 tbsp. [90 ml.] of cold water	45 ml.
¼ lb.	walnuts, chopped (about 1 cup [¼ liter])	125 g.
4 tsp.	fresh lemon juice, pulp strained out	20 ml.
1 cup	confectioners' sugar	¼ liter

Cook the apples in the water until soft, about 15 to 20 minutes. Force the apples through a food mill and measure the

purée; there should be about 2 cups [½ liter]. Combine the purée with the same measure of granulated sugar and add the salt. Stirring constantly to prevent scorching, cook the mixture over medium heat until it thickens, 30 to 40 minutes. Add the softened gelatin, stirring until the gelatin dissolves. Remove the pan from the heat; add the walnuts and lemon juice. Pour the mixture into a buttered pan 8 inches [20 cm.] square.

Let the mixture cool completely, then refrigerate it. When it has set, cut it into 1-inch [2½-cm.] squares. Cool the squares to room temperature and roll them in the confectioners' sugar.

JUNE ROTH
OLD-FASHIONED CANDYMAKING

Fig Jellies

To make about ¾ pound [350 g.]

4 tbsp.	unflavored powdered gelatin	60 ml.
⅔ cup	water	150 ml.
½ cup	granulated sugar	125 ml.
3 to 4 tbsp.	fresh orange juice, pulp strained out	45 to 60 ml.
2 tbsp.	fresh lemon juice, pulp strained out	30 ml.
⅓ cup	chopped dried figs	75 ml.
1 oz.	pistachios or almonds, chopped (about ¼ cup [50 ml.])	30 g.
1 tbsp.	grated orange peel	15 ml.
¼ lb.	angelica	125 g.
½ cup	confectioners' sugar mixed with ½ cup [125 ml.] cornstarch, or ¾ cup [175 ml.] superfine sugar	125 ml.

Soften the gelatin in half of the water. Boil the rest of the water with the sugar, orange juice and lemon juice for 10 minutes. Remove the pan from the heat, and add the figs, nuts and grated orange peel. Boil the mixture for another 10 minutes. Add the softened gelatin, stirring the mixture in one direction only. Boil the mixture for 10 minutes, making 30 minutes cooking time in all.

Pour the jelly mixture into a wet pan 8 by 12 by 1¼ inches [20 by 30 by 3 cm.], and let it set for 24 hours. Cut the jelly into small oval shapes, then cut the angelica into narrow strips to resemble fruit stems and attach them to the ovals. Roll the jellies in the mixture of confectioners' sugar and cornstarch, or dust them liberally on each side with the superfine sugar. Allow the jellies to dry thoroughly before packing them away.

ESMÉ GRAY BOOKER
SWEETS THAT HAVE TEMPTED ME

Candied Fruits, Nuts and Vegetables

Candied Cranberries

To make about ¾ pound [350 g.]

2 cups	firm, fresh, unblemished cranberries	½ liter
4 cups	sugar	1 liter
1 cup	water	¼ liter
	cream of tartar	

Wash the cranberries under cold running water and pat them completely dry with paper towels. With a trussing needle or a small skewer, pierce each berry completely through. Set the berries aside.

In a 2- to 3-quart [2- to 3-liter] enameled or stainless-steel saucepan, combine 3 cups [¾ liter] of the sugar, the water and a pinch of cream of tartar. Stirring constantly, cook over medium heat until the sugar dissolves. Increase the heat, let the syrup come to a boil, and cook briskly, uncovered and undisturbed, for about five minutes more, or until the syrup reaches a temperature of 220° F. [105° C.] on a candy thermometer. Remove the pan from the heat and gently stir the cranberries into the syrup, turning them about with a spoon until the berries are evenly coated. Set them aside at room temperature for at least 12 hours, preferably overnight.

Stirring gently, bring the cranberries and syrup to a simmer over medium heat. Then drain the berries in a sieve or colander set over a bowl, and return the syrup to the pan.

Bring the syrup to a boil over high heat, and cook briskly until it reaches a temperature of 250° F. [121° C.] on a candy thermometer (*hard-ball stage, pages 8-11*).

Remove the pan from the heat, drop the berries into the syrup, and stir gently until they are thoroughly coated and glistening. With a slotted spoon, arrange the berries in one layer on a long strip of wax paper. Discard the remaining syrup. Let the berries cool until lukewarm; if pools of syrup collect around any of the berries, carefully move the berries to a clean part of the paper.

Roll the berries in the remaining cup of sugar two or three at a time, and transfer them to fresh wax paper. Cool the berries completely to room temperature before serving.

FOODS OF THE WORLD/AMERICAN COOKING: NEW ENGLAND

Candied Fruit Peel

Peel keeps almost indefinitely, and may be used diced in baking or served as a confection. Orange and grapefruit peel should not be cooked together: The distinctive flavor of each would be spoiled.

To make about 2 pounds [1 kg.]

3	large grapefruits or 5 large navel oranges	3
2¾ cups	sugar	625 ml.
1 cup	water	¼ liter
1½ tsp.	ground ginger	7 ml.

Cut each fruit in half crosswise. Scrape out and discard the fruit pulp and membranes, but leave the white pith attached to the peel. Cut the peel into long strips ¼ to ½ inch [6 mm. to 1 cm.] wide. Put the strips into a pan, cover them with boiling water, and simmer them for five minutes. Drain the strips. Repeat the process four more times, using fresh boiling water each time and draining the strips well between boilings. This will remove the bitter oils from the peel.

In a heavy saucepan, combine 2 cups [½ liter] of the sugar with the water, add the ginger, and simmer until the sugar dissolves. Add the strips of peel. Cook the mixture slowly, partially covered, for at least 45 minutes, until the strips of peel are soft and have absorbed the syrup. Turn the strips out onto a large sheet of aluminum foil or wax paper, spreading them in a single layer and spacing them well apart to prevent sticking. Let the peels cool thoroughly, then sprinkle them liberally with the remaining sugar. Let them stand uncovered until they are fully dry, about five to seven hours or overnight. Store the peels in a tightly closed jar.

WILLIAM HARLAN HALE AND THE EDITORS OF HORIZON MAGAZINE
THE HORIZON COOKBOOK

Candied Chestnuts

Marrons Glacés

In this recipe, the concentration of the sugar in the syrup is increased by repeatedly boiling the syrup, without adding additional sugar. Each time the syrup is boiled, it must be cooked to a slightly higher temperature; however, do not let the syrup reach the soft-ball stage (pages 8-11)—at which concentration it will merely glaze the chestnuts without penetrating them. Both this method and the method demonstrated on pages 50-51 can be used for crystallizing fruit. The technique of peeling chestnuts is described on page 56.

To make about 1 ½ pounds [¾ kg.]

1 lb.	chestnuts, shelled and peeled (about 2⅓ cups [575 ml.])	½ kg.
2 cups	sugar	½ liter
2 tbsp.	liquid glucose or light corn syrup	30 ml.
about ½ cup	water	about 125 ml.

Cook the peeled chestnuts in enough water to cover until a needle inserted in the base of a chestnut enters without difficulty, about 40 minutes. Drain the chestnuts.

In a separate saucepan, dissolve the sugar and glucose or corn syrup in the water, and cook the mixture over medium heat until the syrup boils and becomes smooth, about 215° F. [101° C.]. Pour the syrup into a heatproof bowl and let it cool; when the syrup is completely cold, add the chestnuts and let them steep for 24 hours.

Put the bowl containing the syrup and chestnuts into a water bath, and gradually heat the syrup. Remove the chestnuts when the syrup reaches the boiling point. Cook the syrup to 216° F. [102° C.]. Remove the bowl from the water bath, return the chestnuts to the syrup, and allow them to steep for 12 hours.

Remove the chestnuts from the syrup, drain them, and put the bowl of syrup back in the water bath. Cook the syrup to 220° F. [104° C.]. Remove the bowl from the water bath, return the chestnuts to the syrup, and leave them in the syrup for another 12 hours.

Remove the chestnuts from the syrup, return the bowl of syrup to the water bath, and cook the syrup to 223° F. [106° C.]. Remove the bowl from the heat, immerse the chestnuts in the syrup, and let them steep for 12 hours.

Finally, remove the chestnuts from the syrup, put the bowl of syrup into the water bath, and cook the syrup to 227° F. [108° C.]. Immerse the chestnuts in the syrup and let them steep for 12 hours. Drain the chestnuts and let them dry in a wire basket or on wire racks. Dry them first in a dry room for 12 hours, then dry them for another 12 hours in a warmer place such as an unlit oven with a pilot light.

GINETTE MATHIOT
LA PÂTISSERIE POUR TOUS

Candied Ginger

To dry fresh ginger, peel it and place it in a 140° F. [60° C.] oven for eight to 10 hours.

To make about 1 pound [½ kg.]

1 lb.	freshly dried ginger, sliced into pieces ¼ inch [6 mm.] thick	½ kg.
about 3 cups	sugar	about ¾ liter
3 tbsp.	water	45 ml.

Put the pieces of ginger into a saucepan and cover them with water. Boil them over medium heat until the ginger is tender—about 30 minutes. Drain the ginger in a colander and let it cool.

When the ginger is cold, measure it in a cup and put it into a pan with an equal amount of sugar and the 3 tablespoons [45 ml.] of water. Stirring often, boil the ginger and sugar slowly until the sugar dissolves, then stir occasionally until the ginger becomes transparent and the liquid has nearly boiled away.

Reduce the heat and stir the candied ginger continually. When it is practically dry, remove the pan from the heat, and use a slotted spoon to put several pieces of ginger at a time into a paper bag containing ½ cup [125 ml.] of sugar. Shake the bag and remove the pieces of ginger with a slotted spoon; lay them on wax paper. Repeat the process until all of the ginger has been sugared. Stored in a glass jar at the back of the cabinet, it will last all winter for nibbles.

GRACE FIRTH
À NATURAL YEAR

Candied Carrots

To make about 2 pounds [1 kg.]

1 cup	granulated sugar	¼ liter
½ cup	water	125 ml.
1 lb.	carrots, sliced ⅛ inch [3 mm.] thick (about 4 cups [1 liter])	½ kg.
½ cup	superfine sugar	125 ml.

In a saucepan, combine the granulated sugar and water over medium heat, stirring until the sugar dissolves. Reduce the heat and simmer the syrup for 15 minutes *(thread stage, pages 8-11)*. Add the carrots and increase the heat to medium. Cook the mixture for about 15 minutes, until the carrots are glazed and have absorbed all of the syrup. Dry the carrot slices on wire racks for several hours, until they feel only slightly sticky. Roll the carrots in the superfine sugar. Leave them until the coating has crystallized. Then store the candied carrots in an airtight jar.

ELIZABETH AHN TOUPIN
HAWAII COOKBOOK AND BACKYARD LUAU

Candied Sweet-Potato Balls

To make 3 pounds [1½ kg.]

6	medium-sized sweet potatoes (about 2 lb. [1 kg.])	6
2 cups	sugar	½ liter
½ cup	water	125 ml.
1 tsp.	vanilla extract	5 ml.

Scoop out little balls from the sweet potatoes with a melon baller. Put the balls into a large pot of lightly salted boiling water, and cook them until they are tender enough to pierce with a toothpick—about 10 to 15 minutes. Remove the pan from the heat and drain the balls.

Dissolve the sugar in the water and cook the syrup to the hard-crack stage *(pages 8-11)*. Add the vanilla extract. Drop in the sweet-potato balls, a few at a time, simmering them in the syrup until they are thickly coated and transparent—about five minutes. Remove the balls one at a time with a skimmer or a fork, and drop them onto wax paper. They will harden on the outside as they dry.

MARY M. WRIGHT
CANDY-MAKING AT HOME

Candied Vegetables

Sliced fresh coconut can be candied in the same way as the vegetables in this recipe.

To make about 1½ pounds [¾ kg.]

1 cup	granulated sugar	¼ liter
½ cup	water	125 ml.
1 lb.	pumpkin, winter squash, carrots, sweet potatoes or other firm-fleshed vegetables, peeled and thinly sliced (about 3 cups [¾ liter])	½ kg.
	superfine sugar	

Put the granulated sugar and water into a saucepan. Stirring, heat them until the mixture starts to boil. Reduce the heat and cook the syrup gently for 15 minutes *(thread stage, pages 8-11)*. Add the vegetable slices to the syrup and cook gently for about 15 minutes, or until they are tender when you poke them with the point of a sharp knife.

With a slotted spoon, lift the slices out of the syrup and spread them out to dry on wire racks that have been set over a piece of wax paper to catch the drips.

After the vegetable slices have been drying for several hours, sprinkle a sheet of wax paper with superfine sugar and roll the vegetable slices in it. Put the slices back on the racks to dry thoroughly.

CAROLYN MEYER
LOTS AND LOTS OF CANDY

Candy Pastes

Apple Balls

Apfelkugeln

To make about 1 pound [½ kg.]

1 cup	sugar	¼ liter
¼ cup	water	50 ml.
2	medium-sized apples, peeled, cored and finely chopped	2
¼ lb.	almonds, blanched, peeled and very finely chopped (about 1 cup [¼ liter])	125 g.
1	lemon, the peel grated, the juice squeezed and its pulp strained out	1
	confectioners' sugar, ground almonds or grated coconut (optional)	

Dissolve the sugar in the water over medium heat, stirring constantly. Stop stirring when the sugar has dissolved, then increase the heat and boil the syrup until it reaches the soft-ball stage *(pages 8-11)*. Reduce the heat and add the apples. Cook the mixture very slowly over very low heat for about 10 minutes. Then add the almonds, lemon peel and lemon juice. Cook for another 10 to 15 minutes, or until a thick paste forms. Spoon the paste onto a work surface coated with confectioners' sugar, and let the paste cool until it can be handled. Roll it into small balls between your palms. Roll the balls in the confectioners' sugar, ground almonds or grated coconut, if using. Serve the balls in individual paper cups.

MÁRIA HAJKOVÁ
MÚČNIKY

Apricot Roll

To make 2 pounds [1 kg.]

2 cups	sugar	½ liter
1 cup	milk	¼ liter
¾ lb.	dried apricots, finely chopped (about 3 cups [¾ liter])	350 g.
1 tbsp.	butter	15 ml.
½ lb.	pecans, chopped (about 2 cups [½ liter])	¼ kg.
1 tsp.	vanilla extract	5 ml.
	salt	

Dissolve the sugar in the milk, stirring constantly, and boil until the mixture thickens—about 236° F. [113° C.] *(soft-*

ball stage, pages 8-11). Add the apricots and boil them until they melt and the mixture reaches about 230° F. [110° C.]. Remove the pan from the heat and beat the mixture hard until it is thick. Add the butter, pecans, vanilla and a pinch of salt. Beat the mixture until it begins to harden.

Pour the mixture onto a wet, smooth cloth and shape it into a long roll. Let it cool; then store the roll in the refrigerator. Cut the roll into thin slices to serve.

JUNIOR LEAGUE OF JACKSON, MISSISSIPPI
SOUTHERN SIDEBOARDS

Banana Candy

Kela Halva

The technique of preparing saffron for use as a coloring is demonstrated on page 15.

To make about 1¾ pounds [875 g.]

6	ripe bananas	6
½ cup	sugar	125 ml.
1¼ cups	water	300 ml.
8 tbsp.	ghee or clarified butter, melted	120 ml.
½ cup	chopped walnuts or almonds	125 ml.
3	whole cardamoms, seeds removed and pulverized	3
¼ tsp.	ground saffron (optional)	1 ml.

Mash the fruit to a pulp and place it in a saucepan with the sugar and water; stir the mixture over low heat until the sugar has dissolved, then boil it rapidly for five minutes. Take the pan off the heat and gradually stir in the *ghee* or clarified butter. Replace the pan on the heat and stir constantly until the mixture begins to form a firm ball in the pan, about 10 to 15 minutes. Stir in the nuts and cardamom seeds. Color the mixture, if desired, with the saffron, and then pour it out onto a lightly oiled flat platter. When cool, cut the candy into 1½-inch [4-cm.] squares.

GOOD HOUSEKEEPING INSTITUTE
GOOD HOUSEKEEPING'S WORLD COOKERY

Pineapple Candy

This candy takes about one hour to cook, but it is worth every minute of it.

Grate the pineapple on the large-holed side of a box grater; you want some bulk here, not just liquid pineapple.

To make about ¾ pound [350 g.]

1 cup	peeled and grated pineapple	¼ liter
¾ cup	honey	175 ml.

In a medium saucepan, cook the fruit and honey together over very low heat, until the mixture reaches the soft-ball

stage *(pages 8-11)*. Stir occasionally at the beginning, but constantly for the last few minutes of cooking. When the mixture is ready, it will look quite thick and all of the free liquid will be gone. Lightly grease a large platter, and spoon half tablespoonfuls of the candy onto it. When the candy has cooled slightly, smooth down any rough edges. When the candy has completely cooled, wrap each piece in wax paper.

STAN AND FLOSS DWORKIN
NATURAL SNACKS 'N' SWEETS

Plum Paste

Confiture de Prunes

Apricot paste can be made in the same way. Fruit pastes make distinguished desserts and keep perfectly from one year to the next.

To make about 5 pounds [2½ kg.]

4 lb.	greengage or other plums, quartered and pitted (about 3½ quarts [3½ liters])	2 kg.
4 cups	granulated sugar	1 liter
2	cinnamon sticks	2
2 cups	superfine sugar	½ liter
2 tsp.	grated lemon peel	10 ml.

Put the plums in an enameled, tinned or stainless-steel pan over very low heat for about 10 minutes, then increase the heat and continue cooking for 10 more minutes, stirring constantly, until the plums are completely soft. Purée the plums through a sieve.

Cook the puréed plums for about 30 minutes, stirring frequently. Measure the purée, and to each cup [¼ liter] of purée add 1 cup of sugar. Stir until the sugar is dissolved, add the cinnamon sticks, bring to a boil, and boil for a minute or two. Remove the cinnamon and pour the paste in a thin layer onto a large, shallow plate. Let it dry beside the stove or in the open air for six to 12 hours, or until the paste is solid enough to be lifted in a piece from the plate.

Mix the superfine sugar with the lemon peel, and use this to sprinkle a pastry board. Roll out 1 pound [½ kg.] of the paste at a time, to a thickness of about ⁄₁₆ inch [1½ mm.], sprinkling with the lemon sugar as you go. Cut the paste into rounds and sprinkle the rounds with lemon sugar. Arrange the rounds in layers in boxes, separating the layers with parchment paper. Repeat until all of the paste and lemon sugar are used. Store in a dry place.

JULES BRETEUIL
LE CUISINIER EUROPÉEN

Peach and Apricot Paste

Persicata ed Albicoccata

To make about 15 pounds [6¾ kg.]

6 to 8 lb.	peaches and apricots, halved and pitted	3 to 4 kg.
1½ quarts	water	1½ liters
about 20 cups	superfine sugar	about 5 liters
12 cups	granulated sugar	3 liters

Put the fruits into an enameled, tinned or stainless-steel pan with 1 quart [1 liter] of the water; bring them to a boil, then simmer them until tender, about 20 minutes. Press the fruits through a sieve and return the purée to medium heat; bring to a boil, and stir continuously with a spatula until the water has evaporated and the purée is thick. Measure the purée and measure an equal volume of superfine sugar.

Dissolve the superfine sugar in 1 cup [¼ liter] of the water over medium heat, and cook the syrup to the hard-ball stage *(pages 8-11)*. Pour the syrup over the fruit purée and, stirring with the spatula, simmer the mixture until it is reduced to a stiff paste. Remove from the heat, and pour it into dampened shallow pans or trays to a depth of about ½ inch [1 cm.]. Leave the paste in a warm, dry place for several days to dry. When the paste is no longer sticky, cut it into strips 1½ inches [3 cm.] long and ½ inch [1 cm.] wide.

Dissolve half of the granulated sugar in the remaining cup of water over medium heat, and cook it to the soft-ball stage. Remove the syrup from the heat and dip the strips of fruit paste in it, one at a time. Roll the strips in the rest of the granulated sugar until they are well coated, then let them dry on wire racks. Store the pieces of fruit paste between sheets of wax paper in a tin with a tight-fitting lid.

GIUSEPPE SORBIATTI
LA GASTRONOMIA MODERNA

Quince and Almond Paste

Lowzina mal Haiwah

To make 10 pounds [4½ kg.]

6 or 7	large quinces (about 6 lb. [3 kg.])	6 or 7
½ cup	water	125 ml.
about 8 cups	sugar	about 2 liters
3 tbsp.	fresh lemon juice, pulp strained out	45 ml.
12 oz.	almonds, blanched, peeled and ground (about 4 cups [1 liter])	350 g.
½ tsp.	ground cardamom (optional)	2 ml.

Wash the unpeeled quinces and cut them into ½-inch [1-cm.] slices. Remove the cores and rinse the quinces again. Put the quinces into a large, heavy stainless-steel saucepan, add the water, cover the pan, and simmer the fruit over low heat for about one and one half hours, or until tender. Stir the fruit occasionally and, if it begins to dry out, add a little more water. Remove the pan from the heat and stir. There should be about 8 cups [2 liters] of fruit pulp.

Cover the pan, and let the fruit stand overnight so that it becomes dark red in color. (If the paste is made immediately, without letting the fruit stand overnight, it will be a pale color and less attractive.)

The next morning, purée the fruit pulp through a food mill to remove the skins. Measure the pulp and add an equal measure of sugar. Cook the mixture over low heat for two and one half to three hours, stirring occasionally with a wooden spoon to prevent sticking and burning. When the paste thickens and comes away from the bottom of the pan, test a spoonful of the mixture on a plate to be sure it holds its shape and is not sticky when it cools. Add the lemon juice and mix well for one to two minutes. Remove the pan from the heat, stirring occasionally, and let the mixture stand until it is almost cold.

Mix the ground almonds with the cardamom, if using, and spread about half of the almonds in an even layer on a large tray or jelly-roll pan. Pour the fruit mixture into the center and spread a handful of the remaining almonds on top. Press the paste by hand or with a rolling pin, adding more almonds to keep the fruit from sticking to your hand or the rolling pin, until the candy is about ½ inch [1 cm.] thick. Spread the remaining almonds on top, cover with wax paper, and let the candy stand overnight.

The next day, cut the paste with a sharp knife into diamond shapes about ½ inch long, then turn the pieces upside down and let them stand for two to three hours to dry thoroughly. Arrange the pieces in tin boxes, placing wax paper between the layers. Cover the boxes tightly and store them in the refrigerator or in the freezer; the frozen candy will keep well for a year if each box is wrapped in a plastic bag.

DAISY INY
THE BEST OF BAGHDAD COOKING

Peach Toffee

Although called a toffee, this candy is really a fruit paste.

To make 1 ½ pounds [¾ kg.]

1 lb.	peaches, halved, pitted, peeled, poached in water for 20 minutes, drained and puréed through a sieve	½ kg.
2 cups	sugar	½ liter
1 tbsp.	almonds, blanched, peeled and slivered	15 ml.
10	whole cardamoms, seeds removed and pulverized	10
1 tbsp.	*ghee* or clarified butter	15 ml.

Heat the fruit gently in a pan until the moisture begins to evaporate and the purée thickens. Stir in the sugar, almonds and cardamom seeds, and continue stirring until the mixture becomes thick and smooth and comes away from the sides of the pan. Add the *ghee* or clarified butter; stir it in well. Pour the mixture into a buttered pan 8 inches [20 cm.] square. Flatten the paste and let it cool. Cut the paste into 1-inch [2½-cm.] squares. Store in an airtight container.

JACK SANTA MARIA
INDIAN SWEET COOKERY

Mulberry or Blackberry Paste

Mûres, Pâte

To make about 4 pounds [2 kg.]

2 lb.	mulberries or blackberries, washed in acidulated water, damaged fruit and stems discarded (about 7 cups [1¾ liters])	1 kg.
about 4 cups	superfine sugar	about 1 liter
about 1 cup	water	about ¼ liter
	granulated sugar (optional)	

Put the fruit through a food mill and measure the pulp. Put the fruit pulp into an enameled, tinned or stainless-steel pan. Add an equal amount of superfine sugar and 1 cup [¼ liter] of water for every 4 cups [1 liter] of fruit pulp. Put the pan on low heat and simmer the mixture, using a skimmer to remove the small seeds that rise to the surface. After the mixture begins to thicken, stir constantly for about 40 minutes, until a wooden spatula leaves a trail as it is moved through the paste.

Pour the fruit paste into an oiled pan 8 inches [20 cm.] square. Cover it with a kitchen towel, and let it set for 48

hours. Unmold the paste. If you want to keep the paste whole, wrap it in aluminum foil. Otherwise, cut it into pieces, roll each piece in granulated sugar, if using, and store the pieces in an airtight container.

CÉLINE VENCE
ENCYCLOPÉDIE HACHETTE DE LA CUISINE RÉGIONALE

Pastilles of Fruit

The technique for making this type of fruit paste is shown on pages 46-47. Other fruits—pears, plums, apricots or raspberries among them—can be used to make pastilles. If berries are used, there is no need to cook them before puréeing them.

To make about 3 pounds [1½ kg.]

3 lb.	quinces or apples, peeled, cored and cut into pieces	1½ kg.
1¼ cups	water	300 ml.
4 cups	granulated sugar	1 liter
2 tbsp.	grated lemon or orange peel	30 ml.
½ tsp.	ground cinnamon	2 ml.
1 cup	ground almonds, hazelnuts, walnuts or pistachios (optional)	¼ liter
	confectioners' sugar	

In a covered pan, stew the quinces or apples in the water until they are soft, about 30 minutes. Keeping the pan covered, let the fruit cool completely. Purée the fruit through a sieve or food mill into a large, shallow pan. Add the granulated sugar. Stirring frequently, simmer the mixture gently over low heat until it becomes very thick and stiff and crackles when a sample is dropped into ice water. This will take from 30 minutes to one hour, depending on the amount of moisture in the fruit. Stir in the lemon or orange peel, the cinnamon and the nuts, if using.

Pour the fruit paste out onto a buttered baking sheet, platter or jelly-roll pan, and spread it in a layer ½ inch [1 cm.] thick. Refrigerate the paste until it sets. Use cookie cutters to cut it into fancy shapes, or use a knife to cut it into 1-inch [2½-cm.] squares. Leftover scraps of paste may be rolled between sheets of wax paper, then cut into shapes or squares. Roll the paste in confectioners' sugar, and store the candy between sheets of wax paper in an airtight container.

WILLIAM HARLAN HALE AND THE EDITORS OF HORIZON MAGAZINE
THE HORIZON COOKBOOK

Quince Candy

Bomboms

To make about 3 pounds [1½ kg.]

2 lb.	quinces, peeled, cored and quartered (about 1¼ quarts [1¼ liters])	1 kg.
1¼ cups	water	300 ml.
about 3½ cups	sugar	about 875 ml.
1 tsp.	vanilla or almond extract	5 ml.

Cook the quinces in the water over low heat until they are tender, about 20 to 30 minutes. Purée the pulp through a sieve and measure it.

In a heavy saucepan, mix the pulp with an equal volume of sugar and, stirring constantly, simmer the mixture until it is quite thick and pulls away from the sides of the pan. Stir in the vanilla or almond extract, and pour the mixture into a buttered pan measuring 8 by 12 by 1¼ inches [20 by 30 by 3 cm.]. Put the pan into a preheated 250° F. [120° C.] oven for about 30 minutes to harden the candy. Cut the candy into ½-inch [1-cm.] squares and wrap the squares in wax paper.

E. DONALD ASSELIN
A PORTUGUESE-AMERICAN COOKBOOK

Carrot Sweetmeat

To make about 1 pound [½ kg.]

3½ cups	milk	875 ml.
2	medium-sized carrots, freshly grated	2
1¼ cups	sugar	300 ml.
6 tbsp.	clarified butter	90 ml.
2 tbsp.	seedless white raisins (optional)	30 ml.
1 tsp.	unsweetened dried coconut	5 ml.
2 tbsp.	finely sliced mixed nuts	30 ml.
1 tsp.	ground cardamom or grated nutmeg	5 ml.

Using a large, heavy frying pan, boil the milk and grated carrots together over medium heat. Stirring constantly, keep boiling until the mixture thickens. This should take about 45 minutes. Add the sugar and keep stirring for another 15 minutes, then add the clarified butter. Reduce the heat, and keep cooking and mixing until almost all of the fat has been absorbed; this should take less than 10 minutes. Add the raisins, if used, and mix thoroughly.

Remove the pan from the heat, and pour the candy into a buttered pan 8 inches [20 cm.] square. Spread the candy evenly, and decorate it with a mixture of the unsweetened dried coconut, mixed nuts, and ground cardamom or grated nutmeg. When cool, cut the candy into about 16 squares.

SAVITRI CHOWDHARI
INDIAN COOKING

Indian Carrot Paste

Gajjar Barfi

To make 1 pound [½ kg.]

8 tbsp.	butter	120 ml.
4	whole cardamoms, seeds removed and pulverized	4
1 lb.	carrots, grated	½ kg.
2½ cups	milk	625 ml.
⅔ cup	sugar	150 ml.
22	almonds, blanched, peeled, halved, 11 of them slivered	22
10	pistachios, chopped	10
¼ cup	seedless white raisins	50 ml.

In a heavy pan over low heat, melt the butter, add the pulverized cardamom seeds and stir for two to three minutes. Add the grated carrots, increase the heat to medium and cover the pan. Cook the mixture until the carrots are soft and the moisture has evaporated, about 15 minutes. Add the milk and continue to cook, stirring constantly to prevent it from boiling over or sticking to the pan, until all of the milk has been absorbed. Add the sugar, the slivered almonds and chopped pistachios, and half of the raisins. Continue to cook, stirring and scraping the sides of the pan, until the mixture becomes very stiff and takes on a shiny appearance.

Spread the mixture evenly onto a buttered platter in a layer about ½ inch [1 cm.] thick. Decorate the mixture with the halved almonds and the rest of the raisins. Let the paste cool completely, then cut it into cubes.

KAILASH PURI
RASOI KALA (COOKERY BOOK)

Carrot Balls

Kulki z Marchwi

To make about 3 pounds [1½ kg.]

2 cups	granulated sugar	½ liter
1 cup	water	¼ liter
2 lb.	carrots, finely grated	1 kg.
1	lemon, the peel grated, the juice squeezed and its pulp strained out	1
about 1 cup	superfine sugar	about ¼ liter

In a heavy pan set over medium heat, dissolve the granulated sugar in ½ cup [125 ml.] of the water. Stir in the grated carrots and cook the mixture, without stirring, until the carrots are tender, about 10 to 15 minutes. Add the rest of the water, the lemon juice and peel, and cook the mixture until it thickens. Pour the mixture onto a lightly oiled work surface and let it cool for a few minutes until it can be handled. Dip your hands in cold water and form the candy into little balls. Roll the balls in superfine sugar and put them into individual paper cups.

JAN CZERNIKOWSKI
CIASTA, CIASTKA, CIASTECZKA

Oriental Apricot Balls

Orientalische Aprikosenkugeln

To stuff these apricot balls, make a deep indentation with your finger in each one and fill the cavity with a mixture of chopped pistachios, ground almonds and sugar. Put the stuffed balls in individual paper cups so that they cannot tip over and spill the stuffing.

To make about 1 ¼ pounds [600 g.]

1 lb.	dried apricots	½ kg.
about 1 ⅓ cups	confectioners' sugar, sifted	about 325 ml.
3 oz.	pistachios, blanched and peeled (about ½ cup [125 ml.])	90 g.

Wipe the apricots with a damp cloth; they should not be soaked or washed, lest they become too moist. Chop the apricots fine and put them in a bowl. Add ¾ cup [175 ml.] of confectioners' sugar, taste the mixture, and add more sugar if desired; the exact amount of sugar required will depend on your taste and the sweetness of the apricots. Wet your hands and knead the mixture until it forms a paste. If necessary to prevent sticking, dip your hands in water while working.

Shape the paste into small balls. Roll the balls in confectioners' sugar and let them dry on racks overnight. Garnish each ball with a pistachio.

MARGRET UHLE AND ANNE BRAKEMEIER
KONFEKT ZUM SELBERMACHEN

Korean Date Balls

To make about 1 pound [½ kg.]

36	dates, pitted (about ½ lb. [¼ kg.])	36
3 tbsp.	sugar	45 ml.
1 tsp.	ground cinnamon	5 ml.
¼ cup	finely crushed pine nuts	50 ml.

Put the dates into the top half of a steamer and steam them over boiling water for 20 minutes. Remove them from the steamer, then mash them or purée them through a sieve. Mix the sugar and cinnamon with the date purée, and shape the mixture into about 18 bite-sized balls. Roll the balls in the crushed pine nuts.

WILLIAM HARLAN HALE AND THE EDITORS OF HORIZON MAGAZINE
THE HORIZON COOKBOOK

Sugared Apricots

Inkoo Mish-Mush

To make about 1 ½ pounds [¾ kg.]

1 lb.	dried apricots, ground in a food grinder or finely chopped	½ kg.
½ cup	water	125 ml.
1 cup	sugar	¼ liter
¼ cup	blanched almonds	50 ml.

Put the apricots in a saucepan and add the water. Cover the pan and simmer the apricots until they form a thick paste—about 20 to 30 minutes. Stir in half of the sugar and cook for 10 minutes longer. Take the pan off the heat and let the paste cool. When it is cold, roll the paste into small balls and flatten them into disks about ½ inch [1 cm.] thick. Press a blanched almond in the center of each disk. Dip the disks into the remaining sugar, coating them all over. Cover the disks with wax paper until you are ready to serve them.

HELEN COREY
THE ART OF SYRIAN COOKERY

Dried-Fruit Candy

Ovochevi Konfeti

The technique of melting chocolate is shown on page 65.

To make about 1 pound [½ kg.]

1 cup	dried prunes, pitted	¼ liter
1 cup	pitted dates	¼ liter
1 cup	raisins	¼ liter
¼ lb.	walnuts or blanched and peeled almonds (about 1 cup [¼ liter])	125 g.
1 tbsp.	honey	15 ml.
about ¾ cup	confectioners' sugar or 2 oz. [60 g.] sweet chocolate	about 175 ml.

Put all of the fruits and nuts through a food mill, using a coarse disk. Add the honey and mix thoroughly. Shape the mixture into small balls and roll the balls in the confectioners' sugar.

Alternatively, line a pan 7 inches [18 cm.] square with wax paper. Pack the fruit-and-nut mixture firmly into the pan to a depth of about ¾ inch [2 cm.]. Melt the chocolate over warm water, and cover the mixture with the melted chocolate. Let it harden, then cut the candy into 1-inch [2½-cm.] squares.

SAVELLA STECHISHIN
TRADITIONAL UKRAINIAN COOKERY

Peach Leather

This is a specialty from Charleston, South Carolina. The strips of fruit paste should be left in a warm, dry place to dehydrate for 12 hours or overnight before you roll them up.

To make 3 pounds [1½ kg.]

2 lb.	dried apricots	1 kg.
1 lb.	dried peaches	½ kg.
about 1½ cups	confectioners' sugar	about 375 ml.

Put the dried fruits through a food grinder twice, using the finest disk. Sprinkle a board thick with confectioners' sugar, and put the fruit mixture on it. Pat and roll the mixture until it is ⅛ inch [3 mm.] thick. Cut it into strips 1¼ by 2 inches [3 by 5 cm.]. When the candy has dried, roll each strip into a tight cylinder. Store the leather in an airtight container.

WILMA LORD PERKINS (EDITOR)
THE FANNIE FARMER COOKBOOK

Fruit Paste

The technique of making fruit paste appears on pages 46-47.

To make about 2½ pounds [1¼ kg.]

2 cups	dried prunes, pitted	½ liter
2 cups	dried apricots or peaches	½ liter
2 cups	dates, pitted	½ liter
about 3 tbsp.	honey	about 45 ml.
about 1 cup	coarse sugar, or about 1½ cups [375 ml.] flaked or shredded coconut, or a mixture of both	about ¼ liter

Grind the fruit through the medium or coarse disk of a food grinder. Mix the fruit well with the honey and, if the mixture seems very dry, add a little more honey. Lightly grease your hands with vegetable oil, and roll the mixture on wax paper or aluminum foil to form long, thin rolls. Roll equal-sized sections of the mixture between the palms of your hands to form balls about ¾ to 1 inch [2 to 2½ cm.] in diameter.

Drop these balls into the coarse sugar or coconut, or drop them into the sugar and then roll them in the coconut. Let the balls stand on wax paper, aluminum foil or cake racks overnight to dry before storing them between sheets of wax paper or foil in airtight containers.

JAMES BEARD
JAMES BEARD'S AMERICAN COOKERY

Fruit and Nut Bars

To make about 1½ pounds [¾ kg.]

¼ lb.	dried apricots, coarsely chopped (about ¾ cup [175 ml.])	125 g.
¼ lb.	dried figs, coarsely chopped (about ¾ cup [175 ml.])	125 g.
¼ lb.	pitted dates, coarsely chopped (about ⅔ cup [150 ml.])	125 g.
½ cup	seedless white raisins	125 ml.
¼ cup	muscat raisins	50 ml.
¼ cup	dried currants	50 ml.
½ lb.	mixed nuts, coarsely chopped (about 2 cups [½ liter])	¼ kg.
	edible rice paper	

Put all of the fruits and nuts through a food grinder twice. Then knead the ingredients thoroughly until a compact mass is formed. Roll out the mixture to a thickness of ¾ inch [2 cm.], keeping the shape well squared off. Cover the top with one sheet of edible rice paper and pat it down firmly.

Using two spatulas, turn the mixture upside down onto a clean work surface or a piece of wax paper; cover this side of the fruit mixture with rice paper, too. Let the candy stand for at least three hours. Then cut it into finger-shaped pieces, each about 4 by 1 inch [10 by 2½ cm.], and wrap each finger in cellophane, twisting the ends to keep out the air.

ESMÉ GRAY BOOKER
SWEETS THAT HAVE TEMPTED ME

Fig Bonbons

Bomboms de Figo

To make about 14 ounces [425 g.]

½ lb.	soft dried figs, finely ground in a food grinder or in a processor, operated in short spurts	¼ kg.
⅓ cup	almonds, blanched, peeled and toasted	75 ml.
about ½ cup	sugar	about 125 ml.

Mix the ground figs and the whole almonds. Shape walnut-sized pieces of the mixture into balls. Roll the balls in the sugar to coat them. Let them stand until the sugar is partly absorbed, about 10 to 15 minutes. Roll the balls in the sugar again. Wrap each bonbon in aluminum foil if you wish.

SHIRLEY SARVIS
A TASTE OF PORTUGAL

Fig Balls

Bolas de Figo

To make about 1 ½ pounds [¾ kg.]

½ lb.	dried figs, stems removed	¼ kg.
½ lb.	almonds, blanched, peeled and toasted (about 1 ½ cups [375 ml.])	¼ kg.
3-inch	strip orange peel	8-cm.
2 oz.	semisweet chocolate, broken into pieces	60 g.
1 cup	sugar	¼ liter
7 tbsp.	water	105 ml.
	superfine sugar	

Put the figs, almonds, orange peel and chocolate through the fine disk of a food grinder or food mill. Dissolve the sugar in the water and boil to a thick syrup *(soft-ball stage, pages 8-11)*. Remove the pan from the heat and mix in the ground ingredients. Let the mixture cool, then form it into little balls and roll the balls in superfine sugar.

CAROL WRIGHT
PORTUGUESE FOOD

Orange Balls

Pallottole d'Aranci

To make about 1 pound [½ kg.]

6	large oranges, the peel only, cut into strips	6
1 cup	granulated sugar	¼ liter
1 tsp.	vanilla extract	5 ml.
	superfine sugar	
¼ lb.	mixed nuts, finely chopped (about 1 ½ cups [375 ml.])	125 g.

Soak the orange peel strips in cold water for 24 hours. Drain; place the peel in a saucepan and cover the strips with cold water. Bring the water to a boil. Cook the strips for about 10 minutes, or until they are soft. Drain them.

Chop the orange peel fine and mix it with the granulated sugar in a saucepan. Stir the mixture slowly over low heat until the sugar dissolves, then continue to cook it for about 10 minutes, or until a small quantity dropped into cold water forms a soft ball *(pages 8-11)*. Remove the pan from the heat. Add the vanilla extract and mix thoroughly. Cool the mixture. Shape it into balls the size of small walnuts. Roll the balls in the superfine sugar and then in the chopped nuts.

MARIA LO PINTO AND MILO MILORADOVICH
THE ART OF ITALIAN COOKING

Prune Sausage

Pflaumenwurst

To make about 1 pound [½ kg.]

1 cup	confectioners' sugar	¼ liter
1 ½ cups	dried prunes, pitted and finely chopped	375 ml.
3 ½ oz.	almonds, blanched, peeled and ground (about 1 ½ cups [375 ml.])	100 g.
2 oz.	candied fruit, finely chopped (about ½ cup [125 ml.])	60 g.
1	egg yolk	1
1 tbsp.	rum	15 ml.
1 tbsp.	vanilla sugar	15 ml.

Mix the confectioners' sugar with the prunes, ground almonds, candied fruit, egg yolk, rum and vanilla sugar, and work the mixture into a paste. Sprinkle a work surface with additional confectioners' sugar, and shape the paste into a sausage. Let it dry out for at least three hours before slicing it for serving.

MÁRIA HAJKOVÁ
MÚČNIKY

Tangerine Creams

To make 6 ounces [175 g.]

2	tangerines, the peel grated, the juice squeezed and the pulp strained out	2
1 ⅓ cups	confectioners' sugar	325 ml.
1 tsp.	fresh lemon juice, pulp strained out	5 ml.

Mix the grated peel with the sugar and lemon juice, and add sufficient tangerine juice to make the mixture into a stiff paste. Knead the paste well. Cut it into small pieces and mold it into small balls or nuggets.

THE KING'S COLLEGE HOSPITAL BOOK OF COOKING RECIPES

Old-fashioned Potato Fondant

This candy may be dipped in chocolate. The technique is demonstrated on pages 74-75.

Uncooked potato fondant is an old pioneer recipe, so old no one knows its source. I received this from an elderly lady in Kentucky, who wrote, "It was given to me by my grandmother, who served it in little frilly cups or used it as a base for mint patties at Christmas time."

To make about 1½ pounds [¾ kg.]

1	small potato, boiled, peeled and mashed (about ½ cup [125 ml.])	1
3 cups	confectioners' sugar, sifted	¾ liter
1 cup	unsweetened dried coconut	¼ liter
1 tsp.	vanilla extract	5 ml.

Combine the mashed potato, sugar, coconut and vanilla in a mixing bowl. Cream the mixture with a wooden spoon or an electric mixer as you would for making a cake. Chill the mixture in the refrigerator for several hours. Turn the mixture onto a damp baking sheet and knead it with your hands until it is creamy, then shape it into 1-inch [2½-cm.] balls. Serve the candy in paper cups. It can be stored in an airtight container for approximately two weeks.

ANITA PRICHARD
ANITA PRICHARD'S COMPLETE CANDY COOKBOOK

Pepper Cakes

This recipe is from a book published anonymously in 1747, but known to have been written by the English cookery writer, Hannah Glasse.

To make 10 ounces [300 g.]

⅓ cup	sweet sherry	75 ml.
1 tsp.	white peppercorns, tied in a muslin or cheesecloth bag	5 ml.
about 2½ cups	confectioners' sugar	about 625 ml.

Take the sherry and white peppercorns, and put them in a small pan. Simmer together for a quarter of an hour, or until the liquid is reduced by about half. Remove the pan from the heat, then take the pepper out and put in as much confectioners' sugar as will make the sherry like a paste. Mix well, then drop the mixture in what shape you please on plates covered with parchment paper, and let it dry.

THE ART OF COOKERY, MADE PLAIN AND EASY

Peppermint Cushions

Pepermuntkussentjes

To make 10 ounces [300 g.]

1	egg white, lightly beaten	1
2¼ cups	confectioners' sugar, sifted	550 ml.
	peppermint extract	

Stir the egg white into 2 cups [½ liter] of confectioners' sugar. Add two or three drops of peppermint extract and continue stirring until the mixture forms a stiff paste.

Dust a board with the remaining confectioners' sugar and pour the paste onto it. Roll the paste into two or three cylinders about 1 inch [2½ cm.] thick. Using oiled scissors, cut the cylinders at ½-inch [1-cm.] intervals to form small cushions. Let the cushions harden in a cool place.

H. H. F. HENDERSON
HET NIEUWE KOOKBOEK

Catalan Candy

Bombones Nuria

Nuria is a village in Catalonia, a region in the northeastern part of Spain.

To make about 3 pounds [1½ kg.]

1¾ cups	granulated sugar	425 ml.
14 oz.	almonds, blanched, peeled, toasted and chopped (about 3½ cups [875 ml.])	425 g.
7 oz.	hazelnuts, toasted, peeled and chopped (about 1¾ cups [425 ml.])	200 g.
14 oz.	semisweet chocolate, grated	425 g.
2	egg yolks, lightly beaten	2
⅔ cup	milk	150 ml.
	confectioners' sugar	

In a saucepan, combine the granulated sugar, chopped almonds and hazelnuts, grated chocolate and egg yolks. Mix thoroughly over low heat. Stirring constantly, gradually add the milk. When the mixture forms a thick paste, remove the pan from the heat and let the mixture cool. When the mixture is cold, form it into small balls. Roll the balls in the confectioners' sugar.

ANA MARIA CALERA
COCINA CATALANA

Raspberry Bars

Other kinds of jam, such as apricot or strawberry, may be used to make this candy. Honey nougat is made in the same way as raspberry nougat, using 3 tablespoons [45 ml.] of honey and a little yellow food coloring in place of raspberry jam and pink food coloring. Melt the honey in a small pan before adding it to the cooled mixture:

To make about 1 ¼ pounds [600 g.]

1¾ cups	sugar	425 ml.
⅔ cup	water	150 ml.
⅓ cup	liquid glucose or light corn syrup	75 ml.
3 tbsp.	raspberry jam, strained through a fine-meshed sieve	45 ml.
	pink food coloring	
3 oz.	almonds, blanched, peeled and roughly chopped (about ¾ cup [175 ml.])	90 g.
	edible rice paper	

Dissolve the sugar in the water. Add the glucose or corn syrup, and boil the mixture until its temperature reaches 244° F. [118° C.] *(firm-ball stage, pages 8-11).*

Remove the pan from the heat. Rinse out a bowl with cold water and pour the syrup into it. Let the syrup cool slightly. Add the jam and the food coloring. Stir the mixture until it is creamy, then knead it until it is a soft paste, working in the almonds as you knead. If the mixture becomes stiff, work in a few drops of tepid water.

Spread the paste in a pan measuring 4 by 6 inches [10 by 15 cm.] that has been lined with edible rice paper. Flatten the surface with your fingers. Dampen the surface of the paste with cold water, and cover it with another sheet of rice paper. Place a piece of stiff cardboard or a thin piece of wood on the top and a 1-to-2-pound [½-to-1-kg.] weight or can on top of that. Let the candy rest overnight. Then unmold it, cut it into bars and wrap the pieces in wax paper.

D. F. HUTTON AND E. M. BODE
SIMPLE SWEETMAKING

Chestnut Balls

Boules aux Marrons

To make the chestnut purée, cut a large cross in the shell on the flat side of each nut. Drop the chestnuts into boiling water, and boil them for two to three minutes. Remove the pan from the heat. Lift the chestnuts out of the water a few at a time, and shell and peel them. Put the shelled chestnuts into a pan and pour in enough milk to barely cover them. Bring the milk to a boil. Simmer the mixture, covered, until the milk has been

absorbed—about 45 minutes. Purée the chestnuts in a food mill or press them through a sieve.

To make about ¾ pound [350 g.]

3½ oz.	semisweet chocolate	100 g.
2 tbsp.	heavy cream	30 ml.
2 tbsp.	butter	30 ml.
½ cup	confectioners' sugar	125 ml.
	vanilla extract	
5 oz.	chestnut purée	150 g.
2 oz.	chocolate sprinkles (about ½ cup [125 ml.])	60 g.

Melt the chocolate with the cream and butter. When the mixture has melted, stir it to obtain a smooth paste.

Remove the pan from the hot water, and stir in the confectioners' sugar, a few drops of vanilla extract and the chestnut purée. Refrigerate the mixture for 24 hours.

Shape the mixture into small balls and roll them in the chocolate sprinkles. Serve the candy very cold in individual paper cups. They will keep for one day.

JACQUELINE GÉRARD
BONNES RECETTES D'AUTREFOIS

Iced Chestnut Balls

Kastanienkugeln

The technique of peeling chestnuts is described on page 56. To purée the peeled chestnuts, first put them in a pan and cover them with milk. Bring the milk to a boil, cover the pan, and simmer the chestnuts until the milk has been absorbed, about 45 minutes. Purée the chestnuts through a sieve or food mill.

To make the chocolate icing, sift 2 cups [½ liter] of confectioners' sugar and 2 tablespoons [30 ml.] of cocoa powder into a bowl. Add 1 to 2 tablespoons [15 to 30 ml.] of warm water to make an icing thick enough to coat the back of a metal spoon.

To make about 1½ pounds [¾ kg.]

1¼ cups	granulated sugar	300 ml.
2 to 3 tbsp.	water	30 to 45 ml.
1¼ lb.	chestnuts, peeled and puréed (about 3 cups [¾ liter])	600 g.
1 cup	confectioners' sugar	¼ liter
	chocolate icing	

In a pan over medium heat, dissolve the granulated sugar in the water, and boil the syrup to the thread stage *(pages 8-11)*. Stir in the peeled and puréed chestnuts. Let the mixture cool until you can handle it, then form it into small balls. Roll the balls in confectioners' sugar and let them dry overnight. The next day, dip them in chocolate icing.

ELEK MAGYAR
DAS KOCHBUCH FÜR FEINSCHMECKER

Chocolate Peanut-Raisin Clusters

To make ¾ pound [350 g.]

½ lb.	semisweet chocolate, cut into pieces	¼ kg.
½ cup	raw Spanish peanuts, shelled and peeled	125 ml.
½ cup	seedless raisins	125 ml.

Melt the chocolate; cool slightly. Add the peanuts and raisins, and mix well. Drop the mixture by spoonfuls onto baking sheets covered with wax paper. Chill until set.

DOROTHY C. FRANK
THE PEANUT COOKBOOK

Cinnamon Fingers

Paluszki Cynamonowe

To make about 1 pound [½ kg.]

5 oz.	walnuts, ground (about 1¾ cups [425 ml.])	150 g.
⅔ cup	superfine sugar	150 ml.
1 tsp.	ground cinnamon	5 ml.
½ tsp.	ground cloves	2 ml.
1	egg, beaten	1
	confectioners' sugar	
	Rum and lemon icing	
1 cup	confectioners' sugar	¼ liter
1 tbsp.	rum	15 ml.
1½ tbsp.	fresh lemon juice, pulp strained out	22 ml.

Mix the walnuts, superfine sugar, cinnamon and cloves together. Bind the mixture with the egg and, on a board sprinkled with confectioners' sugar, knead the mixture until it is smooth. Dust a rolling pin with confectioners' sugar, and roll out the candy into a rectangle about ½ inch [1 cm.] thick. Slice the candy into strips the width and length of a finger.

Lay the cinnamon fingers on a baking sheet covered with parchment paper, and bake them in a preheated 250° F. [120° C.] oven for 10 minutes, or until they are dried out.

Meanwhile, mix the confectioners' sugar, rum and lemon juice together in a bowl. Remove the cinnamon fingers from the oven and ice them with the mixture.

MARJA DISSLOWA
JAK GOTOWAĆ

Polish Walnut Roll

Rolada Orzechowa

To make about 1¾ pounds [875 g.]

1 lb.	walnuts, ground (about 6 cups [1½ liters])	½ kg.
7 oz.	semisweet chocolate, grated	200 g.
2 tbsp.	honey	30 ml.
¼ lb.	almonds, blanched, peeled and chopped (about 1 cup [¼ liter])	125 g.
1	lemon, the peel grated, the juice squeezed and its pulp strained out	1
about 1 cup	confectioners' sugar	about ¼ liter

Stirring continuously, cook the walnuts, chocolate and honey until they form a smooth, thick paste. Stir in the chopped almonds, lemon peel and lemon juice.

Pour the mixture onto an oiled marble slab or wooden board, and let it cool until you can handle it. Form the mixture into a cylindrical roll about 1 inch [2½ cm.] thick. Coat the roll with confectioners' sugar, wrap it in wax paper and chill it. When the roll has set, slice it diagonally into ovals about ½ inch [1 cm.] thick.

JAN CZERNIKOWSKI
CIASTA, CIASTKA, CIASTECZKA

Coconut Tablets

Tablettes Coco

The techniques of grating coconut and making coconut milk are demonstrated on page 13.

To make about 10 ounces [300 g.]

2⅔ cups	freshly grated coconut	650 ml.
⅔ cup	superfine sugar	150 ml.
1 tsp.	ground cinnamon	5 ml.
2 tsp.	grated lime peel	10 ml.
	vanilla extract	
	almond extract	
3 to 4 tbsp.	coconut milk	45 to 60 ml.

In a heavy saucepan, mix the grated coconut, sugar, cinnamon, lime peel, and a few drops each of the vanilla and almond extracts. Stir in the coconut milk. Stirring constantly with a wooden spoon, cook the mixture over low heat until it has the color and consistency of caramel *(pages 8-11)*. Remove the pan from the heat. Pour the mixture out in small pools onto an oiled marble slab or oiled parchment paper.

CHRISTIANE ROY-CAMILLE AND ANNICK MARIE
LES MEILLEURES RECETTES DE LA CUISINE ANTILLAISE

Indian Coconut Paste

Coconut Barfi

The techniques of opening a coconut and grating the flesh are demonstrated on page 13.

To make about ¾ pound [350 g.]

2½ cups	half-and-half cream	625 ml.
1½ cups	freshly grated coconut	375 ml.
⅓ cup	superfine sugar	75 ml.
	pink food coloring	
	vanilla extract	
4	whole cardamoms, seeds removed and pulverized	4

Heat the cream to a boil. Reduce the heat and simmer the cream for 10 to 12 minutes, stirring occasionally to prevent it from boiling over. Add the coconut, and stir and scrape the sides of the pan. Add the sugar, and continue to stir and scrape until the mixture comes away from the sides of the pan and forms a mass. Remove the pan from the heat.

Add the food coloring, three or four drops of vanilla extract and the pulverized cardamom seeds. Spread the candy evenly in a buttered pan 8 inches [20 cm.] square. Smooth the surface with a knife and let the candy cool. When the candy is cold and set, cut it into cubes and store the cubes in an airtight container.

KAILASH PURI
RASOI KALA (COOKERY BOOK)

Coconut Conserves

Raskara

The technique of opening and grating a coconut is demonstrated on page 13. Molasses or dark brown sugar can be substituted for the granulated sugar.

To make about 3 pounds [1½ kg.]

about 2 cups	sugar	about ½ liter
four 1 lb.	coconuts, opened and drained, flesh removed, peeled and grated (about 10 cups [2½ liters])	four ½ kg.
4	whole cardamoms, seeds removed and separated	4

Mix the sugar with the coconut. Cook the mass over gentle heat, stirring constantly, until the mixture forms a soft paste—about 30 minutes. Sprinkle the cardamom seeds into the mixture. Spoon the paste out onto an oiled marble slab or flat dish. When the paste is cool enough to handle, mold it into balls with your hands.

MRS. J. HALDAR
BENGAL SWEETS

Coconut and Almond Candy

To make about 2 pounds [1 kg.]

2 cups	sugar	½ liter
1 cup	hot milk	¼ liter
¼ lb.	almonds, blanched, peeled and chopped (about 1 cup [¼ liter])	125 g.
4 cups	freshly grated coconut	1 liter
6	egg yolks, lightly beaten	6

Mix the sugar into the hot milk and stir over low heat until the sugar dissolves. Bring the syrup to a boil, then add the almonds and stir constantly until the mixture thickens and reaches the thread stage *(pages 8-11)*. Reduce the heat to low, add the coconut and then gradually stir in the egg yolks.

Stir the mixture constantly over low heat until it begins to thicken into a cream, about five to 10 minutes. Remove the pan from the heat and leave it until the cream is cool enough to handle. Then shape the mixture into small balls. Put the balls on wax paper to dry and harden overnight.

CORA, ROSE AND BOB BROWN
THE SOUTH AMERICAN COOK BOOK

Persian Marzipan

Toot

The Iranian cook will enhance the aroma of her almonds by immersing them in narcissus blossoms for several days. If desired, you may place your almonds in an airtight container with one vanilla bean. This candy will not keep for very long because it tends to dry out quickly.

To make about ¾ pound [350 g.]

7 oz.	almonds, blanched, peeled and ground (about 2 cups [½ liter])	200 g.
½ cup	confectioners' sugar	125 ml.
¼ cup	rose water or 2 tsp. [10 ml.] vanilla extract	50 ml.
1 cup	superfine sugar	¼ liter
about 1½ oz.	pistachios, blanched, peeled and slivered (about ½ cup [125 ml.])	about 45 g.

Mix the ground almonds and confectioners' sugar. Add the rose water or vanilla extract, and stir until the mixture forms a stiff, smooth paste. Shape the paste into small balls, then roll each ball between the palms of your hands to lengthen it somewhat into the shape of a white mulberry (*"toot"* in Farsi), which this candy is supposed to resemble. Roll each piece in the superfine sugar, and stick a slivered pistachio in one end to represent the stem. Store the candy in an airtight container.

NESTA RAMAZANI
PERSIAN COOKING

To Make Pine-Nut Candy

Pour Faire le Pignolat en Roche

Michel de Nostredame, or Nostradamus, as he is better known, was a physician who lived in Provence in the early 16th Century. He is famous for his book of prophecies, couched in rather obscure language, many of which appear to have come true. This recipe is from his book of beauty preparations and confections, published in 1552.

An electuary, a term used in this recipe to describe the consistency of boiled sugar, is a thick, medicinal syrup. The sugar-boiling equivalent is the hard-crack stage, 310° F. [154° C.] on a candy thermometer (pages 8-11). Nostradamus suggests decorating this candy with edible gold leaf. He also says that almonds can be candied in the same way.

To make about 3 pounds [1½ kg.]

2½ lb.	pine nuts (about 5 cups [1¼ liters])	1¼ kg.
2 cups	sugar	½ liter
2 to 3 tbsp.	rose water	30 to 45 ml.
1	egg white, lightly beaten	1

Roast the pine nuts in a preheated 250° F. [120° C.] oven for about 15 minutes, or until they are lightly colored.

In a saucepan, dissolve the sugar in the rose water, and bring the mixture to a boil. Cook the syrup until it is as thick as an electuary. In the winter or in wet weather, you will have to boil the syrup for a little longer; in summer, you will find the syrup is ready as soon as it boils without foaming and making a noise. Noise is a sign that there is still some moisture left in the syrup.

Remove the syrup from the heat, dip the pan briefly in cold water to stop the cooking, then rest the base of the pan on a barrel top or other surface that will hold it well.

Use a wooden spoon or spatula to beat the mixture briskly until it turns white. When the mixture begins to cool, add the egg white. Beat the mixture again and set it over low heat. Cook it for two to three minutes, until the moisture from the egg white has evaporated and the mixture is as thick as it was before the white was added.

Add the pine nuts to the thick syrup. Mix them in well. While keeping the pan on low heat so that the mixture does not cool, use a narrow-bladed spatula to remove walnut-sized portions of the mixture. Set these pieces well apart on parchment paper and let them cool.

MICHEL DE NOSTREDAME
EXCELLENT ET MOULT UTILE OPUSCULE

Little Praline Balls

Petits Pains au Pralin

To make about 4 pounds [2 kg.]

2½ lb.	almonds, blanched, peeled, and dried for about 5 minutes in a cool oven (about 7 cups [1¾ liters])	1¼ kg.
6	egg whites, 3 lightly beaten	6
1 cup	superfine sugar	¼ liter
¼ cup	sifted flour	50 ml.
1¼ cups	praline powder (recipe, page 167)	300 ml.
1 tbsp.	vanilla sugar	15 ml.
2 cups	confectioners' sugar	½ liter

Pound the almonds in a large mortar, gradually adding the three unbeaten egg whites. Add the superfine sugar, the flour and the praline powder. Mix well and add the vanilla sugar. Gather the paste into a ball and put it on a marble slab lightly coated with confectioners' sugar.

Roll the paste into a cylinder and cut off pieces about the size of walnuts. Roll the pieces into balls. Dip each ball into the beaten egg whites and roll it in the confectioners' sugar. Place the balls on buttered-and-floured baking sheets, arranging them 1½ inches [4 cm.] apart. Bake in a preheated 250° F. [120° C.] oven for about 15 minutes, or until cracks begin to appear in the balls. Remove them from the oven, let them cool and place them in individual paper cups.

MME. JEANNE SAVARIN (EDITOR)
LA CUISINE DES FAMILLES

Pistachio Marzipan

Les Massepains Ordinaires de Pistaches

The techniques for peeling and grinding nuts are demonstrated on pages 12-13.

To make about 1¾ pounds [875 g.]

1½ cups	granulated sugar	375 ml.
2 to 3 tbsp.	water	30 to 45 ml.
1 lb.	pistachios, blanched, peeled and finely ground (about 6 cups [1½ liters])	½ kg.
Orange royal icing		
1	egg white	1
2¼ cups	confectioners' sugar	550 ml.
	orange-flower water	

Dissolve the granulated sugar in the water and cook this syrup to the soft-ball stage *(pages 8-11)*; stir in the pistachios. Without stirring, cook this paste over low heat for three to four minutes, until it begins to look dry. Sprinkle a work surface with confectioners' sugar. Pour the paste onto the work surface and spread it out to cool.

When this marzipan paste is cold, roll it out to a thickness of about ½ inch [1 cm.]. Cut it into decorative shapes with sharp-edged cookie cutters.

Lay the marzipan shapes on baking sheets covered with parchment paper. Bake them in a preheated 250° F. [120° C.] oven for about 20 minutes, or until the tops of the shapes are dry to the touch. Remove them from the oven and let them cool on the sheets. Turn them over.

Prepare the royal icing by beating the egg white with the confectioners' sugar and a few drops of orange-flower water. The mixture should be stiff but should spread easily. Use this icing to coat the soft top and sides of the marzipan shapes. Return the shapes to the oven at the same temperature to dry out for about 10 minutes.

PIERRE JOSEPH BUC'HOZ
L'ART DE PRÉPARER LES ALIMENTS

Almond Sticks

To make about 2 pounds [1 kg.]

1¼ cup	almond paste (recipe, page 166)	300 ml.
3½ cups	confectioners' sugar	875 ml.
2 tsp.	fresh lime juice, pulp strained out	10 ml.
4	egg whites, lightly beaten	4
½ lb.	almonds, toasted and coarsely chopped (about 2 cups [½ liter])	¼ kg.

Mix the almond paste with the confectioners' sugar and lime juice. Add enough of the beaten egg whites to turn the mixture into a smooth, stiff paste. Roll out the paste about ½ inch [1 cm.] thick, and cut it into sticks. Roll the sticks in the chopped almonds. Arrange the sticks on wire racks set on baking sheets, and place the sticks in a preheated 250° F. [130° C.] oven with the door ajar. Let the sticks dry for one to one and one half hours.

MARY LAND
NEW ORLEANS CUISINE

Sunflower Balls

Although this basic recipe has just two ingredients and is easy and quick to make up, you must be prepared to get a bit of honey on your hands.

Don't hesitate to double this recipe.

To make about ¼ pound [125 g.]

1 cup	sunflower seeds	¼ liter
2 tbsp.	honey	30 ml.

Grind the seeds down to a fine flour in a blender or rotary grater, and empty the seed flour into a bowl. Drip the honey

over the ground seeds, and use a fork to work the two together until you have a cohesive mass. If your seeds won't cohere, work in a bit more honey. When very well mixed, spoon out teaspoonfuls of the mixture and shape them into balls between the palms of your hands. With this little honey, the outsides of the balls should not be really sticky, and they may be placed directly onto a dish for serving.

STAN AND FLOSS DWORKIN
NATURAL SNACKS 'N' SWEETS

Lübeck Marzipan

Lübecker Marzipan

Make sure you do not cook the marzipan for too long: It must be removed from the heat as soon as it loses its stickiness or it will release all of its oil and will no longer be a smooth paste. The technique of making candied orange peel is demonstrated on page 53.

To make 2 pounds [1 kg.]

1 lb.	almonds, blanched, peeled and finely ground (about 6 cups [1½ liters])	½ kg.
2 to 3 tbsp.	orange-flower water	30 to 45 ml.
5 cups	confectioners' sugar, sifted	1¼ liters
	candied flower petals (recipe, page 167)	
	candied orange peel	

In a small saucepan set over low heat, stir the almonds with the orange-flower water and 4 cups [1 liter] of the confectioners' sugar until the mixture no longer sticks to your fingers when you touch it—after about five to eight minutes. Do not let the mixture get any drier than that.

Turn the mixture out onto a board sprinkled with the rest of the confectioners' sugar and roll it out, sprinkling more confectioners' sugar—both over and underneath the marzipan—as you work. The marzipan can either be formed into a large cake or cut into small shapes with a biscuit cutter.

Set the marzipan on a baking sheet dusted with confectioners' sugar. Then put the marzipan in a preheated 250° F. [120° C.] oven for about 15 minutes to dry. It must not become hard or brown, but should remain soft and snow-white. Decorate the marzipan with candied flower petals and candied peel that has been cut into leaf shapes.

HENRIETTE DAVIDIS
PRAKTISCHES KOCHBUCH

Boiled Marzipan

Boiled marzipan is smoother and more plastic than the unboiled variety. If more than one flavoring is used, these should be added, with the appropriate coloring, to separate portions of the marzipan during the kneading stage. Food coloring and flavoring for marzipan are discussed on pages 14-15. The techniques of making marzipan are shown on pages 58-59. If the marzipan becomes hard and inclined to crack after storage, add two or three drops of tepid water and knead the mixture thoroughly until it becomes pliable again.

To make about 2 pounds [1 kg.]		
2 cups	granulated sugar	½ liter
¾ cup	water	175 ml.
12 oz.	almonds, blanched, peeled and ground (about 3 cups [¾ liter])	350 g.
2	egg whites, lightly beaten	2
1 tsp.	orange-flower water (optional)	5 ml.
	confectioners' sugar	
	food coloring and flavoring	

In a pan, gently heat the granulated sugar and water together, stirring constantly, until all of the sugar has dissolved. Stop stirring as soon as the liquid comes to a boil. Increase the heat, and boil the syrup until it reaches a temperature of 240° F. [116° C.]—the soft-ball stage *(pages 8-11)*.

Remove the pan from the heat, and stir the syrup lightly until you observe a faint cloudiness. This means the syrup has begun to grain. Stir in the ground almonds. Add the lightly beaten egg whites and return the pan to low heat. Cook very gently for a minute or two until the marzipan mixture firms up slightly. Add the orange-flower water, if using, and mix well.

Dust a work surface with confectioners' sugar and pour the marzipan onto it. Let the marzipan cool until it can be handled easily. Then knead it until it is smooth and pliable; if the mixture is too moist, work in 2 to 4 tablespoons [30 to 60 ml.] of confectioners' sugar. Divide the marzipan into portions, as required, and flavor and color each portion while it is still warm.

To store the marzipan, wrap each colored piece separately in wax paper or plastic wrap. Place the wrapped marzipan in a plastic bag in an airtight container or in the refrigerator. It should keep for about one month.

HELEN JEROME
SWEET-MAKING FOR ALL

Iced Marzipan

Massepain Glacé

This recipe first appeared in an anonymous book published in 1732. The almonds can be ground in a food processor; in this case, add the egg whites after the almonds are combined with the syrup. The technique of making iced marzipan is shown on pages 62-63. Food coloring and flavoring for marzipan are discussed on page 58. If you prefer a snow-white marzipan and icing, reduce the oven heat to 250° F. [120° C.] and increase the baking time to about 15 minutes, both before and after icing the marzipan.

To make about 6 pounds [3 kg.]		
3 lb.	almonds, blanched and peeled	1½ kg.
4 to 5	egg whites	4 to 5
3 cups	granulated sugar	¾ liter
⅔ cup	water	150 ml.
	confectioners' sugar	
Glacé icing		
5 tbsp.	water	75 ml.
	orange-flower water (optional)	
5 cups	confectioners' sugar	1¼ liters

Pound the almonds to a paste in a mortar, adding some of the egg white from time to time to prevent the nuts from becoming too oily.

Dissolve the granulated sugar in the water over medium heat, and cook the syrup to the soft-ball stage *(pages 8-11)*. Remove the pan from the heat. Add your almonds and blend all of the ingredients with a spatula, carefully scraping the sides of the pan to prevent sticking. You will know that your paste is ready if none sticks to the back of your hand when you touch the marzipan.

Sprinkle a board with confectioners' sugar. Take the paste out of the pan and put it on the board. Sprinkle the marzipan with more confectioners' sugar and let it cool. Roll out the marzipan to a thickness of about ¼ inch [6 mm.], and cut your shapes out of it with cookie cutters. Lay the shapes out on parchment paper, and press them down slightly with the tip of your finger. Bake them in a preheated 400° F. [200° C.] oven for five minutes, or until they are dry.

To make the icing, mix the water and a few drops of orange-flower water or other flavoring with the confectioners' sugar, stirring the mixture until it is thick.

Remove the pieces of marzipan from the oven, gently lift them off the paper, and turn them over. Use a narrow-bladed spatula to spread a little icing on the unbaked side of the pieces. Return the pieces iced side up to the paper, and put them back in the preheated 400° F. oven for five to 10 minutes, or until the icing is dry and lightly browned at the edges. Store the marzipan in an airtight tin.

PROSPER MONTAGNÉ
NEW LAROUSSE GASTRONOMIQUE

Königsberg Marzipan

Königsberger Marzipan

Königsberg marzipan is a German marzipan molded into tiny cup-shapes and filled with fondant (pages 32-33) or, as in this case, candied fruits and candy jellies (pages 48-51). The original version of this recipe called for bitter almonds. To give sweet almonds a slightly bitter flavor, mix them with a few drops of almond extract.

To make about 3 pounds [1 ½ kg.]

¾ cup	granulated sugar	175 ml.
1 lb.	almonds, blanched, peeled and very finely ground (about 6 cups [1 ½ liters])	½ kg.
½ cup	water	125 ml.
3½ cups	confectioners' sugar	875 ml.
1 tsp.	rose water	5 ml.
1 cup	candied fruits or candy jellies, cut into decorative shapes	¼ liter

Put the granulated sugar, almonds and water into a saucepan set over medium heat, and stir with a wooden spoon for five to eight minutes, until the paste is smooth and comes away cleanly from the sides of the pan and a kitchen towel pressed against the paste does not stick to it. Let the paste cool, then put it in a can with a tight-fitting lid and leave it until the following day.

Transfer the paste to a large bowl, and gradually work in about 3 cups [¾ liter] of the confectioners' sugar and the rose water until the mixture is smooth. The marzipan is now ready for use.

Shape the marzipan into disks about 1 inch [2½ cm.] thick and 1 inch in diameter, and make a deep depression in the middle of each disk with your thumb. Arrange the marzipan shapes on a baking sheet covered with parchment paper.

In a separate bowl, mix the rest of the confectioners' sugar with enough tepid water to make a thick syrup. Brush this syrup on the tops and sides of the marzipan disks.

Bake the marzipan on the top shelf of a preheated 400° F. [200° C.] oven for four to five minutes. Remove the marzipan from the oven and let it cool. When the marzipan shapes are cold, fill the depressions in them with the candied fruits or candy jellies.

FRITZ BECKER
DAS KOCHBUCH AUS MECKLENBURG, POMMERN UND OSTPREUSSEN

Marzipan Candy

Massepains

Menon, whose first name is unknown, was a chef at the court of Louis XV. He wrote several cookbooks; the one in which this recipe appears, La Cuisinière Bourgeoise, was published in 1746 and was the most popular French cookbook for more than a hundred years.

The almonds can be ground in a food processor, in which case they should be transferred to a bowl before being mixed with the egg whites. If candied orange-blossom petals are not available, substitute 1 teaspoon [5 ml.] of orange-flower water. The technique of making a cooked fruit paste is shown on pages 46-47.

To make about 3 pounds [1 ½ kg.]

1 lb.	almonds, blanched (about 3 cups [¾ liter])	½ kg.
3	egg whites	3
about ½ cup	thick apricot jam, sieved, or cooked fruit paste, cooled	about 125 ml.
1 tbsp.	candied orange-blossom petals, pounded	15 ml.
about 3½ cups	confectioners' sugar (1 lb. [½ kg.])	about 875 ml.
Lime icing		
1	lime, seeded and finely chopped, including the peel	1
6	egg whites, lightly beaten	6
about 2⅔ cups	confectioners' sugar, sieved	about 650 ml.

Pound the almonds to a paste in a mortar, adding the egg whites a little at a time during the pounding. Mix in the apricot jam or the fruit paste and the orange-blossom petals. Put the almond mixture into a saucepan, add 2 cups [½ liter] of the confectioners' sugar and, stirring constantly, cook over low heat until the paste is stiff.

Pour the paste onto a marble slab and knead it until smooth, adding confectioners' sugar to stop it from sticking to your fingers. Then roll out this marzipan and form it into the shapes you desire.

To make the icing, add the lime to the lightly beaten egg whites. Dip the marzipan shapes into the mixture, then roll them in confectioners' sugar until they are well coated. Arrange the shapes on baking sheets covered with parchment paper. Bake them in a preheated 250° F. [120° C.] oven for about 20 minutes, or until the icing is dry but not browned.

MENON
LA CUISINIÈRE BOURGEOISE

White Sugar Candy

Lowzina b'Shakar

This delectable candy is usually made for weddings; decorated with edible gold leaf, it is sent to relatives and friends by the bride's family.

To make about 12 ounces [350 g.]

1 cup	sugar	¼ liter
½ cup	water	125 ml.
½ tsp.	fresh lemon juice, pulp strained out	2 ml.
1 tsp.	rose water	5 ml.
5 oz.	almonds, blanched, peeled and ground (about 1 cup [¼ liter])	150 g.
2 or 3	cardamom seeds	2 or 3
⅛ tsp.	ground cardamom	½ ml.

Combine the sugar and the water, and cook them over medium heat for seven or eight minutes, or until the syrup spins a long thread when dropped from a spoon *(thread stage, pages 8-11)*. Add the lemon juice and cook for one or two minutes. Add the rose water and let the syrup return to a boil. Remove the pan from the heat and stir with a wooden spoon until the syrup is almost cold. Add ⅔ cup [150 ml.] of the almonds and the whole cardamom seeds. Stir until the candy mixture turns white.

Mix the ground cardamom with the rest of the ground almonds, and sprinkle about half of this mixture in a thin layer on a baking sheet. Spread the candy over this layer. Gradually sprinkle the rest of the ground cardamom mixture over the candy while flattening it evenly until it forms a layer about ½ inch [1 cm.] thick. Let the candy cool and set for about five minutes, then cut it diagonally at 1-inch [2½-cm.] intervals to form diamond shapes. Place the diamonds in a tin box, arranging them in layers separated by wax paper. Cover tightly and refrigerate the candy to preserve its softness and flavor.

DAISY INY
THE BEST OF BAGHDAD COOKING

Spanish Royal Marzipan

Pasta Real

As an alternative to shaping the paste with your fingers, you can roll it out and cut it into shapes with cookie cutters. The technique of coating marzipan with sugar syrup is demonstrated on pages 62-63.

To make 1½ pounds [¾ kg.]

¾ cup	superfine sugar	175 ml.
⅔ cup	water	150 ml.
14 oz.	almonds, blanched, peeled and finely ground (about 5 cups [1¼ liters])	425 g.
10	egg yolks, lightly beaten	10
	confectioners' sugar	

Over medium heat, dissolve the superfine sugar with the water, and bring the syrup to a boil. Add the ground almonds, stirring with a wooden spoon. Cook the mixture, stirring constantly, for approximately five minutes. Remove the pan from the heat.

When the mixture has cooled to lukewarm, gradually stir in the egg yolks. Return the pan to the heat. Stirring constantly, cook the mixture until it comes away from the sides of the pan, about five to 10 minutes.

Pour the paste out onto a wooden surface and let it cool. When it is cold, dust your fingers with confectioners' sugar, and mold the paste into decorative shapes such as stars, hearts or loaves. Let the marzipan shapes dry for at least 12 hours or overnight. On the next day, coat the dried shapes with sugar syrup to give them their customary luster.

LUIS RIPOLL
NUESTRA COCINA

Czech Chocolate Truffles

Schokoladentrüffel

These truffles cannot be stored and should be eaten on the day they are made.

To make about ¾ pound [350 g.]

4 tbsp.	butter	60 ml.
2	egg yolks	2
1½ tbsp.	confectioners' sugar	22 ml.
⅔ cup	cocoa powder	150 ml.
7 oz.	semisweet chocolate, grated	200 g.

Beat the butter with the egg yolks and sugar until the mixture is light and creamy. Add the cocoa powder and 6 ounces [175 g.] of the grated chocolate. Knead the mixture well, form it into small balls, and roll the balls in the reserved grated chocolate.

JOZA BŘÍZOVÁ AND MARYNA KLIMENTOVÁ
TSCHECHISCHE KÜCHE

Chambéry Truffles

Truffes de Chambéry

To make about ½ pound [¼ kg.]

4 oz.	semisweet chocolate	125 g.
2 tbsp.	butter	30 ml.
1 ½ tbsp.	confectioners' sugar	22 ml.
2	egg yolks	2
2 tsp.	rum	10 ml.
	cocoa powder	

Melt the chocolate in a pan over boiling water. Cream together the butter and confectioners' sugar, and add them to the chocolate. Stir until the sugar has dissolved. Remove the pan from the boiling water and add the egg yolks one at a time, stirring constantly. Add the rum and mix thoroughly. Put the mixture in a cool place—not the refrigerator—for 12 hours. Then shape the mixture into small balls and roll these in the cocoa powder. Allow the truffles to harden for at least two hours.

ALICE B. TOKLAS
THE ALICE B. TOKLAS COOK BOOK

Bitter-Chocolate Truffles

To make brandy or rum truffles, the author suggests omitting the vanilla extract, using 2 tablespoons [30 ml.] less cream and adding 2 tablespoons of brandy or rum.

To make about 1 ½ pounds [¾ kg.]

8 tbsp.	butter, softened	120 ml.
1	egg, well beaten	1
3 oz.	unsweetened chocolate	90 g.
1 tbsp.	black coffee	15 ml.
about 3½ cups	confectioners' sugar, sifted (1 lb. [½ kg.])	about 875 ml.
½ cup	heavy cream	125 ml.
1 tbsp.	vanilla extract	15 ml.
4 oz.	chocolate sprinkles or grated semisweet chocolate	125 g.

Mix the butter and the egg. In the top of a double boiler over hot water, melt the unsweetened chocolate with the coffee.

Put 2 cups [½ liter] of the confectioners' sugar into a bowl. Add the butter-and-egg mixture, the melted chocolate, the heavy cream and the vanilla. Stir well. If necessary, add more confectioners' sugar to turn the mixture into a paste stiff enough to handle. Form the paste into balls, about ½ inch [1 cm.] in diameter. To ensure that they are of equal size, use the teaspoon from a set of measuring spoons to measure out the quantity of truffle paste for each ball.

While the truffles are still soft, roll them in the chocolate sprinkles or grated semisweet chocolate. Put them in the refrigerator until they are firm, about two hours.

MARION FLEXNER
OUT OF KENTUCKY KITCHENS

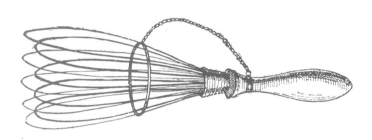

Easter Truffles

Paastruffels

This nest-shaped candy is prepared as a special Easter treat in the Netherlands.

To make about ½ pound [¼ kg.]

¼ cup	cocoa powder	50 ml.
⅔ cup	confectioners' sugar, sifted	150 ml.
4 tbsp.	butter, softened	60 ml.
1 oz.	chocolate sprinkles (about ¼ cup [50 ml.])	30 g.
1 oz.	pink and white sprinkles (about ¼ cup [50 ml.])	30 g.

Beat the cocoa powder, confectioners' sugar and butter together. Refrigerate the mixture for a few hours to stiffen it. Shape the mixture into about 20 small balls. Slightly flatten the balls and, with the handle of a wooden spoon, make a small indentation in each ball to give it the shape of a bird's nest. Roll each nest in the chocolate sprinkles, and sprinkle the indentation in the middle of the nest with the pink and white sprinkles.

H. H. F. HENDERSON
HET NIEUWE KOOKBOEK

Chocolate Rum Balls

Bolitas de Ron

To make about 1 ½ pounds [¾ kg.]

1 cup	heavy cream	¼ liter
18 oz.	semisweet chocolate, 1 lb. [½ kg.] broken into pieces and the rest finely grated	560 g.
⅔ cup	rum	150 ml.
½ lb.	walnuts, chopped (about 1 cup [¼ liter])	¼ kg.

Put the cream in a saucepan, and bring it to a boil over medium heat. Add the 1 pound [½ kg.] of chocolate pieces. Stir the mixture constantly with a wooden spoon until it is smooth and thick. Remove the pan from the heat and let the mixture cool. When it is cold, stir in the rum and chopped nuts. When the mixture becomes firm enough to handle, roll it into balls about the size of walnuts. Roll the balls in the grated chocolate.

MARIA DEL CARMEN CASCANTE
150 RECETAS DE DULCES DE FÁCIL PREPARACIÓN

Coffee Truffles

The technique for making this type of truffle is demonstrated on pages 66-67. If desired, a teaspoon [5 ml.] of rum, brandy or liqueur may be added to the candy. Instead of being shaped into balls, the candy can be piped onto buttered baking sheets or into foil or paper candy cups.

To make 1 ¼ pounds [600 g.]

1 ⅓ cups	confectioners' sugar	325 ml.
8 tbsp.	butter, softened	120 ml.
8 oz.	semisweet chocolate, melted	¼ kg.
	coffee extract	
	chocolate sprinkles or cocoa powder	

Beat the confectioners' sugar and butter together into a paste. Let the melted chocolate cool for about five minutes, then beat in a few drops of the coffee extract and the sugar-butter paste. Continue to stir until the candy is thick and has cooled to tepid. Shape the candy into small balls and roll the balls in the chocolate sprinkles or cocoa powder.

MARY NORWAK
TOFFEES, FUDGES, CHOCOLATES AND SWEETS

Fernand Point's Chocolate Truffles

Truffes au Chocolat

To make about ½ pound [¼ kg.]

¼ lb.	semisweet chocolate, broken into pieces	125 g.
1 tbsp.	water	15 ml.
1 tbsp.	superfine sugar	15 ml.
6 tbsp.	butter	90 ml.
1	egg yolk, lightly beaten	1
	cocoa powder	

Melt the chocolate in a double boiler with the water, sugar and butter. Remove the pan from the heat. When the chocolate has cooled a bit, stir in the egg yolk. Let the mixture cool at room temperature for five hours, then form it into balls and roll them in the cocoa powder.

FERNAND POINT
MA GASTRONOMIE

Filled Chocolate Balls

Gefüllte Schokoladenkugeln

To make about ¾ pound [350 g.]

¾ cup	confectioners' sugar, sifted	175 ml.
1	egg white	1
5 oz.	semisweet chocolate, grated (about 1 ¼ cups [300 ml.])	150 g.
2 tsp.	rum	10 ml.
2 oz.	walnuts, ground (about ⅔ cup [150 ml.])	60 g.
Egg-yolk filling		
1	hard-boiled egg yolk, pressed through a sieve	1
1 tsp.	confectioners' sugar	5 ml.
½ tsp.	butter, softened	2 ml.
	rum	

Mix the sugar with the egg white, 1 cup [¼ liter] of the chocolate, the rum and the ground walnuts. Knead the mixture into a paste, cut it into small, equal-sized pieces, and shape each piece into a small ball.

To make the filling, combine the egg yolk, sugar, butter and a few drops of rum. Put one ball at a time in the palm of your hand, and press the ball with a finger to make a small indentation. Put in a little of the filling, close up the ball again, and roll it in the remaining grated chocolate.

JOZA BŘÍZOVÁ AND MARYNA KLIMENTOVÁ
TSCHECHISCHE KÜCHE

Fine Dutch Truffles

Fijne Chocoladetruffels

Hydrogenated coconut oil is obtainable where Dutch or German foods are sold.

To make about 10 ounces [300 g.]

7 oz.	semisweet baking chocolate, broken into small pieces	200 g.
1 tbsp.	milk or strong black coffee	15 ml.
3 tbsp.	butter or hydrogenated coconut oil	45 ml.
1	egg, beaten	1
¼ cup	confectioners' sugar, sifted	50 ml.
2 tbsp.	superfine sugar mixed with ¼ cup [50 ml.] cocoa powder (optional)	30 ml.
¼ cup	chocolate sprinkles (optional)	50 ml.

In the top of a double boiler set over hot water, melt the chocolate with the milk or coffee. Add the butter or hydrogenated coconut oil, stirring constantly until it melts. Remove the chocolate mixture from the heat and let it cool until lukewarm. Stir the egg into the sifted confectioners' sugar. Beating constantly, gradually add the melted chocolate mixture in a thin stream. Let the candy cool until it is firm. Shape it into balls, and roll each ball immediately either in the mixture of superfine sugar and cocoa powder or in the chocolate sprinkles.

H. H. F. HENDERSON
HET NIEUWE KOOKBOEK

German Chocolate Truffles

Schokoladetrüffel

To make about 6 ounces [175 g.]

4 tbsp.	butter	60 ml.
4 oz.	semisweet chocolate, grated	125 g.
1 tbsp.	rum	15 ml.
	chocolate sprinkles	

Beat the butter with a spoon until it is fluffy; stir in the grated chocolate and the rum. Refrigerate the mixture until it is firm—one to two hours. Shape the mixture into small balls, and roll the balls in the chocolate sprinkles. Place in individual paper cups, and let the truffles dry at room temperature for two to three hours. Store in the refrigerator.

ELIZABETH SCHULER
MEIN KOCHBUCH

French Chocolate Truffles

To make about 2½ pounds [1¼ kg.]

7 oz.	unsweetened chocolate	200 g.
4 tbsp.	butter	60 ml.
¼ cup	honey	50 ml.
1¾ lb.	praline powder (recipe, page 167)	875 g.
½ cup	cocoa powder	125 ml.
½ cup	confectioners' sugar, sifted	125 ml.
2 tbsp.	ground cinnamon	30 ml.

Place the chocolate, butter and honey in the top of a double boiler set over boiling water. Stirring, heat until the chocolate and butter melt. When the mixture is smooth, remove it from the heat and stir in the praline powder. Cool the candy and shape it into balls. Combine the cocoa powder, confectioners' sugar and cinnamon, and roll the balls in this mixture to coat them. Chill the truffles until they are hard. Store them in an airtight container.

JULIETTE ELKON
THE CHOCOLATE COOKBOOK

Finnish Chocolate Drops

Choklad

This candy can also be cooled on parchment or wax paper.

To make about ½ pound [¼ kg.]

6 oz.	semisweet chocolate	175 g.
3 tbsp.	butter	45 ml.
2 tsp.	grated orange peel	10 ml.
1	egg, beaten	1

Warm the chocolate and the butter over very low heat until both have melted. Whisk the chocolate mixture and the orange peel into the beaten egg, a little at a time.

Drop the mixture by teaspoonfuls onto a buttered baking sheet or into little paper cups, and refrigerate the chocolate drops until they are firm.

GUNNEVI BONEKAMP
SCANDINAVIAN COOKING

Michel Oliver's Chocolate Truffles

Truffes au Chocolat

I know that my truffle recipe has a drawback. Because the truffles contain a lot of cream, they remain soft and must be kept in the refrigerator. But, in my opinion, this disadvantage is largely compensated for by fine flavor. You can replace the rum with any alcohol of your choice or you can leave the alcohol out.

To make about 1 pound [½ kg.]

10 oz.	semisweet chocolate, broken into pieces	300 g.
2 tbsp.	water	30 ml.
⅔ cup	*crème fraîche* or heavy cream	150 ml.
1 cup	confectioners' sugar, sifted	¼ liter
1 tbsp.	vanilla sugar	15 ml.
2 tbsp.	rum	30 ml.
2 tbsp.	cocoa powder	30 ml.

Take a large, shallow pan, place a trivet or rack inside it, half-fill the pan with water, set it over medium heat, and bring the water to a simmer.

Put the chocolate pieces into a large, heatproof bowl, add the 2 tablespoons [30 ml.] of water, and put the bowl into the pan of simmering water. Stir the chocolate with a wooden spoon until it has melted completely, then add the cream, the confectioners' sugar, the vanilla sugar and the rum. Stir the mixture with a wooden spoon until it forms a smooth paste. Then pour the paste into a clean bowl and refrigerate it for at least two hours.

Sprinkle the bottom of a large dish with the cocoa powder. Take the bowl containing the truffle paste out of the refrigerator—the paste should now be fairly well set. Take a large tablespoonful of the truffle paste, roll it into a ball between your palms, and roll the ball in the cocoa powder. Do the same with the rest of the truffle paste, making about 12 large truffles. Keep the truffles refrigerated until you are ready to eat them.

MICHEL OLIVER
MES RECETTES

Russian Truffles

The handling of dipping chocolate or chocolate-flavored coating is demonstrated on page 75.

To make about ¾ pound [350 g.]

3 oz.	semisweet chocolate, chopped	90 g.
⅔ cup	heavy cream, whipped	150 ml.
3 tbsp.	confectioners' sugar, sifted	45 ml.
1 tsp.	rum	5 ml.
1 tsp.	vanilla extract	5 ml.
6 oz.	dipping chocolate or chocolate-flavored coating	175 g.
2 oz.	chocolate sprinkles or grated semisweet chocolate (about ½ cup [125 ml.])	60 g.

Melt the chopped chocolate, beat the cream into it and let the mixture cool. When cool, mix it into a paste with the confectioners' sugar. Stir in the rum and vanilla extract, and form the mixture into small balls. Melt and temper the dipping chocolate or melt the chocolate-flavored coating, and dip the rum-flavored balls into it. While they are still damp, roll the balls in the chocolate sprinkles or grated chocolate.

SONIA AGNEW
SWEET-MAKING FOR EVERYWOMAN

Uncooked Chocolate Cream Fudge

Although this candy is called a fudge, the result more closely resembles a truffle paste. The mixture can also be shaped by piping it from a pastry bag.

To make about 1¼ pounds [600 g.]

4 oz.	semisweet chocolate, broken into small pieces	125 g.
4 tbsp.	butter	60 ml.
3 tbsp.	light cream	45 ml.
1 tsp.	vanilla extract	5 ml.
3½ cups	confectioners' sugar, sifted (1 lb. [½ kg.])	875 ml.

Put the chocolate pieces and the butter into a heatproof bowl set over a saucepan of hot water. Leave them until they have melted, stirring once or twice.

Remove the bowl from the saucepan of water, and stir the cream and vanilla into the chocolate mixture. With a wooden spoon, gradually work in the confectioners' sugar. Mix well. Transfer the mixture to a buttered pan 8 inches [20 cm.] square. Leave the fudge in a cool place until it has set, about three hours. Cut it into 1-inch [2½-cm.] squares.

SONIA ALLISON
THE DAIRY BOOK OF HOME COOKERY

Rum Balls

Rumkugeln

To make about 14 ounces [425 g.]

2 oz.	semisweet chocolate, grated	60 g.
5 oz.	hazelnuts, roasted, peeled and ground (about 1¼ cups [300 ml.])	150 g.
about 1 cup	superfine sugar	about 1 liter
1	egg white	1
2 tbsp.	rum	30 ml.
	coarse sugar	

Mix the chocolate with the ground hazelnuts, superfine sugar, egg white and rum. Wet your hands and knead the mixture until it is smooth. Shape the mixture into balls about 1 inch [2½ cm.] in diameter. Roll the balls in the coarse sugar and let them dry out in a warm place for two days.

HEDWIG MARIA STUBER
ICH HELF DIR KOCHEN

Vanilla Truffles

The making of this type of truffle is shown on pages 66-67. The chocolate-and-cream mixture can also be rolled in cocoa powder, grated chocolate, grated coconut, confectioners' sugar, or a mixture of these. Instead of vanilla, the paste may be flavored with 1 teaspoon [5 ml.] of brandy, rum or a liqueur.

To make about ¾ pound [350 g.]

8 oz.	milk or semisweet chocolate, broken into pieces	¼ kg.
4½ tbsp.	heavy or whipping cream	67 ml.
	vanilla extract	
¼ cup	cocoa powder	50 ml.
1 tbsp.	confectioners' sugar	15 ml.

Put the chocolate into a heatproof bowl or the top of a double boiler. Put the bowl or pan into hand-hot water, not exceeding 125° F. [50° C.]. If you use a double boiler or a container in which the water does not reach the bottom of the bowl or pan holding the chocolate, heat the water to the boiling point, then remove it from the heat, and put the bowl or pan of chocolate over the hot water. Stir the chocolate occasionally until it has thoroughly melted.

Put the cream into another saucepan and bring it to a boil. Then let it cool until tepid. Add a few drops of vanilla extract, then tip the cream into the melted chocolate and stir until it is all thoroughly mixed.

Stirring occasionally, let the mixture cool to room temperature—about 65° F. [18° C.]. The paste will now be quite thick but not hard. Stir it with a wooden spoon, or beat it with a whisk or an electric mixer until the paste is lighter in color and fluffy. This process is very important to give the right texture. Refrigerate the paste until it hardens.

Sift the cocoa powder and confectioners' sugar together, and use them to dust a work surface. Use two teaspoons to measure out rough lumps of paste large enough to make ¾- to 1-inch [2- to 2½-cm.] balls. Drop these lumps of paste onto the work surface at regular intervals. Then, dipping your fingers in a little of the sweetened cocoa powder, pick up the lumps and quickly shape them into balls, putting them back on the cocoa-covered board before the paste melts and the balls become sticky.

Refrigerate the truffles again for a short time to chill and firm their surfaces. If the chocolate-and-cream mixture is very moist, the truffles can be kept a day or so before serving to let the outsides dry and a little crust form on each ball.

ALEC LEAVER
MAKING CHOCOLATES

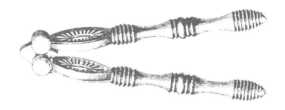

Walnut Balls

Bouchées aux Noix

To make about ½ pound [¼ kg.]

3½ oz.	walnuts, ground (about 1¼ cups [300 ml.])	100 g.
¾ cup	confectioners' sugar	175 ml.
1 tbsp.	butter, softened	15 ml.
2 tbsp.	strong black coffee	30 ml.
¼ cup	granulated sugar	50 ml.

Mix the ground walnuts with the confectioners' sugar, softened butter and coffee. This paste should be firm enough to be kneaded by hand.

Shape the paste into little balls and roll the balls in the granulated sugar. Refrigerate the balls for several hours before serving them. They will keep for two to three days.

JACQUELINE GÉRARD
BONNES RECETTES D'AUTREFOIS

Assemblies

French Candy

French candy, or what was called French candy, was made in Charleston, South Carolina, from an early date. Martha Washington made French candy in Virginia it is said, but hers were creams. This recipe is for a fruit-and-nut candy.

To make 1 ½ pounds [¾ kg.]

3½ cups	confectioners' sugar (1 lb. [½ kg.])	875 ml.
1 tsp.	vanilla extract	5 ml.
2	small egg whites	2
2	large dried figs, cut into ½-inch [1-cm.] pieces	2
3	medium-sized dates, pitted and cut into ½-inch [1-cm.] pieces	3
3	medium-sized dried prunes, pitted and cut into ½-inch [1-cm.] pieces	3
2 oz.	nuts, halved (about ½ cup [125 ml.])	60 g.

In a mixing bowl, combine the confectioners' sugar with the vanilla extract and egg whites to make a stiff paste. Turn the mixture out onto wax paper or a work surface lightly dusted with confectioners' sugar. Roll it out to a thickness of about ⅛ inch [3 mm.]. Cut this sugar "pastry" into squares big enough to wrap around fruit or nut pieces.

To fill the candies, place a fruit or nut piece in the center of each square. With your finger tips, gently press the edges of the sugar paste together around the filling. Store the candies between layers of wax paper in an airtight box lined with wax paper. The candy will keep for a week.

MORTON G. CLARK
FRENCH-AMERICAN COOKING

Apricots Stuffed with Almond Paste

Albicocche Marzapane

To make about 2 pounds [1 kg.]

1 lb.	whole dried apricots	½ kg.
½ lb.	almonds, blanched, peeled and ground (about 3 cups [¾ liter])	¼ kg.
1¾ cups	confectioners' sugar	425 ml.
	almond extract (optional)	
1	egg white, stiffly beaten	1
	fresh lemon juice (optional)	
	superfine sugar	

Soak the apricots in hot water overnight. The next day, cook them over very low heat for about 20 minutes—until they are tender—in the water in which they were soaked. Drain the apricots and let them cool.

Mix together the ground almonds, confectioners' sugar and—if a stronger flavor is liked—two or three drops of almond extract. Add the egg white, mixing it in well. If the paste is too stiff to mold, add a few drops of lemon juice. Fill each apricot with almond paste. Roll the apricots in superfine sugar. Let them dry on racks in a cool place overnight.

BERYL GOULD-MARKS
THE HOME BOOK OF ITALIAN COOKERY

Prunes Stuffed with Pistachios

Pruneaux Farcis

The pine nuts can be replaced by 1 cup [¼ liter] of finely crushed candied chestnuts.

To make about 1 ½ pounds [¾ kg.]

15	large dried prunes	15
2 oz.	pine nuts (about ¼ cup [50 ml.])	60 g.
1	egg white	1
¼ cup	superfine sugar	50 ml.
2 tbsp.	kirsch	30 ml.
15	pistachios	15
1¼ cups	granulated sugar	300 ml.
½ cup	water	125 ml.

Slit each prune on one side, and remove the pit without spoiling the shape of the prune. In a mortar, pound the pine nuts with the egg white. Add the superfine sugar and pound the ingredients together. Add the kirsch and mix, pounding with the pestle. Put this paste into a small saucepan and heat it gently, stirring continuously, until it stiffens slightly. Remove the pan from the heat and let the paste cool.

Shape the paste into 15 small olive-shapes. Stuff the prunes with the paste olives, sticking a whole pistachio into the part of the paste visible through the slit in the prune; the pistachios must be visible.

In a pan, dissolve the granulated sugar in the water and cook it to the hard-crack stage *(pages 8-11)*. Remove the pan from the heat. Put a stuffed prune onto a fork and dip it in the syrup. Slide it off the fork onto an oiled marble slab and let it dry. Repeat the dipping process with the rest of the prunes. When they are cool, put them into individual paper cups.

MME. JEANNE SAVARIN (EDITOR)
LA CUISINE DES FAMILLES

Stuffed Prunes

Prugne Farcite

The technique of making almond paste is shown on pages 56-59. A paste made of 3¾ cups [925 ml.] of freshly grated coconut and 1 cup [¼ liter] of fondant (recipe, page 166) may be substituted for the almond paste, as shown on pages 72-73. The technique of making fondant is shown on pages 30-31.

Make sure the syrup-dipping is done in a nonsteamy kitchen, otherwise the sugar coating will melt and soften.

To make about 4 pounds [2 kg.]		
36	soft dried prunes	36
1 lb.	almond paste *(recipe, page 166)* (about 2 cups [½ liter])	½ kg.
2 cups	sugar	½ liter
½ cup	water	125 ml.
½ tbsp.	light corn syrup	7 ml.

Slit each prune carefully down one side, remove the pit, and fill the cavity with a generous amount of the almond paste, smoothing down the exposed portion of the paste with the back of a dampened spoon.

Cook the sugar, water and corn syrup in a deep, heavy saucepan until the mixture reaches the hard-crack stage *(pages 8-11)*. The moment it is ready, remove the pan from the heat and place it in a large pan filled with cold water to arrest the cooking process, then set it over boiling water to keep the syrup hot. Using tongs or a pair of forks, dip each prune into the syrup. Align the coated prunes on a strip of lightly buttered wax paper, making sure that the prunes do not touch one another. Let them cool for about two hours before placing them in pleated-paper candy cups.

LUIGI CARNACINA
GREAT ITALIAN COOKING

Full Figs

Figos Recheados

You can buy these figs almost anywhere in the Algarve—the southern coast of Portugal—wrapped in fringed paper and strung together into a rope.

To make 24 figs		
24	soft dried figs	24
1 oz.	semisweet chocolate, grated	30 g.
⅓ cup	ground almonds	75 ml.

Snip the stem from each fig and gently pull the fig open to form a cavity in the center. Mix the grated chocolate and ground almonds, and fill the cavities as full as possible with the mixture. Close up the cavities with your fingers.

Place the figs on a baking sheet and bake them in a preheated 300° F. [150° C.] oven for five minutes. Turn the figs over and bake them for another five minutes. Remove them from the oven and let them cool before storing.

SHIRLEY SARVIS
A TASTE OF PORTUGAL

Stuffed Figs

Teen Mihshee

To make about 1¾ pounds [875 g.]		
1 cup	fresh orange juice, pulp strained out	¼ liter
1 tbsp.	fresh lemon juice, pulp strained out	15 ml.
1 tbsp.	grated lemon peel	15 ml.
⅔ cup	sugar	150 ml.
1 lb.	dried figs, stems trimmed	½ kg.
5 oz.	almonds (about 1 cup [¼ liter])	150 g.

In a saucepan, combine the orange juice, lemon juice, lemon peel and 3 tablespoons [45 ml.] of the sugar. Add the figs and heat the mixture to the boiling point. Reduce the heat, cover the pan and simmer the fruit until it is tender—30 minutes to one hour. Drain the figs well and let them cool.

Make an opening at the stem end of each fig with a sharp knife and stuff an almond into the hole; close the opening by pinching the fig with your fingers. Roll the figs in the rest of the sugar. Arrange the figs on racks and dry them overnight before storing them—between layers of wax paper—in an airtight container.

HELEN COREY
THE ART OF SYRIAN COOKERY

Stuffed Dates and Walnuts

Dattes et Noix Farcies

To make about 3½ pounds [1¾ kg.]

1 lb.	almonds, blanched and peeled (about 3 cups [¾ liter])	½ kg.
2 cups	superfine sugar	½ liter
⅓ cup	white rum	75 ml.
	green or pink food coloring	
1 tbsp.	freshly brewed strong black coffee	15 ml.
1 lb.	whole pitted dates	½ kg.
½ lb.	walnuts, halved (about 2 cups [½ liter])	¼ kg.

To make the almond paste, pound the almonds and the superfine sugar together in a mortar or grind them in a processor. If you use a processor, grind only 1 cup [¼ liter] of the mixture at a time.

For the date stuffing, mix 3 tablespoons [45 ml.] of the rum with a few drops of green or pink food coloring, and moisten half of the almond paste with the mixture. For the walnut stuffing, flavor the rest of the paste with the remaining rum and the black coffee. To stuff the dates, roll a little of the green or pink paste into a ball and use it to fill the cavity left by the pit in each date. To stuff the walnuts, roll a little coffee-flavored paste into a ball and sandwich it between two walnut halves.

LOUIS GINIÉS
CUISINE PROVENÇALE

Sugared Walnuts

The author suggests that the walnut halves may be dipped into melted chocolate before they are coated with icing. In this case, the icing should not be baked; instead, the walnuts should be left in a warm, dry place until the icing has dried. The technique of dipping nuts in chocolate is demonstrated on pages 74-75.

To make about ½ pound [¼ kg.]

18	walnuts, halved, blanched and peeled	18
about 1 cup	confectioners' sugar	about ¼ liter
1	egg white, lightly beaten	1

To dry the walnut halves, arrange them on a piece of parchment paper set on a baking sheet and place them in a pre-heated 250° F. [120° C.] oven; leave the door of the oven open. Remove the walnuts after about 20 minutes.

Mix the confectioners' sugar with the egg white to make an icing that will just coat the back of a spoon. Dip the walnut halves in the icing and return them to the baking sheet covered with parchment paper. Place the baking sheet in a preheated 350° F. [180° C.] oven and bake the walnuts until they are light brown in color, about five to 10 minutes. Remove them from the oven, let them cool and, when they are cold, remove them from the paper. Serve the walnuts piled on a glass dish.

OSCAR TSCHIRKY
"OSCAR" OF THE WALDORF'S COOK BOOK

Dipped Candies

Fondant-dipped Cherries

Cerises Déguisées

To make the brandied cherries called for in this recipe, put fresh cherries, with their stems attached, into a glass jar. Cover the cherries with a mixture of brandy and sugar, allowing six times as much brandy as sugar. Close the jar and refrigerate it; shake the jar about once a week. The cherries will be ready for use in four or five months.

Fresh cherries also can be fondant-dipped; substitute sugar syrup (page 8) or water for the liquor specified in the recipe.

In either case, the skins of the fruit must be absolutely dry before the cherries are dipped or the fondant will not cling to them. As soon as excess fondant has drained off, the coated cherries can be dipped in superfine sugar for a glittery finish.

The same recipe can be used for coating other fruits preserved in brandy or spirits. If the fruit has no stem, stick a toothpick into one end. If you do not have paper candy cups, dry the fruit on foil dusted with confectioners' sugar.

To make about 1 pound [½ kg.]

40 to 50	brandied cherries, with stems	40 to 50
½ lb.	fondant (recipe, page 166) (about 1⅓ cups [325 ml.])	¼ kg.
1 or 2 tbsp.	liquor from the brandied cherries	15 or 30 ml.
	pink food coloring	

Drain the cherries, reserving their liquor and taking great care not to detach them from their stalks. Lay the cherries on wire racks, making sure they are not touching one another, to dry for several hours or overnight at room temperature.

In a small saucepan, melt the fondant over very low heat, stirring constantly. Add 1 tablespoon [15 ml.] of the cherry liquor and three or four drops of pink food coloring. The fondant will become very fluid. Do not heat it to more than 113° F. [45° C.]. If at this point the fondant is not fluid enough, add another tablespoon of the liquor.

Remove the pan from the heat. Holding each cherry by its stem, dip it into the fondant so that it is completely coated. Work without haste, putting each cherry into an individual paper cup as it is coated. Let the cherries cool before serving.

JACQUELINE GÉRARD
BONNES RECETTES D'AUTREFOIS

Raspberry Brandies

To make brandied raspberries, put the raspberries into a jar with ¼ cup [50 ml.] of sugar and cover them with about 2½ cups [625 ml.] of brandy. Cover the jar tightly, and leave it in the refrigerator for four to six weeks before opening it. The technique of making raspberry brandies is demonstrated on page 86. The authors recommend storing the candies for four or five days after they have been made to let the centers become well impregnated with the brandy.

To make 1 pound [½ kg.]

24	brandied raspberries	24
8 oz.	dipping chocolate or chocolate-flavored coating	¼ kg.
1 cup	fondant *(page 166)*	¼ liter
2 tsp.	brandy from the raspberries	10 ml.

Drain the raspberries well. Melt and temper the dipping chocolate—or melt the chocolate-flavored coating—and use a teaspoon to pour it into 24 foil candy cups. Swirl the chocolate around inside each cup to coat it completely, and pour off the excess by inverting the cup over the bowl of chocolate. Let the chocolate harden for a few minutes.

In a bowl over hot water, melt the fondant with the brandy. Use a teaspoon to pour a small quantity of fondant into each chocolate cup so that the cup is not more than one third full. Add a brandied raspberry, then fill the cup almost to the rim with more melted fondant. Let the fondant harden for five minutes. Then use a teaspoon to spoon enough of the chocolate over each cup to cover the fondant completely. Swirl the chocolate over the fondant to seal the edges and let the chocolate harden. Serve the chocolates in their foil cups.

L. M. RAITH
HAND-MADE CONTINENTAL CHOCOLATES AND PRALINES

Milan Nut Chocolates

The technique of fondant-dipping is shown on pages 70-71. The handling of dipping chocolate and chocolate-flavored coating is demonstrated on pages 74-75.

To make about 2½ pounds [1¼ kg.]

3½ cups	sugar	875 ml.
1¼ cups	water	300 ml.
½ cup	liquid glucose or light corn syrup	125 ml.
6 oz.	almonds, finely ground (about 2¼ cups [550 ml.])	175 g.
6 oz.	walnuts, finely ground (about 2¼ cups [550 ml.])	175 g.
6 tbsp.	kirsch	90 ml.
1½ lb.	fondant (about 4 cups [1 liter]) *(recipe, page 166)*	¾ kg.
¼ lb.	walnuts, halved, or almonds, blanched, peeled and halved (about 1 cup [¼ liter])	125 g.
6 oz.	dipping chocolate or chocolate-flavored coating	175 g.

Boil the sugar, water, and glucose or corn syrup together until they reach a temperature of 252° F. [122° C.] *(hard-ball stage, pages 8-11)*. Remove the pan from the heat, and stir in the ground almonds and walnuts to make a marzipan. At this stage, the marzipan will be quite soft. Pour the marzipan out onto a marble slab and let it cool.

When the marzipan is cold, it becomes quite hard. Crush it to a powder with a rolling pin, then mix it with 3 to 4 tablespoons [45 to 60 ml.] of kirsch to form a stiff paste. Roll it out to a thickness of about ½ inch [1 cm.]. Cut the marzipan into ovals.

Gently melt the fondant with the rest of the kirsch. When the fondant is well warmed and fluid, remove it from the heat and dip the oval marzipan shapes into the fondant. Immediately place half a walnut or almond on the top of each oval. When the fondant has set, melt and temper the dipping chocolate or melt the chocolate-flavored coating, and dip the bottom half of each piece of candy into the chocolate.

WALTER BACHMANN (EDITOR)
CONTINENTAL CONFECTIONERY

Delicieuse

The handling of dipping milk chocolate and milk-chocolate-flavored coating is demonstrated on pages 74-75.

To make about 3 pounds [1½ kg.]

¾ cup plus 2 tbsp.	heavy cream	200 ml.
1½ cups	sugar	375 ml.
6 or 7	egg yolks	6 or 7
1 cup	butter, softened	¼ liter
1¼ cups	fresh orange juice, pulp strained out	300 ml.
1 tsp.	finely grated orange peel	5 ml.
2 lb.	semisweet chocolate, coarsely chopped	1 kg.
1½ to 2 lb.	dipping milk chocolate or milk-chocolate-flavored coating	¾ to 1 kg.

Heat the cream just to a simmer. Mix the sugar well with the egg yolks, and add the butter. Mix this with the hot cream and the orange juice and orange peel. Stirring constantly, heat the mixture to the boiling point.

Add the chopped semisweet chocolate, stir until the chocolate melts, and pour the mixture out onto parchment paper, holding the mixture in place with confectioners' bars. Let the mixture cool. When it has set, use a circular cutter to cut out 1-inch [2½-cm.] rounds. Melt and temper the dipping milk chocolate or melt the milk-chocolate-flavored coating. Dip the candy in the chocolate.

WALTER BACHMANN (EDITOR)
CONTINENTAL CONFECTIONERY

Crystallized Brandy Liqueurs

Starch-casting is shown on pages 80-83. It is advisable to practice the starch-casting technique before filling the molds with liqueur mixture. After each experiment, the starch must be warmed and sifted onto the tray again. The handling of dipping chocolate and chocolate-flavored coating is demonstrated on pages 74-75.

Rum or whiskey liqueurs are made in the same way. Whatever the spirit or liqueur used, the quantity must be precise, ⅓ cup [75 ml.] to every 2 cups [½ liter] of sugar used to make the syrup. The chocolates can be dipped twice for extra strength.

To make 1½ pounds [¾ kg.]

8 to 10 lb.	cornstarch	4 to 5 kg.
2 cups	sugar	½ liter
½ cup	water	125 ml.
⅓ cup	brandy	75 ml.
8 oz.	dipping chocolate or chocolate-flavored coating	¼ kg.

Sift the cornstarch, and leave it for 10 days in a warm place, such as a gas oven with a pilot light. Stir the cornstarch once or twice during this period. Make the starch molds by sticking equal-sized shapes, or modeling blocks, at regular intervals onto a strip of wood.

Dissolve the sugar in the water, and bring it to a boil in accordance with the sugar-boiling procedure *(pages 8-11)*. When the sugar is completely dissolved, boil it quickly to a temperature of 227° F. [108° C.], the thread stage. When the correct temperature has been reached, dip the base of the pan into cold water to stop the boiling, let the syrup cool for five minutes or so, then pour in the brandy. Cover the pan with a damp cloth and a lid, and let the syrup cool until it is tepid—approximately 120° F. [49° C.]. If desired, the pan can again be dipped into cold water for a few moments.

Use a box or cake pan not more than 1½ inches [4 cm.] deep to make a starch tray. Sift enough of the cornstarch in a mound in the center of the tray to fill the tray completely when the cornstarch is leveled off. Use the back of the starch molds or a ruler to flatten the cornstarch, and make sure the surface is absolutely level. Reserve the surplus cornstarch and keep it warm.

Press the starch molds into the starch tray, spacing the impressions evenly. To keep the impressions sharp, use a swift, upward movement to lift the molds out of the tray. Take care that when a length of molds is pressed into the cornstarch, there is no disturbance that could press the existing impressions out of shape. This can be accomplished by using two sets of molds and keeping one in the impressions while the other one is used to make further impressions in a leapfrog fashion.

Take a heavy, cone-shaped metal funnel and fit the handle of a wooden spoon into its opening. Pour the cooled syrup into the funnel. Fill each of the impressions in the starch tray with the syrup, drop by drop, controlling the flow by means of the spoon handle in the funnel. Use a flour sifter filled with reserved cornstarch to cover the entire surface of the tray with a ¼-inch [6-mm.] layer of warm cornstarch.

Leave the tray undisturbed for at least six hours. By this time, a crystalline shell should have formed at the base of each liqueur and to some extent up the sides, but hardly at all on the top. Therefore, the liqueurs have to be turned upside down so that the shells can be encouraged to form evenly all around. This must be done in one quick flip. A chocolate-dipping fork or ordinary household fork can be used. The liqueurs should be left in the cornstarch for another six hours at least, until they have all formed a complete shell. They can be left for much longer.

Then melt and temper the dipping chocolate or melt the chocolate-flavored coating. Remove each liqueur individually from the starch tray, dust it carefully with a pastry brush, and dip it in the melted chocolate. Be careful not to break the liqueur shell while dipping, as this will ruin the chocolate for future use.

ALEC LEAVER
MAKING CHOCOLATES

———————◆◆———————

Chocolate Chips

The handling of dipping chocolate or chocolate-flavored coating is demonstrated on pages 74-75.

To make about 10 ounces [300 g.]

1 cup	light brown sugar	¼ liter
½ cup	light molasses	125 ml.
1 tbsp.	butter	15 ml.
1½ tsp.	vanilla extract	7 ml.
4 oz.	dipping chocolate or chocolate-flavored coating	125 g.

In a saucepan, place the brown sugar, molasses and butter. Cook over low heat, stirring constantly, until the sugar has dissolved. Bring the mixture to a boil, and boil until it reaches the hard-crack stage *(pages 8-11)*. Remove the pan from the heat and flavor this taffy mixture with 1 teaspoon [5 ml.] of the vanilla extract.

Pour the taffy onto a buttered marble slab or work surface. When the mixture is cool enough to handle, pull it into several long thin strips. Cut the strips into small pieces. Leave them until cold.

When the strips are cold, melt and temper the dipping chocolate or melt the chocolate-flavored coating, and add the rest of the vanilla extract to it. Dip the pieces of taffy into the melted chocolate. Leave them on the marble slab to cool and set before storing.

MARY M. WRIGHT
CANDY-MAKING AT HOME

Eugénies

The technique of candying fruit peel is shown on page 53. The handling of dipping chocolate or chocolate-flavored coating is demonstrated on pages 74-75. The peel can also be served undipped. Instead of being peeled as described below, each orange may be peeled in a single spiral.

You can store this candy for a week in the refrigerator, completely buried in cocoa powder.

To make about 6 ounces [175 g.]

2	large oranges	2
3½ quarts	water	3½ liters
2¾ cups	superfine sugar	675 ml.
5 oz.	dipping chocolate, coarsely chopped, or chocolate-flavored coating	150 g.
½ cup	cocoa powder	125 ml.

With a small, sharp knife, slice both ends off each orange so you can set the oranges on a work surface. Then peel off the skin from top to bottom in strips 1 inch [2½ cm.] wide, taking great care that no white pith comes away with the colored peel. The peeled oranges can be used for some other purpose. Cut the peel strips into diamonds roughly equal in size— about 1 to 1½ inches [2½ to 3 cm.] across.

Bring 1 quart [1 liter] of water to a boil in a saucepan, then blanch the orange-peel diamonds in it for three minutes. Refresh them under cold water. Repeat twice more, using fresh boiling water each time. This blanching is intended to remove as much bitterness as possible from the peel. Drain the peel in a colander.

Empty and rinse the saucepan, and put in the remaining ½ quart [½ liter] of water and the sugar. Bring the mixture to a boil, stirring constantly with a fork to dissolve the sugar. Add the drained orange peel. Cook the mixture for three hours, uncovered, over low heat; the surface of the liquid should be barely shivering.

Take out the orange-peel diamonds with a skimmer, and lay them on a wire rack to drain off excess syrup. Let them stand for three hours, or until they are no longer sticky.

Then melt and temper the dipping chocolate or melt the chocolate-flavored coating. Lift up one piece of candied orange peel at a time on a fork, without piercing it, and dip it in the melted chocolate. Put the coated diamonds on the wire rack to let the chocolate set a little. After a few minutes, roll them in a plateful of the cocoa powder until they are completely coated. Let them cool in the cocoa and pick them out with your fingers, shaking each piece gently to dust off any excess cocoa.

Pile them in a crown shape on a plate covered with a white paper doily, and offer them as an extremely elegant accompaniment to coffee at the end of a meal.

MICHEL GUÉRARD
MICHEL GUÉRARD'S CUISINE GOURMANDE

———————◆◆———————

Chocolate Drops

While making the balls, you can mold an almond into the center of each one and roll the balls in coarse sugar to make delicious cream almonds. Or you can mold unbroken walnut halves into each ball and, when they are cold, dip the balls in the chocolate.

To make about 1½ pounds [¾ kg.]

2½ cups	superfine sugar	625 ml.
½ cup	water	125 ml.
4 oz.	unsweetened chocolate, broken into pieces	125 g.

In a saucepan, dissolve the sugar in the water over medium heat and bring the syrup to a boil. Boil without stirring for about four minutes *(soft-ball stage, pages 8-11)*. Place the saucepan in cold water, and beat until the mixture is cold and thick enough to shape into balls. Make about 80 little balls and let them cool completely.

Grate the chocolate into a bowl and set the bowl over boiling water. When the chocolate melts, use a fork to dip each of the balls into it. Lay them on buttered paper to dry.

THE BUCKEYE COOKBOOK

Honey Nougat Chocolates

The handling of dipping chocolate and chocolate-flavored coating is demonstrated on pages 74-75.

To make about 3 pounds [1½ kg.]

2½ cups	honey	625 ml.
½ cup	liquid glucose or light corn syrup	125 ml.
2 cups	heavy cream	½ liter
1¼ lb.	almonds, blanched, peeled, slivered and lightly toasted (about 3¾ cups [925 ml.])	600 g.
1½ lb.	dipping chocolate or chocolate-flavored coating	¾ kg.
about 1 lb.	almonds, halved and toasted (about 3 cups [¾ liter]) (optional)	about ½ kg.

In a copper pan, heat the honey, glucose or corn syrup, and the cream. Boil the mixture to the firm-ball stage *(pages 8-11)*. Add the slivered almonds and pour the candy onto an oiled marble slab, containing it with confectioners' bars. Melt and temper the dipping chocolate or melt the chocolate-flavored coating. When the candy mixture is almost cold, cut it into small triangles and dip each one in the prepared chocolate. A lightly toasted almond half may be placed on each piece of candy as decoration.

WALTER BACHMANN (EDITOR)
CONTINENTAL CONFECTIONERY

Kentucky Colonels

The handling of dipping chocolate and chocolate-flavored coating is demonstrated on pages 74-75.

To make 1½ pounds [¾ kg.]

4 tbsp.	butter, softened	60 ml.
4 cups	confectioners' sugar, sifted	1 liter
¼ cup	bourbon	50 ml.
½ lb.	pecans, chopped (2 cups [½ liter])	¼ kg.
	dipping chocolate or chocolate-flavored coating	

Place the butter in a mixing bowl. Beat in the sugar, ¼ cup [50 ml.] at a time, alternating it with about 1 teaspoon [5 ml.] of bourbon. Stir in the pecans. Form the mixture into ½-inch [1-cm.] balls, and place them on lightly greased baking sheets. Chill the balls in the refrigerator overnight or for at least four hours.

Then melt and temper the dipping chocolate or melt the chocolate-flavored coating, and dip the candy balls into it.

ANITA PRICHARD
ANITA PRICHARD'S COMPLETE CANDY COOKBOOK

Locarno Rocks

The technique of making marzipan is shown on pages 58-59.

To make about ¾ pound [350 g.]

6 oz.	marzipan (recipe, page 166) (about 1 cup [¼ liter])	175 g.
¼ lb.	candied ginger, finely chopped	125 g.
1 to 2 tbsp.	confectioners' sugar, sifted	15 to 30 ml.
⅔ cup	unsweetened dried coconut	150 ml.
1 oz.	semisweet chocolate, melted	30 g.

Mix the marzipan and ginger together. If the mixture is too sticky to handle easily, add some or all of the confectioners' sugar. Enclose the paste in plastic wrap and leave it in a cool place for 24 hours.

Roll the marzipan mixture into cylinders 1 inch [2½ cm.] thick and cut them into 1-inch sections. Or, if you like, shape the paste into little balls, or roll it out and cut it into triangles, diamonds or rectangles.

Mix the coconut with the melted chocolate. Dip the marzipan shapes into the chocolate-and-coconut mixture to coat the tops. Place the shapes on wax paper to dry and cool.

SONIA AGNEW
SWEET-MAKING FOR EVERYWOMAN

Peanut Butter Cups

To make about 1 ½ pounds [¾ kg.]

12 oz.	semisweet chocolate, chopped	350 g.
6 oz.	milk chocolate, chopped	175 g.
2 tbsp.	butter	30 ml.
1 cup	peanut butter	¼ liter

Melt the chocolates and butter over hot, not boiling, water, stirring the mixture until it is smooth. Melt the peanut butter separately in the same manner.

Pour a scant tablespoon [15 ml.] of the chocolate mixture into each of 16 cupcake liners, and let the chocolate cool. Pour a tablespoon of the melted peanut butter over each chocolate layer, and let this cool. Finally, pour about a tablespoon of the melted chocolate mixture on top. Cool the candy thoroughly, for at least one hour. Trim the excess paper from the tops of the cupcake liners. Store the finished cups in a cool place.

LYDIA SAIGER
THE JUNK FOOD COOKBOOK

Glazed Brandied Cherries

Cerises Glacées au Caramel

To preserve cherries in brandy, pack 1 pound [½ kg.] or 1 quart [1 liter] of sweet cherries into a quart glass jar and pour in 2 cups [½ liter] of brandy and ⅓ cup [75 ml.] of sugar. Seal the jar tightly and shake it once a week. Let the cherries steep for four to five months before using them. The brandy, drained from the cherries being used for this recipe, will become imbued with cherry flavor and can be saved to serve as a liqueur.

To make about 2 pounds [1 kg.]

2½ cups	sugar	625 ml.
1 lb.	brandied cherries, drained, then dried between paper towels	½ kg.
	red food coloring	

Dissolve 1 cup [¼ liter] of the sugar in 1 tablespoon [15 ml.] of water, and cook the syrup to the thread stage *(pages 8-11)*. Let the syrup cool.

Pour the cold sugar syrup into a bowl and add the cherries. Stir the cherries to coat them with the syrup, then drain them. Place the cherries on wire racks, arranging them so that they do not touch one another, and leave them in a warm, dry place until they feel barely sticky to the touch.

Boil the rest of the sugar and ⅔ cup [150 ml.] of water to the hard-crack stage *(pages 8-11)*, and remove this syrup from the heat. Add a few drops of food coloring. Stick a wood-en pick into each cherry and, holding the cherry by the pick, dip it into the hot syrup, then lay it on a lightly oiled baking sheet. Let the cherries dry for at least 10 minutes. When they are cold and dry, remove the picks and put the cherries into small, round candy cups.

JULES GOUFFÉ
THE BOOK OF PRESERVES

Glacéed Orange Segments

Spicchi di Arance Canditi

These glacéed orange segments should be served no more than three or four hours after they have been dipped in the syrup; otherwise, dampness will cause the coating to melt. For the same reason, do not refrigerate them. They are perfect served with vanilla ice cream.

To make about 2½ pounds [1 ¼ kg.]

3 cups	sugar	¾ liter
1 cup	water	¼ liter
1 tbsp.	light corn syrup	15 ml.
4	navel or temple oranges, peeled, separated into segments, and the white membrane removed	4

Combine the sugar, water and corn syrup in a small, deep, heavy saucepan. Place the pan over medium heat and stir until the sugar is dissolved. Let this syrup cook until it almost caramelizes—it should reach a temperature of 290° F. [143° C.] on a candy thermometer. Remove the pan from the heat, and place it in a larger pan filled with cold water to arrest the cooking process; then set it over boiling water to keep the syrup hot and liquid. Using tongs or a fork, dip one orange segment at a time into the hot syrup, coating it well. Align the dipped segments on a lightly oiled baking sheet. Serve the orange segments as soon as the sugar coating has hardened and cooled.

LUIGI CARNACINA
GREAT ITALIAN COOKING

Caramelized Dates

Dattes Glacées au Caramel

To make about 1 pound [½ kg.]

1 cup	confectioners' sugar	¼ liter
4 oz.	blanched almonds (about ¾ cup [175 ml.])	125 g.
	kirsch	
	green food coloring	
½ lb.	dried dates, partially slit open and pitted	¼ kg.
1 ½ cups	granulated sugar	375 ml.
⅔ cup	water	150 ml.
about 1 cup	brown or confectioners' sugar	about ¼ liter

In a mortar, pound the 1 cup [¼ liter] of confectioners' sugar and the almonds together, moistening the mixture with sufficient kirsch to produce a stiffish paste; color the paste with a little green food coloring to give it a light green tint. Rub the mixture through a fine sieve.

Place some of this paste inside each date and fold the halves together in such a way as to show a ¼-inch [6-mm.] strip of green paste along the slit. Stick a toothpick into each date. Dissolve the granulated sugar in the water to make a sugar syrup, and boil it to the hard-crack stage *(pages 8-11)*. Dip the dates in the syrup. Dry the dates in the air by sticking the toothpick ends into a bowl of sifted brown or confectioners' sugar, arranging them so that the toothpicks rest on the bowl's rim and the dates drain outside the bowl.

When the dates are dry and have cooled completely, remove them from the toothpicks and put them into individual oval paper bonbon cups.

JULES GOUFFÉ
THE BOOK OF PRESERVES

Glazed Chestnuts

Kasztany w Cukrze

Walnuts, pecans, hazelnuts, brazil nuts and almonds can be glazed in the same way. These nuts, of course, need no cook-

ing. The technique of shelling and peeling chestnuts is described on page 56.

The glaze will not keep longer than 24 to 48 hours; the chestnuts must therefore be prepared for immediate use.

To make 1 ½ pounds [¾ kg.]

2 cups	sugar	½ liter
½ cup	water	125 ml.
1 lb.	chestnuts, shelled, peeled, simmered in water for 40 minutes, and drained (about 2⅓ cups [575 ml.])	½ kg.

Over medium heat, dissolve the sugar in the water and cook the syrup to a pale caramel *(pages 8-11)*. Stick a toothpick into each chestnut and dip it into the syrup, then immediately into a bowl of ice water. Place the chestnuts on buttered baking sheets and allow the glaze to dry; this takes approximately five minutes.

MARJA OCHOROWICZ-MONATOWA
POLISH COOKERY

Candied Walnuts

Noci al caramello

The technique of making candied walnuts is demonstrated on pages 72-73.

To make 2 ½ pounds [1 ¼ kg.]

1 cup	nut paste, made with almonds *(recipe, page 166)*	¼ liter
	green food coloring	
½ lb.	walnuts, halved (about 2 cups [½ liter])	¼ kg.
2 cups	sugar	½ liter
½ cup	water	125 ml.
2 tsp.	light corn syrup or a pinch of cream of tartar	10 ml.

Knead the nut paste with a few drops of green food coloring to tint it pale green. Shape the nut paste into small balls the size of cherries, and place each ball between two walnut halves, pressing the halves together firmly.

In a small, heavy saucepan, dissolve the sugar in the water with the corn syrup or cream of tartar, and cook the sugar syrup to the hard-crack or light-caramel stage *(pages 8-11)*. Remove the pan from the heat and dip the walnut sandwiches one at a time into the syrup. Align the walnuts on buttered wax paper or a buttered baking sheet, and let them dry and cool completely; then place the walnuts in paper candy cups.

LUIGI CARNACINA
GREAT ITALIAN COOKING

Strawberry Delight

Deser-e Toot Farangi

To make about 3½ pounds [1½ kg.]

2½ lb.	strawberries, stems left on (about 2 quarts [2 liters])	1¼ kg.
2 cups	sugar	½ liter
½ cup	water	125 ml.
2 tbsp.	rose water or 2 tsp. [10 ml.] vanilla extract	30 ml.

Wash the strawberries and drain them on paper towels. Spread the berries out on two or three baking sheets lined with wax paper.

Dissolve the sugar in the water over medium heat. Add the rose water or vanilla extract and, with a slotted spoon, skim any foam from the surface. When the syrup reaches the soft-ball stage *(pages 8-11)*, pour 1 teaspoon [5 ml.] of syrup over each strawberry. When the berries have cooled, loosen each one from the wax paper with the tip of a knife. Arrange the strawberries on paper doilies.

NESTA RAMAZANI
PERSIAN COOKING

Toffee Apples

Any toffee mixture boiled to the hard-crack stage can be used to coat apples in the manner described here.

To make 8 apples

2 cups	Demerara or turbinado sugar	½ liter
⅔ cup	molasses	150 ml.
8 tbsp.	butter	120 ml.
1 tbsp.	vinegar	15 ml.
8	apples	8

Stirring constantly, cook the sugar, molasses, butter and vinegar over medium heat until the sugar dissolves and the butter melts. Then boil the toffee mixture to the hard-crack stage *(pages 8-11)*.

Push sticks into the apple cores from the stem ends. Dip the apples into the toffee, twirl them around for a few seconds, then remove the apples and let them cool, sticks in the air, on a buttered baking sheet or on buttered wax paper.

LIZZIE BOYD (EDITOR)
BRITISH COOKERY

Pistachio Olives

Les Pistaches en Olive

If you do not have a fine-screen rack for drying the candies, the toothpicks used to hold them can be stuck into a potato, a piece of polystyrene foam or any similar material that will support the candies.

To make about 1¼ pounds [600 g.]

½ lb.	pistachios, blanched, peeled and finely ground (about 3 cups [¾ liter])	¼ kg.
1½ cups	superfine sugar	375 ml.
	confectioners' sugar	
2 to 3 tbsp.	water	30 to 45 ml.

Put the pistachios in a pan with ½ cup [125 ml.] of the superfine sugar. Gently heat the mixture, stirring and beating it with a wooden spoon until the paste no longer sticks to the sides of the pan. Spoon the paste onto a piece of wax paper dusted with confectioners' sugar; let the paste cool until it is just warm to the touch. Pinch off small pieces one at a time, and roll them between your palms into olive shapes. Stick a toothpick into one end of each olive-shaped candy.

In a pan over medium heat, cook the remaining 1 cup [¼ liter] of sugar in the water, stirring until the sugar dissolves. Increase the heat and boil the syrup until it begins to caramelize *(light caramel stage, pages 8-11)*. Remove the pan from the heat. Dip each candy into the caramel and stick the free end of each toothpick into the mesh of a fine-screen rack, so that the candies can dry in the air. Serve the candies in a porcelain dish decorated with a paper doily.

PIERRE JOSEPH BUC'HOZ
L'ART DE PRÉPARER LES ALIMENTS

Standard Preparations

Fondant

If the fondant is to be made into candies *(pages 32 and 33)*, cook it until a candy thermometer registers 240° F. [116° C.]. If the fondant is to be used for dipping, cook it to 236° F. [113° C.]. Food coloring and flavoring suitable for fondant are explained on page 14.

To make about ¾ pound [350 g.]

2 cups	sugar	½ liter
½ cup	water	125 ml.
2 tbsp.	liquid glucose or light corn syrup, or ⅛ tsp. [½ ml.] cream of tartar	30 ml.

Put the ingredients into a heavy pan, preferably one made of untinned copper, and stir them over medium heat. While the sugar is dissolving, use a wet pastry brush to brush down any crystals that form on the sides of the pan; alternatively, put a lid on the pan for a minute to let the steam from the syrup wash down the sides of the pan. As soon as the sugar has completely dissolved, stop stirring and put a candy thermometer in the pan. Bring the syrup to a boil over high heat and cook it to the soft-ball stage *(pages 8-11)*. Remove the pan from the heat and quickly dip the base into cold water to stop the cooking process.

Pour the syrup onto a marble slab or large baking pan that has been sprinkled with water. Let the syrup cool for three to four minutes. With a dampened metal scraper, turn the sides of the mixture toward the middle to ensure that the syrup cools evenly. When the syrup has a yellowish tinge and becomes viscous, work it with the scraper or a wooden spatula, using a figure-8 motion. The syrup will thicken and become whiter. Work the syrup until it becomes completely opaque and crumbly. Wet your hands and gather the mixture into a ball. Knead it with your hands for about 10 minutes until it is smooth, white and malleable.

Cover the fondant with a damp cloth and let it ripen for at least 12 hours before using it. Wrapped in wax paper or plastic wrap and stored in a tightly sealed jar, the fondant can be kept in the refrigerator for up to four months.

Lollipops

To make fruit lollipops, replace the water, corn syrup, flavoring and coloring with ⅔ cup [150 ml.] of fruit juice. Juicy fruits such as blackberries, blueberries, cherries, grapes, mulberries, chopped pineapple, or raspberries are all suitable for making lollipops. Gently heat the fruit in an enameled or stainless-steel pan until its juice begins to flow. Strain the juice through a jelly bag. Do not allow the temperature of the syrup to rise above 290° F. [143° C.]; otherwise, the syrup may discolor.

Lollipop sticks are sold at candymaking supply stores.

To make 1 pound [½ kg.]

2 cups	sugar	½ liter
1 tbsp.	light corn syrup	15 ml.
⅔ cup	water	150 ml.
	food coloring and flavoring	

In a heavy saucepan, combine the sugar, corn syrup and water. Stir over medium heat until the sugar is completely dissolved. Remove any stray sugar crystals from the sides of the pan with a dampened pastry brush. Continue stirring until the syrup begins to boil. Place a candy thermometer in the pan and boil until the temperature reaches 290° F. [143° C.]—just below the hard-crack stage *(pages 8-11)*.

Remove the pan from the heat and briefly dip it into cold water to arrest cooking. Add a few drops of food coloring and flavoring to the syrup. Using a large metal spoon, immediately pour pools of syrup onto an oiled marble slab or baking sheet. Push a lollipop stick into each pool of syrup while it is still soft. Working quickly but carefully, make lollipops in this manner until only a few spoonfuls of syrup are left. Dab a little of the remaining syrup onto the embedded end of each stick before the lollipops have completely set.

As soon as the syrup has hardened, wrap the lollipops in cellophane or wax paper.

Nut Paste

Nut paste can be made from most kinds of untreated (that is, not roasted, salted or dyed) nuts: almonds, beechnuts, Brazil nuts, hazelnuts, hickory nuts, pistachios, pecans, walnuts or a mixture of these; only coconuts and peanuts are not suitable. When made entirely from almonds, a cooked nut paste is called marzipan. The ratio of sugar to nuts can be increased or decreased according to taste, and can be as high as two parts of sugar to one part of nuts. One variation is to use equal parts of ground nuts and soft dark brown sugar.

Nut pastes can be bound with egg yolks or whole eggs instead of egg whites. Yolks or whole eggs will make the paste richer and darker in color; pastes made this way can be stored no longer than one week. Suitable flavorings for nut pastes include vanilla, brandy, rum, liqueur or a teaspoon

[5 ml.] of finely grated orange peel. Food coloring and flavoring are discussed on pages 14-15.

	To make about 2 pounds [1 kg.]	
3½ cups	confectioners' sugar, sifted (1 lb. [½ kg.])	875 ml.
½ lb.	almonds, blanched, peeled and ground (about 3 cups [¾ liter])	¼ kg.
½ lb.	hazelnuts, blanched, peeled and ground (about 3 cups [¾ liter])	¼ kg.
2 or 3	egg whites, lightly beaten	2 or 3
	food coloring and flavoring (optional)	

In a large bowl, mix the confectioners' sugar and ground nuts. Stirring constantly, gradually add enough of the egg whites to make the mixture moist and cohesive. Knead the mixture gently with your hands until it is smooth and thick. To store the paste, wrap it well in layers of wax paper or plastic wrap, and refrigerate it. It will keep for three weeks.

If you wish to flavor and color the paste, dust a cool surface with more sifted confectioners' sugar and put the paste on it. Knead in a few drops of the desired coloring and flavoring. If the mixture becomes too moist, knead in a little more confectioners' sugar; if the mixture dries out during kneading, add a little lightly beaten egg white. To use the paste for making candy, roll it out with a rolling pin lightly dusted with confectioners' sugar, then cut it into shapes or mold it by hand.

Marzipan. Use granulated sugar instead of confectioners' sugar. Boil 2 cups [½ liter] sugar with ¾ cup [175 ml.] water until the syrup reaches the soft-ball stage *(pages 8-11)*. Remove the pan from the heat, and stir in the almonds and egg whites as called for above. Over low heat, continue to cook the mixture, stirring constantly, until the paste thickens. For storing, coloring and flavoring the marzipan, proceed as for nut paste.

Nut Brittle

Brittle can be made with any hard, dry nuts such as almonds, hazelnuts, peanuts, pecans or pistachios. The nuts may be plain or toasted, peeled or unpeeled, and may be chopped, halved or left whole. When made with peeled nuts and pulverized after it has set, brittle is called praline powder, and is used as an ingredient in other candy recipes.

	To make about 1¾ pounds [875 g.]	
¾ lb.	nuts	350 g.
2 cups	sugar	½ liter
⅔ cup	water	150 ml.

Spread the nuts on a baking sheet in a single layer, and put them in a preheated 350° F. [180° C.] oven for about five minutes to warm. Thoroughly oil or butter a marble slab or two pans measuring 8 by 12 inches [20 by 30 cm.] each.

In a heavy saucepan over medium heat, dissolve the sugar in the water, stirring constantly. Use a wet pastry brush to brush down any crystals that form on the sides of the pan; alternatively, place a lid on the pan for a short time to let the steam from the syrup wash down the crystals. As soon as the sugar has dissolved, stop stirring and put a candy thermometer in the pan.

Bring the syrup to a boil over high heat and boil it to a light caramel color—320° to 330° F. [160° to 165° C.]. Remove the pan from the heat and immediately dip the base into cold water to stop the cooking process.

Immediately add the warmed nuts, and very gently stir the mixture to mix the nuts into the syrup. Pour the mixture onto the oiled or buttered slab or into the pans. With an oiled spatula, spread the mixture evenly. As soon as the brittle is cool enough to touch, generously coat your hands with oil or butter and gently stretch the solidifying mixture from the edges, pulling it until it forms a thin sheet. When the brittle is completely cold, it can be broken into pieces.

Praline powder. Make brittle with peeled nuts. When it is cold, put a few pieces into a plastic bag and crush them with a rolling pin. Alternatively, drop a few pieces into the bowl of a food processor equipped with a metal blade. Grind the pieces into ¼-inch [6-mm.] fragments by operating the machine in short bursts. Then let the machine run steadily until the brittle is pulverized.

Candied Flowers

Clover, chrysanthemums, crab-apple blossoms, day lilies, daisies, dandelions, elderberry blossoms, freesias, geraniums, gladioluses, lilacs, marigolds, nasturtiums, orange blossoms, pansies, primroses, roses and violets may be candied in this manner. Use only unsprayed flowers, freshly picked and dry. Small flowers such as violets should be candied whole; candy the individual petals of larger flowers.

	To make about ½ pound [¼ kg.]	
1 cup	flowers	¼ liter
2	egg whites, lightly beaten	2
about 2 cups	superfine sugar	about ½ liter

Using a soft brush, coat each flower petal with egg white. Dip the flowers in superfine sugar and place them on a rack to dry. If dipping does not coat the flower surfaces thoroughly, sift a little additional sugar over them.

Recipe Index

All recipes in the index that follows are listed by English titles except in cases where a dish of foreign origin, such as penuche or halvah, is universally recognized by its source name. Entries are organized in separate categories by the type of candy and also by the major ingredients specified in the recipe titles. Foreign recipes are listed under the country or region of origin. Recipe credits appear on pages 173-176.

79; tempering dipping chocolate, 74, 75

Dipping fork, 7, 69; for candies dipped in fondant, 70, 71; for clusters, 79; decorating chocolate-dipped candies, 76, 77; dipping candy centers in chocolate, 74, 75; molding candy centers, 82; oiling, 72

Dried fruit: coating filled fruit with a sugar syrup, 72, 73; stuffing prunes and dates with fondant and grated coconut, 72-73; using to make a fruit paste, 46

Easter egg, 68, 84-85; coating the mold with chocolate-flavored coating, 84-85; decorating, 85; joining two halves, 85; unmolding, 84

Edinburgh rock: crystallization, 26

Egg: binding nut pastes with, 55, 56

Egg whites: aerating sugar syrup to make nougat, 42-43; beating in copper bowl, 40; binding uncooked nut pastes with, 55, 56-57; in marzipan, 58; stabilizing with cream of tartar, 40

English golden syrup: *a mild molasses syrup from England, available at specialty food stores.*

Equipment: candy thermometer, 7, 8, 9, 10, 11; confectioners' bars, 7, 18, 19, 37, 42, 43; dipping fork, 7, 69, 72, 74, 75, 76, 77; improvising molds, 7; marble work surface, 7; nonreactive pans, 7; for starch-casting, 7, 80-83

Extracts: lemon, 33; made by steeping fruit peel in vodka, 14; peppermint, 26, 31; vanilla, 14

Fats: as interfering agents, 7, 8

Firm-ball stage: adding cream to make caramel candies, 36-37; consistency, 11; temperature of, 10

Flavorings, 14. *See also* Chocolate; Liqueur, orange; Vanilla

Fondant, 30-33; adding corn syrup, 30; adding saffron, 33; centers for chocolate cups, 86; centers for dipped candies, 74-75; coating balls with almonds and pistachio nuts, 32; coating fondant centers with fondant, 70-71; coloring with spinach extract, 31; controlling graining, 8, 21; cooking sugar syrup to soft-ball stage, 30; dipping in chocolate, 74; dipping fresh fruit in, 70-71; filling for prunes and dates, 72-73; kneading, 30; melted and poured into chocolate cups, 86; melting, 33; pouring into molds, 33; resting, 30, 31; shaping by hand, 30, 32, 70; temperature for dipping, 70; working syrup, 31

Fructose, 6

Fruit: candying citrus peel, 53; choosing fruits to be candied, 50; citrus peels as flavoring, 14; coating candied, 52; candying, 50-51; dipping fresh fruit in fondant, 70-71; drops made with flavored syrup, 23; extracts made by steeping peel in vodka, 14; filled fruit coated with syrup, 72-73; icing, 52; jelly, 48-49; lollipops made with juice of fresh

raspberries, 22-23; pastes, 46-47. *See also names of individual fruits*

Fruit candies: candied citrus peel, 53; candied pineapple, 50-51; coating candied pineapple, 52; dried-fruit paste, 46-47; fresh-fruit paste, 46-47; fruits for, 45, 46; jellies made with juices of oranges and raspberries, 45, 48-49; sugar in, 45

Fruit drops, 22

Fruit juices: citrus, 48; extracting juice from berries, 48; flavoring, 14; fruit drops made with fruit syrup, 22; making lollipops from, 22-23; pulled candy made with fruit syrup, 28-29; set with gelatin to make candy jellies, 48-49

Fruit pastes: binding agents, 46; binding with honey, 46-47; coating with confectioners' sugar, 47; made with dried fruits, 46-47; made with fresh fruit (apples), 46-47; and pectin, 46; shaping by hand, 46, 47; storing, 46

Fudge: beating while hot, 39; controlling graining, 8, 21; cooking to soft-ball stage, 38; cooling before beating, 38; firm and grainy, 38-39; flavorings, 38; making a smooth fudge, 38-39; oiling pan, 18; vanilla sugar in, 38

Gelatin: adding body to sugar syrup to make marshmallows, 40; dissolving in fruit juice, 48; setting fruit jellies, 48-49; soaking powdered gelatin, 40, 48

Ghee: *clarified yak butter, available at stores specializing in Indian foods. Clarified butter may be substituted.*

Glucose, 6; adding to sugar syrup, 8; as interfering agent, 7, 8

Granulated sugar: in nut paste, 56; refining raw sugar, 6

Grapes: dipping in fondant, 70-71

Hard-ball stage: consistency, 11; for marshmallows, 40-41; temperature of, 10

Hard-crack stage: consistency, 11; cooking syrup for coating, 72-73; folding and twisting syrup into barley sugar, 24-25; for lollipops, 22-23; syrup for fruit drops, 22; temperature of, 10

Hazelnuts: grinding for uncooked nut paste, 56-57; making a nut brittle, 78; roasting and peeling, 12, 13

Honey: adding to nougat, 42; binding dried-fruit paste, 46-47; as interfering agent, 7, 36, 42; as sweetener, 5, 6

Horehound: flavoring candy with, 14

Humbugs: brown-sugar syrup cooked to soft-crack stage, 28; cutting rope, 29; twisting contrasting ropes, 28-29

Icing: for candied fruit, 52

Interfering agents: acids, 7, 8; adding to sugar syrup, 6-7, 8; corn syrup, 7, 8; fats, 7, 8; glucose, 7, 8; honey, 7; sweeteners, 7, 8

Invert sugar, 7

Jellies: dampening mold with water, 18; dissolving sugar and corn syrup in the fruit juice, 48; extracting juice for, 48; fruits to use, 48; made with juices of oranges and raspberries, 48-49; pouring into molds, 48; setting in layers, 48-49

Juice. *See* Fruit juices

Lactose: caramelization of, 36

Lemon extract: flavoring melted fondant, 33

Lemon juice: in barley sugar, 24; in butterscotch, 35; controlling crystallization with, in a sugar syrup, 7, 8

Liqueur, orange: as flavoring agent, 14; in marzipan, 72; in uncooked nut paste, 56

Lollipops: boiling syrup to hard-crack stage, 23; effect of weather, 22; extracting juice for, 22; made with juice of fresh raspberries, 22-23; pouring onto marble, 23; sticks, 23

Maple sugar, 6

Marble: work surface, 7, 22, 23, 30, 56, 57

Marshmallows, 40-41; cooking syrup to hard-ball stage, 40; dipping in chocolate, 40; dipping in melted fondant, 40; dusting pan with cornstarch and confectioners' sugar, 18-19, 41; flavoring with orange-flower water, 40; soaking gelatin, 40

Marzipan: baking, 62-63; bull's-eyes, 60; checkerboard design, 60-61; coffee flavoring, 59; colored with saffron, 58; colored with spinach, 58, 60; cooked, made with ground almonds, 58-59; cooking sugar syrup, 58; crystallizing syrup, 58; filling walnuts, 72-73; firmed by egg whites, 58; flavored with orange liqueur, 72; flavorings and colorings for, 58, 59; glazing baked candies with confectioners' sugar, 63; kneading, 59; layered with chocolate paste and dipped in chocolate, 77; methods of making, 55; rolling into sheets, 58; shaping, 58; stacking layers, 58; steeping candies in sugar syrup, 62-63; storing, 58

Milk solids and fats: as interfering agents, 8

Modeling block: for starch-casting, 7, 80-83

Molasses: production, 6

Molded candies: brandy-flavored syrup molded in cornstarch and dipped in chocolate, 80-83; chocolate coatings for molding, 69; chocolate cups in foil candy cups, 86; chocolate Easter egg, 68, 84-85; fondant, 33

Molds: for chocolate Easter egg, 84-85; dampening pans with water, 18; dusting pans with cornstarch and powdered sugar, 18-19; foil candy cups, 86; homemade modeling block, 80; lining pans with paper, 18; preparing pans for molding, 18

Nougat: adding nuts, 42, 43;

aerating sugar syrup with egg whites, 42; boiling syrup, 42; combining syrup with egg whites, 42-43; ingredients for, 42; interfering agents, 42; weighting, 42

Nut brittle: cooking syrup to light caramel stage, 35; made from hazelnuts, 78; made with peanuts, 35; nuts for, 34; rolling chocolate truffles in, and dipping in chocolate, 78-79; stretching, 35; warming nuts, 34

Nut paste (uncooked): binding with eggs, 55, 56; coating with sugar, 55; cutting shapes, 56; flavoring with candied orange peel and orange liqueur, 56; kneading, 56, 57; mixture of ground nuts, sugar and egg, 56-57. *See also* Marzipan

Nuts: in chocolate clusters, 78-79; chopping, 12; coating fondant balls, 32; coating with sugar syrup, 72-73; cooked marzipan, 58-59; cracking and grating coconuts, 13; dipping in chocolate, 74-75; glazed and baked marzipan, 62-63; grinding in food processor, 12; marzipan candies, 58-63; parboiling and peeling, 12; paste of ground almonds and hazelnuts, 56, 57; pounding in a mortar, 12; roasting and peeling, 12, 13. *See also names of individual nuts*

Orange: fruit jelly made with juice, 48-49; liqueur, 14, 56, 72; simmering peel in sugar syrup to candy, 53

Orange-flower water: *a flavoring made by distilling oil extracted from orange blossoms. It is available at pharmacies and specialty food stores;* 14, 40

Pastes: chocolate, 55, 64-65, 66-67; fruit, 46-47; nut, 55, 56-57, 58-63. *See also* Marzipan; Truffles

Peanuts: nut brittle made with, 34, 35

Peels, citrus: candied, 53; candied orange peel in coated chocolate clusters, 78-79; flavoring nut paste with candied orange peel, 56

Peppermint extract: flavoring taffy with, 26; in fondant, 31

Pine nuts: *the small, cream-colored, slightly oil-flavored kernels from the cones of the stone pine. They are often marketed under their Italian name, pignola, and are available at specialty food stores.*

Pineapple: coating with superfine sugar, 52; dipping candied segments in syrup, 52; poaching in water, 50; preparing for candying, 50; saturating in sugar syrup (candying), 50-51; softening the candied fruit, 52

Piping: chocolate paste, 64, 65; decorating chocolate-dipped candies, 76; making a bag from parchment paper, 16-17; with melted chocolate, 76; on molded chocolate Easter egg, 85

Pistachios: chopping, 12; in nougat, 42-43; parboiling and

cipe Credits

sources for the recipes in this volume are shown below. e references in parentheses indicate where the recipes ear in the anthology.

new, Sonia, *Sweet-Making for Everywoman.* Pub-ed in 1936 by Herbert Joseph Ltd., London. By permis- of Herbert Joseph(107, 154, 162).
son, Sonia, *The Dairy Book of Home Cookery.* © Milk rketing Board of England and Wales 1977. Published he Milk Marketing Board, Surrey, England. By permis- of the Milk Marketing Board of(107, 108, 154).
erican Heritage, the editors of, *The American Heri-e Cookbook.* Copyright © 1964 by American Heritage

Publishing Co., Inc. Published by American Heritage Pub-lishing Co., Inc., New York. By permission of American Heritage Publishing Co., Inc.(90, 96, 115).
The Art of Cookery, Made Plain and Easy. By a Lady. London, 1747(142).
Artusi, Pellegrino, *La Scienza in Cucina e l'Arte di Mangiar Bene.* Copyright © 1970 Giulio Einaudi Editore S.p.A., Torino. Published by Giulio Einaudi Editore S.p.A.(102).
Asselin, E. Donald, M. D., *A Portuguese-American Cookbook.* Copyright in Japan, 1966, by The Charles E. Tuttle Company, Inc. Published by The Charles E. Tuttle Company, Inc., Tokyo. By permission of The Charles E. Tuttle Company, Inc.(138).
Bachmann, Walter (Editor), *Continental Confectionery.* First edition 1955. Published by Maclaren & Sons Ltd., Lon-don(159, 160, 162).

Beard, James, *James Beard's American Cookery.* Copy-right © 1972 by James A. Beard. First published by Little, Brown and Company, Boston. Published in 1974 by Hart-Davis MacGibbon Ltd./Granada Publishing Ltd., Hertford-shire, England. By permission of Granada Publishing Ltd.(140).
Becker, Fritz, *Das Kochbuch aus Mecklenburg, Pommern & Ostpreussen.* Copyright © 1976 by Verlagsteam Wolf-gang Hölker. Published by Verlag Wolfgang Hölker. Pub-lished by permission of Verlag Wolfgang Hölker(149).
Bellin, Mildred Grosberg, *The Jewish Cook Book.* Copyright 1941 by Bloch Publishing Co., Inc. Published by Bloch Publishing Co., Inc., New York, 1947. By permission of Bloch Publishing Co., Inc.(103, 122).
Blanquet, Mme. Rosalie, *Le Pâtissier des Ménages.* Librairie de Théodore Lefèvre et Cie./Émile Guérin, Éditeur, Paris, 1878(91).

Bonekamp, Gunnevi, *Scandinavian Cooking.* Copyright © 1973 Spectator Publications Ltd., London. Published by Spectator Publications Ltd. By permission of Spectator Publications Ltd.(109, 113, 153).
A Book of Famous Old New Orleans Recipes. Copyright Peerless Printing Co., Inc., New Orleans. Published by Peerless Printing Co., Inc. By permission of Peerless Publishing Co., Inc.(103, 104).
Booker, Esmé Gray, *Sweets That Have Tempted Me.* © Esmé Gray Booker 1959. Published by Mills & Boon Ltd., London. By permission of Mills & Boon Ltd.(123, 131, 140).
Bookmeyer, Mary B., *Candy and Candy-Making.* Published by Chas. A. Bennett Co., Inc., c. 1930. By permission of The University of Nebraska Foundation, Lincoln(129).
Borer, Eva Maria, *Tante Heidi's Swiss Kitchen.* English text copyright © 1965 by Nicholas Kaye Ltd. Published by Kaye & Ward Ltd., London. First published under the title *Die echte Schweizer Küche* by Mary Hahns Kochbuchverlag, Berlin W., 1963. By permission of Kaye & Ward Ltd.(111).
Boyd, Lizzie (Editor), *British Cookery.* © 1976 by British Tourist Authority and British Farm Produce Council. Published by Croom Helm Ltd., London. By permission of the British Tourist Authority, London(165).
Brand, Mildred, *Ideals Candy Cookbook.* Copyright © 1979 by Mildred Brand. By permission of Ideals Publishing Corporation(89, 98).
Breteuil, Jules, *Le Cuisinier Européen.* Published by Garnier Frères Libraires-Éditeurs c. 1860(135).
Břízová, Joza and Maryna Klimentová, *Tschechische Küche.* Published by PRÁCE, Prague and Verlag für die Frau, Leipzig, 1977. Translated by permission of DILIA, Theatrical and Literary Agency, Prague, for the authors(150, 152).
Brown, Cora, Rose and Bob, *The South American Cook Book.* First published by Doubleday, Doran & Company, Inc. in 1939. Republished in 1971 by Dover Publications, Inc., New York(115, 145).
Buc'hoz, Pierre Joseph, *L'Art de Préparer les Aliments.* Second edition. Published by the author, Paris, 1787(146, 165).
The Buckeye Cookbook: Traditional American Recipes. As published by the Buckeye Publishing Company in 1883. Republished in 1975 by Dover Publications, Inc., New York(113, 162).
Byron, May (Editor), *Puddings, Pastries, and Sweet Dishes.* Published in 1929 by Hodder & Stoughton Ltd., London. By permission of Hodder & Stoughton Ltd.(90, 92).
Calera, Ana Maria, *Cocina Catalana.* © Ana Maria Calera 1974. Published in 1974 by Editorial Bruguera, S.A., Barcelona. Translated by permission of Editorial Bruguera S.A.(127, 142).
Carnacina, Luigi, *Great Italian Cooking.* Edited by Michael Sonino. Published in English by Abradale Press Inc., New York, and The Hamlyn Publishing Group Ltd., London. By permission of Aldo Barzanti Editore S.p.A.(157, 163, 164).
Cascante, Maria del Carmen, *150 Recetas de Dulces de Fácil Preparación.* © Editorial De Vecchi, S.A., 1975. Published by Editorial De Vecchi, S.A., Barcelona. Translated by permission of Editorial De Vecchi, S.A.(152).
Cavalcanti, Ippolito, Duca di Buonvicino, *Cucina Teorico-Pratica.* Tipografia de G. Palma, Naples. Second edition, 1839(89).
Chenoweth, Walter W., *How to Make Candy.* Copyright 1936 by The Macmillan Company. Published in 1936 by The Macmillan Company, New York(93, 94, 98).
Chowdhary, Savitri, *Indian Cooking.* Copyright © Savitri Chowdhary 1954, 1975. First published 1954 by André Deutsch Ltd., London. Revised edition published by Pan Books Ltd., London, 1975. By permission of André Deutsch Ltd.(138).
Clark, Morton G., *French-American Cooking.* Copyright © 1967 by Morton G. Clark. By permission of Harper & Row, Publishers, Inc., New York(156).
Cohen, Rona, *Recipes to Rona.* By permission of Kitchen Bazaar, Div. of Sherman Distributors of Maryland, Inc.(100).

Colquitt, Harriet Ross (Editor), *The Savannah Cook Book.* © 1933 by Harriet Ross Colquitt. © 1960 by Harriet Ross Colquitt. Eighth edition 1974, published by Colonial Publishers, Charleston, S.C. By permission of Colonial Publishers(123).
Corey, Helen, *The Art of Syrian Cookery.* Copyright © 1962 by Helen Corey. Published by Doubleday & Company, Inc., Garden City, New York. By permission of Doubleday & Company, Inc.(139, 157).
Czernikowski, Jan, *Ciasta, Ciastka, Ciasteczka.* Published by Wydawnictwo Przemyslu Lekkiego i Spozywczego, Warsaw, 1958. Translated by permission of Agencja Autorska, Warsaw, for the heiress to the author(106, 138, 144).
Davidis, Henriette, *Praktisches Kochbuch.* Newly revised by Luise Holle. Published in Bielefeld and Leipzig, 1898(99, 147).
de Groot, Roy Andries. *The Auberge of the Flowering Hearth.* Copyright © 1973 by Roy Andries de Groot. Published by The Bobbs-Merrill Company, Inc., Indianapolis/New York. By permission of Robert Cornfield Literary Agency, New York(159).
de Nostredame, Michel. *Excellent Et Moult Utile Opuscule.* Published by Antoine Volant, Lyons, 1556(146).
Disslowa, Marja, *Jak Gotować.* Published by Wydawnictwo Polskie R. Wegnera, Poznań, 1938. Translated by permission of Agencja Autorska, Warsaw, for the author(144).
Dworkin, Stan and Floss, *Natural Snacks 'n' Sweets.* Reprinted from The Good Goodies © 1974 by Stan and Floss Dworkin. Permission granted by Rodale Press, Inc., Emmaus, Pa.(94, 135, 147).
Elkon, Juliette, *The Chocolate Cookbook.* Copyright © 1973 by Juliette Elkon. Published by The Bobbs-Merrill Co., Inc. By permission of The Bobbs-Merrill Co., Inc.(100, 153).
The Fannie Farmer Cookbook. Eleventh edition, revised by Wilma Lord Perkins. Copyright 1896, 1900, 1901, 1902, 1903, 1904, 1905, 1906, 1912, 1914 by Fannie Merritt Farmer. Copyright 1915, 1918, 1923, 1924, 1928, 1929 by Cora D. Perkins. Copyright 1930, 1931, 1932, 1933, 1934, 1936, 1941, 1942, 1946, 1951 by Dexter Perkins. Copyright © 1959, 1965 by Dexter and Wilma Lord Perkins. Published by Little, Brown & Company, Boston. By permission of The Fannie Farmer Cookbook Corporation(103, 140).
Firth, Grace, *A Natural Year.* Copyright © 1972 by Grace Firth. Published by Simon & Schuster, New York. By permission of Simon & Schuster, a division of Gulf & Western Corporation(89, 133).
Flexner, Marion, *Out of Kentucky Kitchens.* © Copyright 1949 by Marion Flexner. Published by Bramhall House, a division of Clarkson N. Potter, Inc., by arrangement with Franklin Watts, Inc., New York. By permission of Franklin Watts, Inc.(95, 115, 122, 151).
Foods of the World, *American Cooking: New England.* Copyright © 1970 Time Inc.(132).
Frank, Dorothy C., *Cooking with Nuts.* © 1979 by Dorothy C. Frank. By permission of Clarkson N. Potter, Inc.(109). *The Peanut Cookbook.* Copyright © 1976 by Dorothy C. Frank. By permission of Clarkson N. Potter, Inc.(144).
Gaspero, Josh (Editor), *Hershey's 1934 Cookbook.* Copyright © 1971 by Hershey Foods Corporation. Published by Hershey Foods Corporation, Hershey, Pa. By permission of Hershey Foods Corporation(114, 116).
Gérard, Jacqueline, *Bonnes Recettes d'Autrefois.* © Librairie Larousse, 1980. Published by Librairie Larousse, Paris. Translated by permission of Société Encyclopédique Universelle, Paris(143, 155, 158).
Gillette, Mrs. Fanny Lemira and Hugo Ziemann, *The White House Cookbook.* (Edited and new material supplied by Frances R. Grossman.) New material copyright © 1976 by David McKay Company, Inc. Published by David McKay Company, Inc., New York. By permission of Frances R. Grossman(96).
Giniés, Louis, *Cuisine Provençale.* Sixth edition. Published by U.N.I.D.E., Paris, 1976. Translated by permission of U.N.I.D.E.(101, 158).
Good Housekeeping Institute, *Good Housekeeping's Basic Cookery.* Published by the National Magazine Company Ltd., London. Revised edition 1954. By permission of the National Magazine Company Ltd.(90). *Good Housekeeping's World Cookery.* © The National Magazine Company Limited, England 1962. Published by Octopus Books Limited, London, 1972. By permission of The National Magazine Company Limited(135).
Gouffé, Jules, *The Book of Preserves.* Translated from the French *Le Livre de Conserves* by Alphonse Gouffé. Published by Sampson, Low, Son, and Marston, London, 1871(163, 164).
Gould-Marks, Beryl, *The Home Book of Italian Cookery.* © Beryl Gould-Marks 1969. Published by Faber & Faber Ltd., London. By permission of Faber & Faber Ltd.(127, 129, 156).
Graham, Winifred, *Chocolates and Candies for Pleasure and Profit.* Copyright © Winifred Graham 1977. Published by White Lion Publishers Limited, London. By permission of Severn House Publishers Ltd., London(108, 130).
Guérard, Michel, *Michel Guérard's Cuisine Gourmande.* English translation Copyright © 1979 by William Morrow and Company, Inc. Originally published in French under the title *La Cuisine Gourmande.* Copyright © 1978 by Editions Robert Laffont, S.A. By permission of William Morrow(161).
Haitsma Mulier-van Beusekom, C. A. H. (Editor), *Culinaire Encyclopédie.* Published by Elsevier 1957. Revised edition 1971 by Elsevier Nederland B.V. and E. H. A. Nakken-Rövekamp. Translated by permission of Elsevier Nederland B.V.(109).
Hajková, Mária, *Múčniky.* © Mária Hajková 1974. Published by PRÁCA, Bratislava and Verlag für die Frau, Leipzig. German translation *Backbuch* © 1974 by PRÁCA, Bratislava, CSSR and Verlag für die Frau, DDR-701 Leipzig. By permission of LITA Slovak Agency, Bratislava(134, 141).
Haldar, Mrs. J., *Bengal Sweets.* Fifth edition. Published by Industry Publishers Ltd., Calcutta, 1947(163, 164).
Hale, William Harlan and the editors of Horizon Magazine, *The Horizon Cookbook.* © 1968 by American Publishing Co., Inc. Published by American Heritage Publishing Co., Inc., New York. By permission of American Heritage Publishing Co., Inc.(132, 137, 139).
Hall, Dorothy, *The Book of Herbs.* © Dorothy Hall 1972. First published 1972 by Angus & Robertson Publishers, London. Published in 1976 by Pan Books Ltd., London. By permission of Angus & Robertson (UK) Ltd.(88).
Hartwig, Daphne Metaxas, *Make Your Own Groceries.* Copyright © 1979 by Daphne Metaxas Hartwig, reprinted by permission of The Bobbs-Merrill Co., Inc.(130).
Heaton, Nell (Editor), *Home-made Sweets.* Copyright Nell Heaton 1949. Published by Faber & Faber Ltd., London, 1949. By permission of Faber & Faber Ltd.(92).
Henderson, H. H. F., *Het Nieuwe Kookboek.* © 1948/1972 Zomer & Keuning-Wageningen. Published by Zomer & Keuning-Wageningen. Translated by permission of Zomer & Keuning B.V., Ede(142, 151, 153).
Herrmann, Martin K., *The Art of Making Good Candies at Home.* Copyright © 1966 by Martin K. Herrmann. Reprinted by permission of Doubleday & Company, Inc.(88).
Hewitt, Jean, *The New York Times Southern Heritage Cookbook.* Reprinted by permission of G. P. Putnam's Sons. Copyright © 1976 by The New York Times(120).
Horváth, Maria, *Balkan-Küche.* Copyright © 1963 by Wilhelm Heyne Verlag, München. Published by Wilhelm Heyne Verlag, Munich. Translated by permission of Wilhelm Heyne Verlag(127, 128).
How to Make Candy. Published by N. P. Fletcher and Company, Hartford, Conn., 1875(90).
Hutton, D. F. and E. M. Bode, *Simple Sweetmaking.* © D. F. Hutton and E. M. Bode 1965. Published by Faber & Faber Ltd., London, 1965. By permission of Faber & Faber Ltd.(88, 99, 111, 143).
Iny, Daisy, *The Best of Baghdad Cooking.* Copyright © 1976 by Daisy Iny. Published by Saturday Review Press/E. P. Dutton & Co. Inc., New York. By permission of Jean V. Naggar Literary Agency, for the author(105, 136, 150).
Irwin, Florence, *The Cookin' Woman.* Published by Oliver and Boyd, London, 1949(96, 108).

ome, Helen, *Sweet-making for All.* Published by
omas Nelson & Sons Ltd., London, 1955. By permission
Thomas Nelson & Sons Ltd.(124, 148).

e Junior League of Jackson, Mississippi, *South-
Sideboards.* Copyright © 1978 by Junior League of
kson, Mississippi. Including recipes from *The Southern
ior League Cookbook* © 1977 by Junior League of Jack-
, Mississippi. By permission of Junior League of Jack-
(110, 120, 134).

e Junior League of New Orleans, *The Plantation
okbook.* Copyright © 1972 by The Junior League of
w Orleans, Inc. Published by Doubleday & Company,
, Garden City, New York. By permission of Doubleday
Company, Inc.(120).

nder, Mrs. Simon (Editor), *The Settlement Cook
ok.* Copyright © 1965, 1976 by The Settlement Cook-
ok Company. By permission of Simon & Schuster, a divi-
n of Gulf & Western Corporation, New York(93).

sdan, Sara, *Love and Knishes: An Irrepressible Guide
ewish Cooking.* By permission of the publisher, Van-
ard Press, Inc., Copyright © 1956 by Sara Kasdan(105,
, 108, 110).

e King's College Hospital Book of Cooking
cipes *(Being a Collection of Recipes Contributed by
ends of the Hospital).* Published by Longmans, Green
d Co., London, 1911. By permission of Friends of King's
llege Hospital(110, 130, 141).

list, E. J., *French Pastry, Confectionery and Sweets.*
lished by Cassell & Company Ltd., London, 1929(100).

d, Mary, *New Orleans Cuisine.* © 1969 by A. S.
rnes & Co., Inc. Published by A. S. Barnes & Co., Inc.,
uth Brunswick and New York. By permission of A. S.
rnes & Co., Inc., San Diego(119, 120, 147).

aver, Alec, *Making Chocolates.* © 1975 by Alec Leav-
Published by Michael Joseph Ltd., London. By permis-
n of Michael Joseph Ltd.(155, 160).

el, Mrs. C. F., and Miss Olga Hartley, *The Gen-
Art of Cookery.* Copyright The Executors of the Estate
Mrs. C. F. Leyel 1925. Published by Chatto & Windus
, London, 1925. By permission of Chatto & Windus
(114).

Pinto, Maria and Milo Miloradovich, *The Art of
an Cooking.* Copyright 1948 by Doubleday & Com-
ny, Inc. By permission of McIntosh & Otis, Inc., New
k(141).

venberg, Miriam, *Creative Candy Making.* Copy-
t © 1979 by Ottenheimer Publishers, Inc. Published
athervane Books under arrangement with Ottenheimer
blishers, Inc. By permission of Ottenheimer Publishers,
, Baltimore(91, 106, 116).

Bride, Mary Margaret, *Harvest of American Cook-
*© 1956, 1957 by Mary Margaret McBride. Published
G. P. Putnam's Sons, New York. By permission of G. P.
nam's Sons(94, 121).

Cormick's Spices of the World Cookbook.
pyright © 1979 by McCormick & Co., Inc. Published by
Graw-Hill Book Company, New York. By permission
McGraw-Hill Book Company(123).

gyar, Elek, *Das Kochbuch für Feinschmecker.* © Dr.
gyar Bálint. © Dr. Magyar Pál. Originally published in
7 under the title *AzInyesmester Szakácskönyve* by Cor-
a, Budapest. Translated by permission of Artisjus, Liter-
Agency, Budapest(143).

nders, Beatrice and E. M. Millner, *The Art of
eet-Making,* Fourth edition, greatly enlarged and re-
d. Published by the Confectionery and Cookery
ol, London, 1923(91,92).

rtin, Faye, *Rodale's Naturally Delicious Desserts and
cks.* © 1978 by Rodale Press, Inc. Permission granted
Rodale Press, Inc., Emmaus, Pa.(102).

thiot, Ginette, *La Pâtisserie pour Tous.* © 1938 Albin
hel, Éditeur, Paris. Published by Albin Michel, Éditeur.
nslated by permission of Éditions Albin Michel(133).

nichetti, Piero Luigi, and Luciana Menichetti
fili, *Vecchia Cucina Eugubina.* Published by Tipolito-
fia Rubini & Petruzzi, Città di Castello, 1976. Translated
permission of Piero Luigi Menichetti, Gubbio(104).

non, *La Cuisinière Bourgeoise.* Published by Guillyn,
is, 1746(149).

Meyer, Carolyn, *Lots and Lots of Candy.* Text copyright
© 1976 by Carolyn Meyer. Published by Harcourt Brace
Jovanovich, Inc., New York. By permission of Harcourt
Brace Jovanovich, Inc.(125, 134).

Miller, Amy Bess and Persis W. Fuller, *The Best of
Shaker Cooking.* Reprinted with permission of Macmillan
Publishing Co., Inc. Copyright © 1970 by Shaker Commu-
nity, Inc.(106).

Montagné, Prosper, *New Larousse Gastronomique.*
Originally published under the title *Nouveau Larousse
Gastronomique.* © Copyright Librairie Larousse, Paris, 1960.
© Copyright English text The Hamlyn Publishing Group
Limited 1977. Published by The Hamlyn Publishing Group
Limited, London. By permission of The Hamlyn Publishing
Group Limited(148).

Nichols, Nell B. (Editor), *Homemade Candy.* Copyright
© 1970 by Farm Journal, Inc. Published by Barnes & Noble
Books, a division of Harper & Row, Publishers, by arrangement with Doubleday & Co., Inc., 1974. By permission of
Farm Journal, Inc., Philadelphia(114, 117, 118, 122).

Norberg, Inga (Editor), *Good Food from Sweden.* Published by Chatto & Windus, London, 1935. By permission
of Curtis Brown Ltd., London, agents for the author(107).

Norwak, Mary, *Toffees, Fudges, Chocolates and Sweets.*
© Mary Norwak 1977. Published by Pelham Books Ltd.,
London, 1977. By permission of Pelham Books Ltd./Mi-
chael Joseph Ltd., London(116, 152).

Nouvelle Instruction pour les Confitures, les Liqueurs et les Fruits. Attributed to Massialot. Second
edition, Paris, 1698(100).

Ochorowicz-Monatowa, Marja, *Polish Cookery.*
Translated by Jean Karsavina. © 1958 by Crown Publishers, Inc. Published by Crown Publishers, Inc., New York. By
permission of Crown Publishers, Inc.(164).

Oliver, Michel, *Mes Recettes.* © Plon, 1975. Published by
Librairie Plon, Département des Presses de la Cité, Paris.
Translated by permission of Librairie Plon(154).

Petits Propos Culinaires VI, October 1980. © Prospect Books 1980. Published by Prospect Books, London
and Washington, D.C. By permission of the publisher(112).

Philippou, Margaret Joy, *101 Arabian Delights.*
Copyright © Margaret Joy Philippou. Published in 1969 by
Clifton Books, Brighton and London(105).

The Picayune's Creole Cook Book. Copyright,
1900, by The Picayune, New Orleans(99, 103, 104, 119).

Point, Fernand, *Ma Gastronomie.* Translated and
adapted by Frank Kulla and Patricia Shannon Kulla. English language edition © 1974, Lyceum Books, Inc., Wilton,
Conn. Published by Lyceum Books, Inc. By permission of
Lyceum Books, Inc.(152).

Pope, Antoinette and François, *Antoinette Pope
School New Candy Cookbook.* Reprinted with permission
of Macmillan Publishing Co., Inc. Copyright 1949, 1956,
1967 by Antoinette Pope and François Pope, renewed
1977 by Antoinette Pope(97).

Prescott, Allen, *The Wifesaver's Candy Recipes.* Published by Blue Ribbon Books, New York, 1934(102).

Prichard, Anita, *Anita Prichard's Complete Candy Cookbook.* Copyright © 1978 by Anita Prichard. Used by permission of Harmony Books(142, 162).

Puri, Kailash, *Rasoi Kala (Cookery Book).* First edition,
1959. Published by Hind Publishers Ltd., Jullundur, Punjab,
India. Translated by permission of the author(138,145).

Raith, L. M., *Hand-made Continental Chocolates and Pra-
lines.* Translated from the original by *The British Baker* staff.
By permission of Applied Science Publishers Ltd.,
London(159).

Ramazani, Nesta, *Persian Cooking.* Copyright © 1974
by Nesta Ramazani. Published by Quadrangle/The New
York Times Book Company, New York. By permission of
the author(101, 145, 165).

Rattray, Mrs. M. E., *Sweetmeat-Making at Home.* Published by C. Arthur Pearson, Ltd., London, 1904. By permission of The Hamlyn Publishing Group Ltd., Middlesex,
England.(112).

Ripoll, Luis, *Nuestra Cocina: 600 Recetas de Mallorca,
Menorca, Ibiza y Formentera.* © by Luis Ripoll. Published by
Editorial H.M.B., S.A., Barcelona, 1978. Translated by per-
mission of the author(150).

Roth, June, *Old-Fashioned Candymaking.* Copyright ©
1974 by June Spienwak Roth. Published by Henry Regnery
Company, Chicago. By permission of Toni Mendez, Inc.,
New York, for the author(131).

Roy-Camille, Christiane, and Annick Marie, *Les
Meilleures Recettes de la Cuisine Antillaise.* © Jean-Pierre
Delarge, Éditions Universitaires, 1978. Published by Jean-
Pierre Delarge, Éditeur, Paris. Translated by permission of
Jean-Pierre Delarge, Éditeur(144).

Sahni, Julie, *Classic Indian Cooking.* Text Copyright ©
1980 by Julie Sahni. By permission of William Morrow &
Company, Inc.(105, 117, 118, 121).

Saiger, Lydia, *The Junk Food Cookbook.* Copyright ©
1979 by Lydia Saiger. Reprinted by permission of Jove
Publications, Inc.(107, 163).

Santa Maria, Jack, *Indian Sweet Cookery.* © Jack Santa Maria 1979. Published by Rider & Co., London. By permission of Rider & Co.(119, 137).

Sarvis, Shirley, *A Taste of Portugal.* Copyright © 1967
Shirley Sarvis. Published by Charles Scribner's Sons, New
York. By permission of the author(140, 157).

Savarin, Mme. Jeanne (Editor), *La Cuisine des Familles*
(Magazine). July 16, 1905; February 9, 1908; March 8,
1908(88, 146, 156).

Schuler, Elizabeth, *Mein Kochbuch.* © Copyright 1948
by Schuler-Verlag, Stuttgart-N. Translated by permission of
Schuler Verlagsgesellschaft mbH., Herrsching(121, 153).

Skuse's Complete Confectioner. Tenth edition. Published by W. J. Bush & Co., Ltd., London, c. 1920(112).

Sorbiatti, Giuseppe, *La Gastronomia Moderna.*
Second edition. Published by Tip. Boniardi-Pogliadi di
Ermenegildo Besozzi, Milan, 1866(136).

Southern Living Magazine, the editors of, *The Cookies and Candy Cookbook.* Copyright © 1976 Oxmoor
House, Inc. Published by Oxmoor House, Inc., Birming-
ham, Alabama. By permission of Oxmoor House,
Inc.(126).

Stechishin, Savella, *Traditional Ukrainian Cookery.*
Copyright 1957, 1959 by Savella Stechishin. Tenth edition,
1979. Published by Trident Press Ltd., Winnipeg, Canada.
By permission of Trident Press Ltd.(101, 126, 139).

Stuber, Hedwig Maria, *Ich Helf dir Kochen.* © BLV Verlagsgesellschaft mbH., München, 1976. Published by BLV
Verlagsgesellschaft mbH., Munich. Translated by permission of BLV Verlagsgesellschaft mbH.(155).

Szathmáry, Louis (Editor), *Fifty Years of Prairie Cooking.* Copyright © 1973 by Arno Press Inc. Published by
Arno Press Inc., a New York Times Company, New York,
1973. By permission of Arno Press Inc.(104, 124).

Taylor, Demetria, *Apple Kitchen Cook Book.* Copyright
© 1966, 1971 by International Apple Institute. Published by
Popular Library, The Fawcett Books Group of CBS Inc.,
New York. By permission of The Fawcett Books Group of
CBS Inc.(131).

Tibbott, S. Minwel, *Welsh Fare.* © National Museum of
Wales, Welsh Folk Museum. Published by National Museum of Wales, Welsh Folk Museum, St. Fagans, Cardiff,
1976. By permission of National Museum of Wales, Welsh
Folk Museum(95, 97).

Toklas, Alice B., *The Alice B. Toklas Cook Book.* Copyright 1954 by Alice B. Toklas. By permission of Harper &
Row, Publishers, Inc., New York(151).

Toupin, Elizabeth Ahn, *Hawaii Cookbook and Backyard Luau.* © 1964, 1967 by Elizabeth Ahn Toupin. © 1967
by Silvermine Publishers, Inc. Published by Bantam Books,
1967, by arrangement with Silvermine Publishers, Inc. By
permission of Silvermine Publishers, Inc., Norwalk,
Conn.(133).

Tschirky, Oscar, *"Oscar" of the Waldorf's Cook Book.*
Published in 1973 by Dover Publications, Inc., New York.
First published by The Werner Company in 1896 under the
title *The Cook Book by 'Oscar' of the Waldorf*(128, 158).

Uhle, Margret and Anne Brakemeier, *Konfekt zum
Selbermachen.* © Droemersche Verlagsanstalt Th. Knaur
Nachf., München/Zürich 1976. Translated by permission of
Droemersche Verlagsanstalt Th. Knaur Nachf. GmbH. &
Co., Munich(98, 128, 139).

Van Arsdale, May B. and Ruth Parrish Casa
Emellos, *Candy Recipes & Other Confections.* Published

by Dover Publications, Inc., New York, in 1975. First published in 1941 by M. Barrows & Company, Inc. under the title *Our Candy Recipes & Other Confections.* By permission of Dover Publications, Inc.(102, 117, 118, 125).
Vence, Céline, *Encyclopédie Hachette de la Cuisine Régionale.* © Hachette 1979. Published by Hachette, Paris. Translated by permission of Hachette(113, 137).
Wakefield, Ruth Graves, *Toll House Tried and True Recipes.* Published by Dover Publications, Inc., 1977(123).
Wannée, C. J. (Editor), *Kookboek van de Amsterdamse Huishoudschool.* Published by H. J. W. Becht's Uitgevers

Mij., Amsterdam. Translated by permission of H. J. W. Becht's Uitgevers Mij. B.V.(94, 96).
Widenfelt, Sam (Editor), *Favorite Swedish Recipes.* Published by Dover Publications, Inc., New York, 1975. By permission of Dover Publications, Inc.(93).
Woman's Day Collector's Cook Book. (Prepared and edited by the Editors of Woman's Day.) Copyright © 1970, 1973 by Fawcett Publications, Inc. Published by Simon & Schuster, New York. By permission of CBS Publications, New York(113, 122, 125, 126).
Woodroof, Jasper Guy, *Coconuts: Production Process-*

ing Products. © Copyright 1970 by The Avi Publishing Co Inc., Westport, Connecticut. Published by The Avi Publishing Co., Inc., second edition, 1979. By permission of The Avi Publishing Co., Inc.(118).
Wright, Carol, *Portuguese Food.* © Text, Carol Wright, 1969. Published by J. M. Dent & Sons Ltd., London. By permission of Deborah Rogers Ltd., Literary Agency (141).
Wright, Mary M., *Candy-Making at Home.* Copyright 1915 by The Penn Publishing Company. Published by The Penn Publishing Company, Philadelphia, 1915(134, 161).

Acknowledgments

The indexes for this book were prepared by Louise W. Hedberg. The editors are particularly indebted to Reg Groves, Knechtel Laboratories, Skokie, Illinois; Werner Krattiger, London; Albert Kumin, Albert Kumin & Associates, Inc., Rhinebeck, New York; Ann O'Sullivan, Majorca, Spain; Dr. R. H. Smith, Aberdeen, Scotland.

The editors also wish to thank: Herb Anhaltzer, S & W Fine Foods, San Mateo, California; Mary Attenborough, Essex, England; The British Sugar Bureau, London; Butterfield Laboratories Ltd., Norfolk, England; Lesley Coates, Essex, England; Emma Codrington, Surrey, England; Neyla Freeman, London; Fritzsche Dodge & Olcott, Ltd., Northamptonshire, England; Annie Hall, London; Mary Harron, London; Maggie Heinz, London; International Flavours & Fragrances Ltd., Suffolk, England; Elisabeth Lamers, Accokeek, Maryland; Kervin Martin, Bill Medlicott Jr., Wilbur Chocolate Co., Lititz, Pennsylvania; Earl Merwin, McCormick and Company, Hunt Valley, Maryland; Pippa Millard, London; Sonya Mills, Kent, England; Donald G. Mitchell, Milford, Delaware; Wendy Morris, London; Elizabeth Pickford, Long Ashton Research Station, Bristol, England; Karl Seibt, Seibt's Konditorei, McLean, Virginia; Baker Smith Ltd., Surrey, England; Fiona Tillett, London; Betty Veley, Ingredients & Equipment, Inc., Radnor, Pennsylvania; Tina Walker, London; Fran Wheeler, Fran's Cake and Candy Supplies, Annandale, Virginia; Williams Ltd., Middlesex, England.

Picture Credits

The sources for the pictures in this book are listed below. Credits for each of the photographers and illustrators are listed by page number in sequence with successive pages indicated by hyphens; where necessary, the locations of pictures within pages are also indicated—separated from page numbers by dashes.

Photographs by Tom Belshaw: 8-10, 11—except top left, 12-13, 15—right, 16—bottom right, 17—top and bottom center, 18—except bottom left, 19, 24—top left, 26-29, 33—top, 34-35, 38, 39—except bottom right, 40-41, 42—top left, 46-47—top, 48-49, 58-59, 60—top, 61, 64-68, 70—bottom, 71—top right, 72-74, 75—bottom, 76-77, 78—bottom, 79—bottom left, 80-84, 85—except bottom center, 86.
Other photographs (alphabetically): Alan Duns, cover, 15—left and center, 16—left and center, 17—bottom left and bottom right, 18—bottom left, 20, 30-32, 39—bottom right, 44, 51—bottom right, 52—except bottom right, 71—top left, 79—bottom right. John Elliott, 11—top left, 78-79—top, 85—bottom center. Louis Klein, 2. Bob Komar, 4, 22—bottom, 23—except top left, 24—except top left, 25, 33—bottom, 36-37, 42—except top left, 43, 47—bottom right, 51—top center, top right and bottom left, 52—bottom right, 53-57, 60—bottom, 62-63, 70—top, 71—bottom. Aldo Tutino, 22—top, 23—top left, 46—bottom, 47—bottom left and bottom center, 50, 51—top left, 75—top.

Illustrations: From the Mary Evans Picture Library and private sources and *Food & Drink: A Pictorial Archive from Nineteenth Century Sources* by Jim Harter, published by Dover Publications, Inc., 1979, 6, 89-166.

Library of Congress Cataloguing in Publication Data
Main entry under title:
  Candy.
  (The Good cook, techniques & recipes)
  Includes index.
  1. Confectionery. I. Time-Life Books.
II. Series: Good cook, techniques & recipes.
TX791.C29   641.8'53   81-5061
ISBN 0-8094-2914-4   AACR2
ISBN 0-8094-2913-6 (lib. bdg.)
ISBN 0-8094-2912-8 (retail ed.)